After Identity

Social and political theorists have traced in detail how individuals come to possess gender, sex, and racial identities. This book examines the nature of these identities. Georgia Warnke aruges that identities, in general, are interpretations and, as such, have more in common with textual understanding than we commonly acknowledge. A racial, sexed, or gendered understanding of who we and others are is neither exhaustive of the "meanings" we can be said to have, nor uniquely correct. We are neither always, nor only, black or white, men or women, or males or females. Rather, all identities have a restricted scope and can lead to injustices and contradictions when they are employed beyond that scope. In concluding her argument, Warnke considers the legal and policy implications that follow for affirmative action, childbearing leave, the position of gays in the military, and marriage between same-sex partners.

GEORGIA WARNKE is Professor of Philosophy and Associate Dean for Arts and Humanities at the University of California, Riverside.

CONTEMPORARY POLITICAL THEORY

As the twenty-first century begins, major new political challenges have arisen at the same time as some of the most enduring dilemmas of political association remain unresolved. The collapse of communism and the end of the Cold War reflect a victory for democratic and liberal values, yet in many of the Western countries that nurtured those values there are severe problems of urban decay, class and racial conflict, and failing political legitimacy. Enduring global injustice and inequality seem compounded by environmental problems, disease, the oppression of women, racial, ethnic and religious minorities, and the relentless growth of the world's population. In such circumstances, the need for creative thinking about the fundamentals of human political association is manifest. This new series in contemporary political theory is needed to foster such systematic normative reflection.

The series proceeds in the belief that the time is ripe for a reassertion of the importance of problem-driven political theory. It is concerned, that is, with works that are motivated by the impulse to understand, think critically about, and address the problems in the world, rather than issues that are thrown up primarily in academic debate. Books in the series may be interdisciplinary in character, ranging over issues conventionally dealt with in philosophy, law, history, and the human sciences. The range of materials and the methods of proceeding should be dictated by the problem at hand, not the conventional debates or disciplinary divisions of academia.

Other books in the series
Ian Shapiro and Casiano Hacker-Cordón (eds.)
Democracy's Value

After Identity

Rethinking Race, Sex, and Gender

GEORGIA WARNKE

CAMBRIDGE
UNIVERSITY PRESS

CAMBRIDGE UNIVERSITY PRESS
Cambridge, New York, Melbourne, Madrid, Cape Town,
Singapore, São Paulo, Delhi, Tokyo, Mexico City

Cambridge University Press
The Edinburgh Building, Cambridge CB2 8RU, UK

Published in the United States of America by Cambridge University Press, New York

www.cambridge.org
Information on this title: www.cambridge.org/9780521709293

First published 2007

A catalogue record for this publication is available from the British Library

ISBN 978-0-521-88281-1 Hardback
ISBN 978-0-521-70929-3 Paperback

To the memory of my parents
Paul C. Warnke, 1920–2001, and
Jean R. Warnke, 1923–2003

Contents

Acknowledgments

My parents were Washington, DC liberals and condemned racism and sexism in all its forms. As we grew up, they expected us to do our part. Like other liberal parents in Washington, they forbade us certain brands of juice and candy, which were associated with the John Birch Society. They also kept us out of certain stores, movie theaters, and the local amusement park, which even in the early 1960s remained segregated. When a nursery school teacher told me I could not be both a mother and a lawyer, my mother said that was the stupidest thing she'd ever heard. When my sister and I failed to show keen enough interest in preparing for our careers immediately after college, my mother sent away for our graduate school applications herself.

Nevertheless, neither of my parents would have been particularly interested in the issues of racial, sex, and gender identity I raise in this book. Nor would they necessarily have thought that trying to understand what these identities are is an important part of overcoming racism and sexism. I dedicate this book to them anyway. I was proud of them, and for the most part they were pleased with me.

I would like to thank the National Humanities Center for the John Medlin Jr. Fellowship it awarded me for the 2004–5 academic year. I would also like to thank the staff of the Center and the members of my "class" of fellows, especially Wendy Allanbrook, Tom Cogswell, Betsy Dain, Deb Harkness, Greg Mitman, Kent Mulliken, Kevin Ohi, Cara Robertson, and Pete Sigal. I very much appreciate the support of Ian Shapiro as well as the members of the Department of Philosophy at the University of California, Riverside and of the past and present graduate students in the Motley Crew

Workshop. I am grateful to Beth Silverstein for the index, to my oldest friend, Rosamond Pittman Casey, for the cover, and to John Haslam, Carrie Cheek, Joanna Breeze, and Barbara Docherty for all their work on the book.

My sons and the other members of my family know what they mean to me.

Table of cases

Introduction: reading individuals

David Reimer's doctors thought that without a penis he could not be a boy. His parents and psychologists worried that he was not really a girl. At the age of three, James Morris decided that he was not a boy. The Texas Supreme Court concluded that Christie Littleton was not really a woman and the Kansas Supreme Court had the same view about J'Noel Ball. The International Olympic Committee decided Maria Patiño was a man while the United States Tennis Association (USTA) decided that Renée Richards was a woman. What are these decisions? How do we determine whether we and others are or are not men and women? What does it mean to be either?

The sense of these questions as I ask them here is different from the sense they have within discussions in moral psychology. Moral psychologists focus on the question of which descriptions of others or ourselves constitute depictions of our identities. The issue here is which sorts of properties that a person possesses count as parts of his or her identity and which sorts contribute only to trivial descriptions of the person. Thus, if it counts as part of one's identity that one is a man or a woman – if, in other words, this fact is not simply a trivial description – the question moral psychology asks is: Why? What constitutes possessing any particular identity? David Copp answers these questions in a way that highlights their difference from the questions I want to ask. He proposes that a person's identity consists in the set of propositions that a person believes of him or herself and that grounds his or her negative or positive emotions of self-esteem. Hence, if a person believes that he is homosexual and this fact grounds positive or negative emotions of self-esteem, then being homosexual is part of the person's identity. Copp thinks that given the issues surrounding homosexuality in our culture, it would be difficult for a person *not* to identify as a homosexual in either a positive or negative way. He adds that "For similar reasons, it is likely that most African Americans identify as such, that most women identify as such, that most Jews who know that they are Jewish identify as such."[1] Copp includes caveats. First, if a set of propositions is to compose an identity, the emotions it grounds must be relatively stable. One might weep at a missed opportunity and the fact that one wept might cause one to feel ashamed. Yet, unless this shame endures, it does not positively or negatively affect one's self-esteem and hence does not ground an identity as a weeper. Second, identities are affected by particular cultures and histories so that "were it not for racism and the history of slavery, for example, it is unlikely that such a high proportion of African Americans would have the fact that they are black as part of their identity."[2]

In the course of this book, I shall question the first caveat and supplement the second. Nevertheless, I want here simply to use Copp's analysis to clarify the initial question I shall ask. Copp's analysis is not interested in the question of what it is to be or to be identified as a homosexual, an African American or a woman. Rather, the question he asks is what role these identities play in our moral psychology. The question I want to ask, however, is just what these identities and identifications are. This question is more interpretive than psychological. Whereas Copp is interested in developing a theory that will determine the sets of propositions that can be identities for us, I am interested in what seems to me to be a prior question: namely, if "a high proportion of African Americans ... have the fact that they are black as part of their identity," what constitutes "the fact that they are black"? Similarly, if a high proportion of women have the fact that they are female as part of their identity, what constitutes the fact that they are female?

---

[1] David Copp, "Social Unity and the Identity of Persons," *Journal of Political Philosophy*, 10 (4), 2002, p. 372.

[2] Copp, "Social Unity and the Identity of Persons," p. 369.

To the extent that being a black or African American in the United States is often more and other than being either the color black or from Africa, it might seem clear how being black and African American can be confusing identities to possess and identifications to make. Less clear, perhaps, is how being female or identifying someone else as female can be problematic. Instead, questions here about being female or identifying others as female may seem to bring my inquiry close to another discussion. This discussion involves the terms "sex" and "gender." While "sex" and "female" have come to be used to designate fundamental biological facts, the terms "gender" and "women" have come to be used to designate the culturally variable ways in which that biology can be expressed. This distinction goes back to Simone de Beauvoir's, *The Second Sex*. Although Beauvoir does not herself use the terms "sex" and "gender," her book's most famous line, "One is not born, but rather becomes a woman"[3] suggests a distinction between a female sex with which one is born and a feminine gender which one acquires. The importance of the difference between what one is born with and what one acquires lies in its separation of what are supposed to be invariable biological circumstances from what are meant to be the entirely variable forms those aspects can take in different cultures and societies.[4]

Nevertheless, the distinction is not without its dissenters. On one side are those that dispute the claim that biology is causally irrelevant to social and cultural roles.[5] Men and women are naturally inclined to different functions for evolutionary reasons insofar as natural and sexual selection have led to differences in intelligences, attitudes, and behaviors. Hence sex causes gender. On another side are those that insist that the causal connection moves in the other

---

[3] Simone de Beauvoir, *The Second Sex* (1949), H. M. Parshley trans. and ed. (New York:" Knopf, Everyman's Library, 1993), p. 281.

[4] See Gayle Rubin's 1975 account, "The Traffic in Women: Notes on the "Political Economy of Sex," in *The Second Wave: A Reader in Feminist Theory*, Linda Nicholson, ed. (New York: Routledge, 1997), pp. 27–62.

[5] See Robert Wright, *The Moral Animal: Evolutionary Psychology and Everyday Life* (New York: Vintage Books, 1995).

direction: conceptions of biological sex are themselves culturally conditioned by conceptions of gender and gender classifications already construct the framework for sex-based classifications.[6] Thus, Monique Wittig claims that gender classifications are part of labor and political economy[7]; Judith Butler attributes them to a "compulsory heterosexual" cultural discourse[8]; and, following Lacan, Juliet Mitchell traces them to the psychoanalytic "law of the father."[9] And on yet a third side are those who claim that nature and culture are too entwined to pull apart in any clear or unidirectional way.

Despite their differences, it is noteworthy, at least for my purposes, that the theorists and scientists on the various sides of the sex–biology or nature–culture debate agree in focusing mainly on causal issues. They ask how the biology of bodies is causally related to traits exhibited by men and women or they ask how gender socialization succeeds in dividing bodies into male and female, or, finally, they ask how biology and society work together to construct males and females, men and women. Yet, in addition to the question of how males, females, men and women come to be, we might also ask what they are. What are we getting at or trying to get at when we attribute either a sex or a gender to another person or to ourselves? Copp's interest is in showing how and when conceiving of oneself as a female or a woman becomes an identity one possesses; others are interested in discovering whether one is first a female and then a woman or first a woman and then a female. For my part, I am interested in what females and women are and how we decide whether a given individual is one.

[6] See, for example, John Macionis, *Sociology* (Englewood Cliffs, NJ: Prentice Hall, 1993).
[7] Monique Wittig, "One Is Not Born a Woman," in Nicholson, ed., *The Second Wave*, pp. 265–272.
[8] Judith Butler, *Gender Trouble: Feminism and the Subversion of Identity* (New York: Routledge, 1990).
[9] Juliet Mitchell, "Introduction – I," in Juliet Mitchell and Jacqueline Rose, eds., *Feminine Sexuality: Jacques Lacan and the école freudienne* (New York: W. W. Norton and Pantheon Books, 1985).

In chapter 1 of this book I ask whether any one knows. For, more frequently than we might suspect, medical experts, legal authorities, and psychosexual researchers disagree both with each other and with themselves. Sometimes authorities rely on chromosomal make-up. One is a woman if one has XX chromosomes and one is not a woman if one has XY chromosomes. Yet, what of individuals who have sex-reassignment surgery or individuals born with an insensitivity to androgens so that, although they have XY chromosomes, they look like women? Identity as a woman sometimes ignores chromosomes and refers to the appearance of the genitalia. At other times it refers to the set of activities and behaviors that the individual enjoys, or to the person's own ideas of who or what he or she is.

Such differences in accounts of who is a woman and in determinations of what counts as female recall similar differences in legal determinations of who was a black in the nineteenth and twentieth centuries. State and federal courts investigated the boundaries of US racial divisions in a variety of contexts. Slave laws prohibited the enslavement of whites and from the late 1600s on also prohibited the enslavement of American Indians. After the Civil War, bans on interracial marriage prevented whites from marrying non-whites. Until 1952, naturalization laws precluded citizenship for all those who were neither black nor white. Until at least the mid-1960s Jim Crow laws limited the access of blacks to almost all public services and institutions. But how were courts to decide who was what? Just as the medical, legal, and psychosexual communities disagree on the criteria for being a woman today, different courts came to different conclusions about race. Indeed, sometimes the same court came to different conclusions at different times and many courts contradicted themselves whenever it was necessary to maintain the racial status quo.

Do these cases have any implications for the determination of sex and gender? Quandaries in racial identification and identity have led to the now widely accepted account of race as a social construction; certainly many conceive of sex and gender as social constructions as well. Part of the point of the present book, however, is to ask whether a different conception of racial, sex, and gender identities might not be equally important. For surely the way we identify ourselves and others is a way of understanding who or what we and they are. That is, it may be that the identities we take seriously today are ones with social and historical causes that constructed people as certain kinds of people. Yet, identities are also simply interpretations of who people are, interpretations that select among the various possibilities in our culture and tradition for saying who and what people are. As ways of understanding, however, identities possess the same features as understanding in general and the same features, in particular, as understanding texts. When we ask who someone is, we are asking the same sort of question we ask when we want to know what the meaning of a particular text is; we are trying to understand the person's "meaning."

Textual understanding has at least three characteristics that are important for thinking through the questions of identities. First, our understanding of texts is situated. We do not come at our texts with a fresh eye but instead with one that is pre-oriented towards the text in a certain way because of the culture and traditions in which we have been socialized. Second, our understanding of texts is purposeful. When we understand a text, we do so not only from a certain perspective and not only within a certain framework of assumptions and concerns. In addition, we have certain hopes and expectations for the text, certain reasons for reading it, and particular worries we would like it to address. Third, because we recognize ourselves as situated and purposefully oriented, we are prepared for different interpretations of the text's meaning. We assume that others have and will understand it differently than we do and, moreover, that we may bring a different framework of attitudes, expectations, and concerns to it at different points of our life. In this book, I want to suggest that our understanding of a person's identity is likewise situated, purposefully oriented, and partial. As Copp's work suggests, it is not novel to assert that understanding another person or oneself as a black is possible only because of the particular history out of which we have emerged. The same holds of races in general: we can understand people as raced individuals only because of and within limited historical and cultural contexts. Indeed, a particular person can be a black in the United States and a white in Latin America and the possibility of his or her being either black or not-black depends upon the particular histories of the particular racial traditions involved. Nevertheless, I also want to make a further claim: even within the historical and cultural settings in which we can be understood as black, white, Asian or Latino/a and in which we can be understood as females or males, men or women, we cannot only or always be understood in any of these ways. Particular historical and cultural contexts may give rise to racial, sexed, and gendered identities. It is a further point to say that only particular contexts within those broader historical and cultural frameworks can include raced, sexed, or gendered individuals as intelligible "parts."

The contradictions in identity attribution that I explore in chapter 1 and 2 of this book are the result of ignoring these sorts of limits on intelligibility. Just like texts, people have different meanings in different contexts and the meanings they have depend upon the relations, situations, and frameworks in terms of which we are trying to understand them. When we understand who a person or ourselves is, we do so only from a certain perspective and only within a certain framework of assumptions and concerns. Hence, our understanding of ourselves and others is always partial and perspectival. An identity is never either the whole of who we are or who we always are. Rather, who we are depends upon the context in which the question arises and the purposes for which it is asked. The source of contradictions in legal, social, and medical accounts of which race, sex, or gender a given person has stems from a failure to recognize that identities are always situationally curtailed. In chapters 6 and 7 of this book I try to make this point clear by looking at debates over the politics of recognition, marriage between same-sex partners, and gays in the military. For, in each of these cases, particular identities overflow the arenas only within which they make sense.

Much of what I say in this book touches on two other important issues. The first involves our assumptions about the binary nature of

sexes and genders and the second asks what is excluded in our use of
the category of "women." In the hope of further clarifying my own
focus, I want to look briefly at both discussions.

The issue of the binary nature of sex and gender raises the
question as to whether we must or even should sort people into one
or the other of two and only two sets: male or female, man or woman.
Are there two and only two sexes coordinated with two and only two
genders? Adding intersexed individuals to our current binary system,
Anne Fausto-Sterling once somewhat facetiously proposed what she
called a five-sex system consisting of men, women, herms (intersexuals with equal portions of male and female attributes), ferms
(intersexuals with a high proportion of female attributes), and
merms (intersexuals with a higher proportion of male attributes).[10]
In contrast, according to Thomas Laqueur, Europe used a one-sex
model until the latter part of the eighteenth century.[11] Metaphysical
commitments about the hierarchy of nature required that men and
women belong to the same order so that men could be placed above
women in the scheme of things. The scheme did not require physicians to overlook all differences between men and women. These they
saw in terms of oppositions between cold and heat, moist and dry.
Nevertheless, they tended to think that the oppositions occurred
within a single sex: female bodies were outside-in male bodies, as
Aristotle and Galen said, possessing the same *telos* as men but without sufficient heat to take the male form to its perfect completion.[12] It
followed from this view that women with too much bodily heat could
produce semen and that if women became entirely too hot through
exercise they might suddenly sprout penises.[13]

[10] See Anne Fausto-Sterling, *Sexing the Body: Gender Politics and the Construction of Sexuality* (New York: Basic Books, 2000), p. 78.

[11] Thomas M. Laqueur, *Making Sex: The Body and Gender from the Greeks to Freud* (Cambridge, MA: Harvard University Press, 1990).

[12] *Ibid.*, p. 4.

[13] *Ibid.*, pp. 123–126. Also see Merry E. Wiesner, *Women and Gender in Early Modern Europe*, 2nd edn. (Cambridge: Cambridge University Press, 2000), p. 54.

Despite the apparent eccentricity of such beliefs, Laqueur does not think that they can be explained simply as the result of inadequate medical and scientific knowledge. The discovery of the clitoris during the Renaissance could have been used to undermine these beliefs because it meant that the model had to deal with two penis analogues: the vagina and the clitoris.[14] Conversely, the discovery of "a morphologically androgynous embryo"[15] in the nineteenth century could have been used to support a one-sex model. Laqueur therefore cites extra-scientific causes for the move to a two-sex model. The premodern and early-modern body occupied a different conceptual space from the modern one. It was not the bedrock material substance on which various attributes could be hung. Instead, it was an illustration of the cosmic order in which microcosm and macrocosm were mapped onto one another and in which men and women had their proper places as two genders hierarchically positioned along a single body.

Numerous historical and anthropological investigations indicate that we need not be content with only two genders, however. Randolph Trumbach argues that "mollies," or adult, transvestite, effeminate homosexuals constituted a third gender in England and Northwestern Europe in the eighteenth century and that "sapphists" or lesbians constituted a fourth gender in the nineteenth century.[16] In regions of the Balkans, at least up to the early twentieth century, daughters were sometimes raised as sons and women sometimes lived as men, receiving certain male privileges and answering to male pronouns.[17] Perhaps the most famous of the additional genders, however, are the *berdaches* or Two-Spirits of certain American Indian

[14] Laqueur, *Making Sex*, p. 65.   [15] *Ibid.*, p. 10.

[16] Randolph Trumbach, "London's Sapphists: From Three Sexes to Four Genders in the Making of Modern Culture," in Gilbert Herdt, ed., *Third Sex, Third Gender: Beyond Sexual Dimorphism in Culture and History* (New York: Zone Books, 1993), pp. 111–136.

[17] See, for example, "Woman Becomes Man in the Balkans," in Herdt, ed., *Third Sex, Third Gender*, pp. 241–281.

cultures.[18] Early studies of *berdaches* often saw them as homosexuals or "sissies," who the studies defined as men who had shown cowardice on the field of battle and were thus condemned to live as women. However, more recent studies suggest that they were either a mixed gender of man–woman[19] or a third gender,[20] or even, in some cases where the status includes *berdaches* mixing a female anatomy with a masculine life, a fourth gender.[21]

In addition to questioning the number of sexes and genders, theorists have also been interested in the intersections of the sexes and genders we currently recognize with other forms of identity, particularly race and class. The perplexities that surround sex and gender thus do not limit themselves to the question of how sex and gender are themselves interrelated, but how they are related to other categories of identity and how these other identities can affect the identities of particular individuals. As Linda Martin Alcoff puts the point, the "expressions" an individual's race take depend upon that individual's class and gender; the "expressions" an individual's gender take depend upon that individual's class and race; and the "expressions" an individual's class take depend upon that individual's race and gender.[22] Consequently, specifications of the category of women pose what Sally Haslanger calls commonality and normativity problems.[23] Because of their different races and classes, there are no characteristics that all women possess. Furthermore, if we look for commonalities, we are in danger not only of overlooking differences between women but also of establishing normative standards for the

---

[18] Sabine Lang, *Men as Women, Women as Men: Changing Gender in Native American Cultures*, John L. Vantine, trans. (Austin, TX: University of Texas Press, 1998), p. 10.

[19] See Lang, *Men as Women, Women as Men*.

[20] See, for example, Will Roscoe, "How to Become a Berdache: Toward a Unified Analysis of Gender Diversity," in Herdt, ed., *Third Sex, Third Gender*, pp. 329–372.

[21] See, for example, Roscoe, "How to Become a Berdache," p. 370.

[22] See Linda Martin Alcoff, "The Contrasting Ontologies of Race and Gender," Paper delivered at the Pacific meetings of the American Philosophical Association, 2003.

[23] Sally Haslanger, "Gender and Race: (What) Are They? (What) Do We Want Them To Be?," *Nous*, 34 (1), 2000, p. 37.

category of women that define certain women out of it. Ignoring differences in women due to race and class raises the risk of over-generalizing from the experiences and identity-characteristics of white, middle-class American and European women. In addition, ignoring these differences marginalizes other women and militates against the possibility of acknowledging their potentially very different experiences and concerns. This problem is already clear in a speech Sojourner Truth reportedly made to the women's rights convention in Akron, Ohio, in 1851.[24] Although she may never have actually delivered the speech attributed to her, its point is clear:

> That man over there says that women need to be helped into carriages, and lifted over ditches, and to have the best place everywhere. Nobody ever helps me into carriages, or over mud-puddles, or gives me any best place! And ain't I a woman? Look at me! Look at my arm? I have ploughed and planted and gathered into barns, and no man could head me! And ain't I a woman? I could work as much and eat as much as a man – when I could get it – and bear the lash as well! And ain't I a woman? I have borne thirteen children, and seen them most all sold off to slavery, and when I cried out with my mother's grief, none but Jesus heard me! And ain't I a woman?[25]

The statement responds to claims that women are too tender and softhearted to engage in politics and too fragile to vote. Yet it also shows how variable identifications of individuals as women are once these identifications are combined with racial attributions and with the attributions of social and economic class. Indeed, the very characteristics that underwrite the identification of one group as women are those that a different intersection of race and gender denies another. White women's gender status involves a physical weakness that differentiates them from men; black women's gender status involves the

---

[24] See Deborah Gray White, *Ar'nt I a Woman: Female Slaves in the Plantation South*, rev. edn. (New York: W. W. Norton, 1999), p. 5.

[25] *Ibid.*, p. 14, transliteration altered.

expectation of physical brawn. If men are meant to take care of white women, black women are meant to take care of men. White women are mothers; black women are not allowed to be.[26]

Studies and histories of alternative sex and gender schemes challenge our own culture's insistence on two sorts of sexed bodies more or less tightly connected to two sorts of gendered person. For their part, the issues of intersectionality raise questions of which individuals belong centrally to a given category of identity, how intersections of race and class with sex and gender undermine the uniformity of women as a group, and what exclusions are implied in defining women primarily in terms of the characteristics of white middle-class women. Nevertheless, adding or subtracting sexes and genders would not answer the questions I want to ask. For those questions are less concerned with which or how many sexes or genders there are than with the hermeneutic conditions of our understanding of individuals as any of them. To the extent that questions of intersectionality highlight the variability in our conceptions of gender, they are more connected to the issues I want to explore in this book. I want to examine the conditions under which we can intelligibly understand someone or ourselves as a man or a woman, a female or a male. The contradiction in identifying women with fragility while supposing some women capable of, or even peculiarly suited to, back-breaking work indicates a problem with the identity of women, in my view, one that emerges when it overshoots its boundaries. The question is what the scope and conditions are in which it makes sense to call someone a woman or a man, a female or a male. How far does the understanding of an individual as a woman or man go and what are the contexts in which it is plausible or adequate as an understanding of who he or she is? If we identify a person as a "woman," "man," or *berdache* what do we thereby illuminate and under what conditions?

[26] Also see Kimberle Crenshaw, "Mapping the Margins: Intersectionality, Identity Politics and Violence Against Women," *Stanford Law Review*, 43 (6), 1991, p. 1252.

The question here is the same for sex, gender, and race. We often take race and sex, if not gender, to be facts about us whether or not we adopt them, in Copp's language, as part of our self-esteem identity. We think we can decide whether to make being a woman part of that identity, just as we can decide whether to make our identities and identifications as scholars, conservatives and poker-players, for example, fundamental to who we take ourselves to be. Yet, we assume that there are differences here in that being a poker-player seems to exist on a shallower level than being a woman. One seems to be necessarily a woman but only contingently a poker-player, or really a woman and a poker-player just for now. Being a poker-player, scholar, or a conservative is also somewhat vague as an identity, since it is not clear exactly how much reading and writing is necessary to status as a scholar or what precise opinions mark one as a conservative. Thus while individuals sometimes say, "I guess you could call me a conservative," they rarely say, "I guess you could call me a woman." Finally, identities as poker-players, scholars, and conservatives are partial. They answer only to certain questions about who and what we are – those that involve what we do, what we believe, and, in the case of poker-players, how we amuse ourselves. In contrast, we tend to conceive of identifications and identities as men and women and whites and non-whites as possessing a more general scope and a deeper reality. Adrian Piper writes about the awkwardness and even outrage that attends those social interactions in which acquaintances who previously thought she was white decide on the basis of facts about her heritage that she is black. She also writes about the awkwardness and even outrage that attends those social interactions in which acquaintances who previously thought she was black decide on the basis of her appearance that she is white.[27] Yet, it is difficult to imagine a similar outrage or awkwardness were acquaintances to decide that she was a poker-player instead of an ice-skater. Even if they were to decide that

---

[27] See Adrian Piper, "Passing for White, Passing for Black", *Transitions*, 58. (1992), pp. 28–29.

she was a conservative instead of a liberal, the awkwardness and outrage, if they arose at all, would be different. They would refer to what
they viewed as her political naïveté or wrong-headedness instead of to
what appears to them in the race case as a deep inauthenticity.

I want to argue against the meaningfulness of this conception of
inauthenticity. Our self-identities and the ways we identify others are
modes of reading individuals. As such, they possess the same conditions and scope as our readings of texts do. At best, these readings are
illuminating rather than canonical, inclusive of other readings rather
than exclusive and the results of particular interpretive frameworks
rather than non-circumscribed understandings. Our understanding of
the text can be plausible and compelling without being uniquely true
of it. In addition, it can allow for other plausible understandings that
reflect alternative interpretive approaches and pick up on different
meanings. Our readings of individuals are similarly scoped. At best,
they illuminate certain identities and do so for the purposes of certain
horizons of concern. We are not always intelligible as either blacks or
whites, Latinos/as or Asians and we are not always intelligible as men
or women. It is not just that these identities are irrelevant in most
circumstances. It is, instead, that they are misunderstandings of who
and what we are.

I   The tragedy of David Reimer

✦

In 1966, at the age of eight months, Bruce Reimer and his twin brother, Brian, were admitted to the hospital for circumcisions that were meant to cure difficulties both were having in urinating.[1] Yet Brian never underwent the procedure because Bruce's circumcision went disastrously awry. The general practitioner used an electrocautery machine to perform the procedure and something went wrong. The machine so severely burned the baby's penis that within days it dried and broke off in pieces. Unsure of what to do, Bruce's parents consulted a variety of doctors and eventually made contact with Dr. John Money at the Johns Hopkins Medical School. In addition to being a respected researcher and clinician, Money had made a name for himself as an expert in the treatment of infants born with intersexual conditions that made it unclear whether they should be brought up as girls or boys. Parents and doctors, he counseled, possessed a "degree" of freedom in deciding which sex and gender to assign to such infants, although this freedom "progressively" shrank between eighteen and thirty months and disappeared altogether at about three years.[2] Still, as long as a definitive sex and gender assignment was made early enough in a child's life, appropriate surgical

---

[1] See John Colapinto, *As Nature Made Him: The Boy Who Was Raised as a Girl* (New York: HarperCollins Perennial Books Edn., 2001); Milton Diamond and Keith Sigmundson, "Sex Reassignment at Birth: Long-Term Review and Clinical Implications," *Archives of Pediatrics and Adolescent Medicine*, 151, 1997, pp. 298–304, Web-based version at www.hawaii.edu/PCSS/online_artcls/intersex/mdfnl.html; John Money and Anke Ehrhardt, *Man and Woman, Boy and Girl: The Differentiation and Dimorphism of Gender Identity from Conception to Maturity* (Baltimore, MD: Johns Hopkins University Press, 1972), pp. 118–123; "Dateline NBC," February 8, 2000. Also see Judith Butler's article on the case, "Doing Justice to Someone: Sex Reassignment and Allegories of Transsexuality," in Judith Butler, *Undoing Gender* (New York: Routledge, 2004).

[2] Ehrhardt, *Man and Woman, Boy and Girl*, p. 176.

interventions could be made to shape the genitals in one way or the other; the condition could be further treated with hormones and the child could be brought up as either a girl or a boy. In either case, Money insisted, the child would develop the appropriate "gender identity," by which he meant "the sameness, unity, and persistence" of the child's sense of him or herself "as male, female, or ambivalent."[3] Treatment of infants with intersexed conditions, then, could be based on assessments of which sex assignment was likely to lead to the best surgical results or preserve reproductive abilities. At the same time, parents could be instructed in child-rearing methods that would reinforce gender identity and help create a well-adjusted child.

Although Bruce had not been born an intersexed infant, Money was confident that the same treatment could be used on him. His parents took his advice. Accordingly, when Bruce was seventeen months old they began to let his hair grow and changed his name to Brenda.[4] Then, when Brenda was twenty-two months old, doctors performed a bilateral orchidectomy that removed both testicles. The Reimers continued to bring Brenda up to think of herself and to act as a girl and they also withheld from her all information about her birth or genital surgery. Throughout Brenda's childhood, Money continued to monitor and to assess her development, meeting with both her and Brian once a year and publishing reports that led the psychological profession at large to believe that the gender reassignment had been an unmitigated success. Indeed, because it had apparently worked so well, it provided a strong argument for the importance of environment and nurture over biology and nature in the on-going debate about the origins of gender identity. Assignments as girls or boys, the case seemed to prove, were malleable, not only for intersexed children but also for those born with unambiguous organs and genitalia. If non-intersexed children were the victims of accidents similar to Bruce's, their anatomies could be reconstructed and they could be

---

[3] *Ibid.*, p. 13.

[4] When David is Brenda, I use "she", when David is Bruce or David, I use "he", when David is in transition, I use "he/she."

brought up to think of themselves as girls or boys in ways appropriate
to their new bodies. Hence, nurture was more important than nature
in a child's gender identity.

Yet, while Money's scientific reports and the book he published
in 1972 with Anke A. Ehrhardt[5] proclaimed Bruce's sex and gender
reassignment a success, later reports suggested that the case was not
so clear. Brenda was a handful. She was an outcast and under-achiever
in school; she did not play with dolls, ripped off the dresses her mother
put on her, and occasionally even tried to urinate while standing.[6] She
walked "like a guy," according to her twin brother and "Sat with her
legs apart. She talked about guy things, didn't give a crap about cleaning house, getting married, wearing make up. We both wanted to play
with guys, build forts and have snowball fights and play army. She'd
get a skipping rope for a gift, and the only thing we'd use that for was to
tie people up, whip people with it."[7] Brenda was sometimes more
interested in Brian's toys than he was. She was a good shot with his
pellet rifle, a gun to which he was himself indifferent, and she would
fight him over some of his other toys, usually winning. In their yearly
meetings with Money, Brian could describe the activity of playing
with dolls better than Brenda could. Indeed, Brian's aunt and uncle
claimed that when he was apart from Brenda he was a quiet and gentle
child, quite different from the rowdy Brenda. About her, relatives and
teachers claimed, "There was a rough-and-tumble rowdiness, an assertive, pressing dominance, and a complete lack of any demonstrable
feminine interests."[8] Sometimes, Brenda would try to be tidy, her
mother said, but for the most part, if she arrived at school, "very
clean and cutely dressed," she would be "grubby, fighting with kids
and playing in the dirt," within minutes.[9]

Brenda's behavior took its toll on the family. She was sent to
numerous psychologists and psychiatrists throughout her childhood
and adolescence; her father became an alcoholic and her mother

[5] *Ibid.*, p. 4.
[6] Diamond and Sigmundson, "Sex Reassignment at Birth," Web-based version.
[7] Colapinto, *As Nature Made Him*, p. 57.   [8] *Ibid.*, p. 61.   [9] *Ibid.*, p. 63.

suffered severe depressions, once attempting suicide. After years of turmoil, a final crisis began when Brenda refused to undergo a series of operations that were meant to construct a faux-vagina for her. Various psychiatrists entered the battle to support Money and Brenda's parents in their efforts to convince Brenda of the necessity of the operation but the standoff continued for four and a half years. Finally, faced with her complete intransigence, the Reimers gave up the fight and informed Brenda of the surgery and gender reassignment she had undergone as an infant. She/he immediately stopped the hormones that her parents had been requiring her to take and began taking testosterone instead. In 1980 she/he underwent a double mastectomy and later underwent various operations to begin building a penis. She/he took the name of David, married and adopted his new wife's children. In June of 2004, now separated from his wife and jobless, David Reimer killed himself.

David Reimer's case became public in an article and later a book by John Colapinto.[10] Colapinto also documented the role that the case had already had in scientific controversies over the question of the respective influences of biology and socialization in the development of gender traits and in the acquisition of a successful gender identity. These controversies continue. Nevertheless, despite their differences over the respective role of nature and nurture in gender identity, both sides in the David Reimer debate share important ideas about what it is to be a girl or a boy, about which traits reflect one's gender identity, and how they mark the success or failure of gender assignments. In this chapter, I want to explore these shared ideas to begin to assess the peculiarities of our identities and attributions as men and women.[11] The ideas contradict a number of legal decisions in the United States and other countries and these decisions also contradict one another. The question, then, is what gender identity is meant to be.

[10] "The True Story of John/Joan," *The Rolling Stone*, December 11, 1997, pp. 54–97 and Colapinto, *As Nature Made Him*.

[11] I make a great deal of use in what follows of John Colapinto's reconstruction of the case because I am interested in the way that it was popularly and culturally understood.

BRUCE/BRENDA/DAVID REIMER

The conclusions to which two psychiatrists involved in Brenda
Reimer's case, Milton Diamond and Keith Sigmundson, came are
diametrically opposed to the sanguine reports Money gave during the
length of Brenda's girlhood.[12] Sigmundson was the head of the psychiatry department in Brenda's hometown to which her case was
referred and Diamond was a consultant initially brought in by the
BBC for a documentary on the case. Whereas Money claimed that
Brenda had successfully taken up identity as a girl, both Diamond
and Sigmundson argued that she/he had not. Instead, they claimed
that David's original, biological sex continued to assert itself throughout his childhood and was the cause of his resistance to reassignment
efforts. Moreover, they argued that Money had miscalculated the
respective weights of biology and socialization. Neither sex nor gender
identity can be altered at will, they said. Rather, "The evidence seems
overwhelming that normal humans are not psychosexually neutral at
birth but are, in keeping with their mammalian heritage, predisposed
and biased to interact with environmental, familial and social forces
in either a male or a female mode."[13] In his popular history of David
Reimer's case, John Colapinto agrees. Brenda, he thinks, remained a
boy and his tragic childhood was simply a series of failed attempts to
brainwash him into believing he was a girl.[14]

What is the evidence to which Money points to proclaim the
success of the reassignment and what is the evidence to which
Colapinto, Diamond, and Sigmundson point prove its failure? What
is noteworthy here is that both sides have the same ideas about what
would constitute success and failure in sex and gender identity. That
is, despite their differences on what the appropriate weights are to
assign to biology and socialization, respectively, Money and his critics
agree in their accounts of what it is to be a boy or a girl and what

[12] Diamond and Sigmundson, "Sex Reassignment at Birth," Web-based version.
[13] Ibid. Also cited in Anne Fausto-Sterling, *Sexing the Body: Gender Politics and the
Construction of Sexuality* (New York: Basic Books, 2000), p. 70.
[14] Colapinto, *As Nature Made Him.*

evidence indicates which one is. Those who criticized Money asked the same questions about Brenda Reimer that Money himself asked and these questions concerned the roles Brenda adopted, her preferences, interests, behaviors and her probable sexual orientation.

Yet, suppose alien anthropologists dropped down from Mars to try to figure out what men and women are for Earthlings. I have in mind here the same sort of anthropologists who tried to figure out what *berdaches* are in Native American cultures.[15] What sorts of methods and evidence do they use to decide whether *berdaches* are homosexuals, sissies, or something else entirely? The early studies of *berdaches* that tried to equate them with homosexuals failed to notice that *berdaches* often had different sexual orientations: some were homosexual but others were bisexual and heterosexual. Likewise, the studies that called them "sissies" or men who had shown cowardice on the field of battle could not account for those who, although demoted from a warrior role, did not become *berdaches*. Nor could they make sense out of *berdaches* who were successful warriors.[16] Later studies also differentiate *berdache* status from a series of other identities: from transvestites, feminine men, masculine women, and "warrior" women who crossed gender boundaries (by fighting, for example) but who retained their original gender identity. In trying to understand identity as a *berdache*, then, anthropologists figure out how it works, what behaviors, attitudes, and activities are and are not characteristic of it, what aspects of life and culture contribute to it, and, in turn, how it fits in with life and culture.

Using the same procedures to understand status as a man or woman on Earth, alien anthropologists might have initially inferred from Bruce's surgery, name-change, and gendered upbringing that identity as a boy as a boy or girl on Earth depended on anatomy and, specifically, that it depended on the presence or absence of a

---

[15] See introduction, p. 9.
[16] Will Roscoe, "How to Become a Berdache: Toward a Unified Analysis of Gender Diversity," in Gilbert Herdt, ed., *Third Sex, Third Gender: Beyond Sexual Dimorphism in Culture and History* (New York: Zone Books, 1993), p. 336.

penis. Because Bruce lost his penis, he could not be a boy. Yet, if they had come to this conclusion, they would have been perplexed by the continuing questions that participants on both sides of the nature–nurture debate asked. For despite Brenda's lack of a penis, both sides in the debate appeared fixated on her roles, preferences, and interests. Why?

ROLES, PREFERENCES, INTERESTS, AND SEX AND GENDER IDENTITY

Colapinto insists that Brenda Reimer grew up in an atmosphere free of rigid views about gender roles.[17] Nevertheless, one of Mrs. Reimer's earliest interviews with Money emphasizes the feminine clothing in which she dressed her, "little pink slacks and frilly blouses." A year and a half later, Money writes, "the mother ... made a special effort at keeping her girl in dresses, almost exclusively."[18] Indeed, Brenda was required to wear dresses even in cold Winnipeg winters when other little girls were wearing warm pants. In a noteworthy incident, Brenda and her brother both wanted to pretend to shave with their father as he got ready for work but Brenda was told to go play with her mother's make-up instead.[19] In Diamond and Sigmundson's account of the incident, in which Joan is the pseudonym they use to protect Brenda Reimer's identity, the demand that she adhere to strict gender roles is explicit: "It was also more common that she, much more than the twin brother, would mimic Father," they write. "One incident Mother related was typical: When the twins were about 4 or 5 they were watching their parents. Father was shaving and Mother applying makeup. Joan applied shaving cream and pretended to shave. When Joan *was corrected and told* to put on lipstick and makeup like Mother, Joan said: "No, I don't want no makeup, I want to shave."[20]

---

[17] See Colapinto, *As Nature Made Him*, p. 250.
[18] Ehrhardt, *Man and Woman, Girl and Boy*, p. 119.
[19] Colapinto, *As Nature Made Him*, p. 56.
[20] Diamond and Sigmundson, "Sex Reassignment at Birth," Web-based version, emphasis added.

Colapinto's claims to the contrary, then, Brenda's parents seem to have thought that if Brenda were to be a girl she would need to take on certain, quite rigidly conceived roles in her make-believe play and, moreover, that she ought not to take on others. Moreover, Diamond and Sigmundson agree, although for them the incident is less about normative lessons than about empirical proof that the sex and gender reassignment had failed. Their point in retelling the shaving story is not to criticize the "correction" Brenda's parents made in her behavior but rather to emphasize that Brenda's mimicking of her father and reluctance to engage in play more appropriate to her putative gender meant that that gender was not hers. For Brenda's parents, identity as a girl requires that one plays in certain ways and not others; for Diamond and Sigmundson, identity as a girl means that one plays in certain ways and not others.

The same holds for the toys with which one plays. Money assured the scientific community that Brenda played with dolls; his adversaries insisted that she did not and stressed the fascination she had for Brian's toys, especially his gun. Despite their differences on the facts, both sides link identity as a girl to the same preferences: liking dolls and not liking guns. They differed only on the question of whether Brenda did or did not have the appropriate likes and dislikes. They same held for chores: Brenda's family and acquaintances found it telling that she showed no interest in cleaning house; Money found it equally telling that she told him that she loved "sewing, cleaning, dusting and doing dishes."[21] While Money's critics cited Brenda's failure to adopt certain interests and pursuits as proof of her inability to be a girl, Money pointed to the same evidence to show that she was adapting to her female identity well.

Neither Money nor his critics limit this link between interests and gender identity to David Reimer's case. In fact, despite their emphasis on the influence of post-natal upbringing on gender identity, Money and Ehrhardt are equally interested in the gender effects of

[21] Colapinto, *As Nature Made Him*, p. 81.

pre-natal hormones. In *Man and Woman, Boy and Girl*, they explore the behaviors of children who are being raised as girls but have been exposed to excessive amounts of fetal androgens, whether naturally or as a consequence of medication their mothers took to avoid miscarriage. When compared to girls who have not been exposed to these hormones *in utero*, Money and Ehrhardt find what they identify as significant forms of "tomboyish" behavior: including "vigorous activity, especially outdoors," a "perfunctory attitude toward motherhood and a lack of interest in either dolls or baby-sitting."[22] The suggestions here are that normal girls, meaning those not unduly affected by fetal androgens, are interested in children and that girls who are interested in outdoor pursuits or vigorous activities are interested in male behaviors. These suggestions do not rely on statistics that show that more girls than boys like children or that more men than women enjoy outdoor pursuits. Rather, children and outdoor pursuits are themselves gendered: interests in children are feminine interests and interests in the outdoors are masculine ones. If boys like children they are effeminate and if girls like the outdoors they are tomboys. These gender-crossing interests reflect the effects of pre-natal exposure to testosterone in the cases Money and Erhardt study and display the failure of Brenda's reassignment in the view of Money's critics. David Reimer agrees. Looking back at his childhood, he remarks: "I looked at myself and said I don't like this type of clothing, I don't like the types of toys I was always being given, I like hanging around with the guys and climbing trees and stuff like that and girls don't do any of that stuff."[23]

BEHAVIOR AND GENDER

In clarifying his decision to castrate Bruce and bring him up as a girl, Bruce's father said, "You know how little boys are. Who can pee the

---

[22] Ehrhardt, *Man and Woman, Boy and Girl*, pp. 10, 98–105. Also see, Anke Ehrhardt and Heinz F.L. Meyer-Bahlburg, "Effects of Pre-natal Sex Hormones on Gender-Related Behavior," *Science*, 211, 1981), pp. 1312–1318.

[23] Diamond and Sigmundson, "Sex Reassignment at Birth," Web-based version.

furthest? Whip out the wiener and whiz against the fence. Bruce wouldn't be able to do that, and the other kids would wonder why."[24] The ability to engage in peeing contests is apparently crucial enough to one's sex status and gender identity that not being able to engage in this behavior is a reason not to try to be a boy. Perhaps this association of gender and urination also explains the consternation caused by Brenda's attempts to urinate from a standing position. Money's critics take this behavior as unambiguous evidence that Brenda was unable to surrender her identity as a boy and even the guilt-ridden Mrs. Reimer complained about the additional toilet cleaning Brenda's attempts required.[25] Yet, after Bruce's castration, Brenda's urine flowed from her body at a 90-degree angle. Money himself admits that "because after surgery the girl's urethral opening was so positioned that urine sometimes would overshoot the seat of the toilet," Brenda needed "more training than usual" to urinate sitting down and that she had to use "slight pressure from the fingers" to "direct the urinary stream downwards."[26] Under these circumstances, one might think that standing to urinate would be at least as efficient as sitting. Indeed, one might think that Brenda's behavior was evidence less of her gender identity than of an admirable effort to find a plausible way of using the toilet given the problems with her redesigned anatomy. Nevertheless, neither side in the David Reimer debate interprets her behavior in this way; rather, all understand it as an aspect of her "real" sex and her "real" gender identity, whether they take that reality to be male or female. The same holds for the scrutiny of the way that Brenda walked and sat. Brian Reimer suggests that because Brenda sat with her legs apart, she was doing a "guy" thing.[27]

Other aspects of Brenda's behavior are also meant to count for or against her identity as a girl. Money often asked the Reimer twins who was the boss in their relationship. In one such interview Brian

[24] Colapinto, *As Nature Made Him*, p. 52. [25] *Ibid.*, p. 61.
[26] Ehrhardt, *Man and Woman, Boy and Girl*, p. 120.
[27] Colapinto, *As Nature Made Him*, p. 57.

demurred so Brenda challenged him, "Are you the boss … Do you want to be the boss? I don't think so. OK, *I'll* be the boss."[28] Colapinto cites this exchange as further proof that Brenda had a male gender identity and thinks further corroboration arises in the same interview when the twins talked about their fights. Money asked Brian if he fought with "other boys" and was told that he did not, that he fought only with girls. Indeed, both twins suggested that Brenda not only defended him when he got in trouble but could easily beat him up.[29] Money seemed delighted when the twins told him that Brenda threw like a girl but his own observation of her throwing motion disappointed him.[30] In reviewing the transcripts of these sessions Colapinto claims that Money wanted to hear certain answers and that Brenda sometimes obliged him by cataloging her performances of feminine behaviors. Nevertheless, Colapinto thinks that the answers are forced. Brenda was the boss in her relationship with Brian, she fought him and won, and she threw like a boy. If Money was privately disappointed with these behaviors, Colapinto takes them as firm indications of problems with Brenda's reassignment as a girl: "Brenda could not consciously articulate her feelings of not being a girl, but as Money's notes show, those feelings were clear in her interviews."[31]

SEXUALITY AND GENDER

Immediately after Bruce's initial circumcision accident the plastic surgeon at the hospital, Dr. Desmond Kernahan, told the Reimers that a penis constructed out of flesh from Bruce's thigh or abdomen would not be adequate. Although it would be able to pass urine, it would not resemble a "normal" organ "in color, texture or erectile capacity."[32] Dr. G. L. Adamson, the head of the Department of Neurology and Psychiatry at the Winnipeg clinic where Bruce's condition was evaluated, offered the following assessment of a life without treatment: "One can predict that he will be unable to live a normal

[28] *Ibid.*, p. 83.   [29] *Ibid.*, p. 84.   [30] *Ibid.*, p. 84.   [31] *Ibid.*, p. 81.   [32] *Ibid.*, p. 15.

sexual life from the time of adolescence: that he will be unable to consummate marriage or have normal heterosexual relations, in that he will have to recognize that he is incomplete, physically defective and that he must live apart."[33]

It is not clear how being unable to consummate marriage translates into a requirement that one "live apart." Nor is it clear what Adamson means by denying that Bruce would be able to engage in a "normal sexual life" or "normal heterosexual relations." Does he mean that only heterosexual relations are normal or that normal heterosexual relations and a normal sexual life would require functions that a reconstructed penis would not be able to perform? The former inference precludes normal homosexuals while the latter rather unimaginatively limits normal sexual life to the intercourse of penis and vagina. Nevertheless, whatever Adamson meant with his comment, some of Money's own remarks indicate that he agrees with the first inference. A successful gender identity or persistence of one's individuality as male or female requires a heterosexual choice of erotic objects. In *Man and Woman, Boy and Girl*, he writes that "A child upon whom a sex reassignment is imposed during this formative period [eighteen months to the ages of three or four] does not as a rule, fare well in psychosexual differentiation, and may never differentiate the appropriate new gender identity so as eventually to fall in love in agreement with it."[34] In reflecting upon his consultations with the Reimers he reaffirms this view: "The child was still young enough so that whichever assignment was made, erotic interest would almost certainly direct itself toward the opposite sex later on."[35]

Money's adversaries agree with this link between sexuality and gender identity. Indeed, if they needed any more proof of Brenda's failure to take on a female gender identity, they suggest that it exists in her discomfort around boys in romantic or sexual situations. Even as a teenager, she claimed that dancing or pairing off with boys never

---

[33] *Ibid.*, p. 15–6. [34] Ehrhardt, *Man and Woman, Boy and Girl*, p. 16.
[35] Colapinto, *As Nature Made Him*, p. 51.

felt right to her.[36] Colapinto also expresses doubt about the interpretation that Kenneth Zucker and his co-authors give of a case similar to David Reimer's. In this case, the child lost his penis in similar circumstances, in a botched circumcision using an electrocautery device, and, like David Reimer, he was castrated and brought up as a girl. Zucker interviewed "the patient" at the ages of sixteen and twenty-six and reported that she "was living socially as a woman. She denied any uncertainty about being female from as far back as she could remember and did not report any dysphoric feelings about being a woman."[37] At the same time, "she recalled that during childhood ... she self-identified as a 'tomboy' and enjoyed stereotypically masculine toys and games." She was also bisexual and was currently living with a woman. In addition, she worked in a blue-collar job. Colapinto insists that these admissions mean that "the case could not be deemed an unalloyed example of the efficacy of sex reassignment."[38]

IMPLICATIONS OF THE REIMER CASE

The psychologists who condemn David Reimer's castration and upbringing as a girl do so because his natural sex doomed him to

---

[36] *Ibid.*, pp. 126–127.

[37] S. J. Bradley, G. D. Oliver, A. B. Chernick, and K. J. Zucker, "Experiment of Nurture: ablatio penis at 2 months, Sex Reassignment at 7 months, and a Psychosexual Follow-up in Young Adulthood," *Pediatrics*, 102, July 10, 1998, Web version at http://pediatrics.aappublications.org/cgi/content.

[38] Colapinto, *As Nature Made Him*, pp. 250–251. Jeffrey Eugenides' novel, *Middlesex* (New York: Farrar, Stroud & Giroux, 2002) concurs with this link between a person's sex and gender and his or her sexuality. Eugenides' protagonist, Cal Stephanides, has a condition called 5-reductase deficiency in which infants with XY chromosomes are born looking like girls. At puberty, however, they develop male characteristics. Cal is attracted to girls when he still thinks of himself as a girl. He explains that this circumstance did not lead to any doubt on his part that he was a girl, since he thought he might just be a lesbian. Nevertheless when he learns of his condition he flees the genital surgery his parents plan for him and begins to live as a man, driven, he says, by "desire." Cal says he conforms to neither the nurture nor the nature side of the debate. He did not feel "out of place" as a girl; nor did he feel "entirely at home among men" (p. 479). Yet, because he was attracted to women, he decided to live as a man. With this decision, Eugenides expresses his agreement with the psychologists we have discussed in this chapter: somehow gender identity and sexuality are mixed up together so that desiring women is masculine and it is more natural to be a man desiring women than a woman desiring women.

failure in any attempt to develop the appropriate roles, interests, activities, and sexual orientations. If David's original doctors assumed that he could be a boy only if he had the anatomy to do particular things, their critics assumed that he could be a girl only if he had the desire to do particular things. Because Bruce could not successfully perform a few of the activities, both sexual and non-sexual, that boys are supposed to be able to perform, the proponents of his castration denied that he could really be a boy. Although Brenda had the reconstructed anatomy associated with being a girl, because she did not have the interests, activities, and sexual orientation that girls are supposed to have, the critics of her castration denied that she could really be a girl.

Yet, when we follow the suggestions of the participants on either side of the David Reimer controversy we find that, despite their differences, they share identical conceptions of what girls, boys, men, and women are. The possession of a specific sex and a specific gender is not simply a question of anatomy but also involves differentiated sets of roles, preferences, interests, and behaviors as well as heterosexual orientations. For all those involved in the Reimer case, identity as a girl or woman requires that one be sexually attracted to men; play a submissive role in relation to them; possess interests in activities such as house-cleaning, playing with dolls, and getting married; and have a quiet and peaceful demeanor.[39] For its part, identity as a boy and man requires that one be sexually attracted to women; indeed, one cannot really be a man unless one can penetrate a vagina with an attached penis and has an interest in doing so. In addition, one must take the lead in social interactions with girls and

---

[39] Here those commenting on David Reimer's case echo medical practitioners at the end of the nineteenth century who tried to diagnose the "true" sex of hermaphrodites by taking into account both gonadal tissue if they could find it and "the general signs offered by the subject, like the hair, beard, breasts, the development of the hips, the voice, the instincts etc." Nor should one be fooled by female dress if a hermaphrodite "had the whole allure, the unself-consciousness of a man in his gaze, his gestures, and his walk." See Alice Domurat Dreger, *Hermaphrodites and the Medical Invention of Sex* (Cambridge, MA.: Harvard University Press, 1998), p. 88.

women, enjoy rough-housing and violent play, sit with one's legs apart and urinate from a standing position.

Of course, the interests and activities with which both sides in the debate define the female sex and gender are spectacularly dreary. Yet, if we return to our Martian anthropologists, we can expect them to decide that, on Earth, being a man or a woman is a matter of the right anatomy coordinated with the right set of attitudes, behaviors, and sexual desires. Nevertheless, we can also expect them to be perplexed by at least two asymmetries in attributions of masculine and feminine identity. In the first place, suppose that the twins had been born with clitorises instead of penises and suppose that one of these clitorises had been accidentally destroyed. This accident surely would not have led doctors to suppose that the infant should not be brought up as a girl. Indeed, some cultures require just this procedure in order for girls to attain the status of "real" women. Why, then, is a penis crucial to identity as a man, although a clitoris is not crucial to identity as a woman and in some cultures even precludes it?

In the second place, all the participants in the debate scrutinize Brenda's roles, interests, behaviors, and probable sexual orientation and all ask whether these attributes reflect the success or failure of her female sex and gender assignment. Yet, not one participant asks whether Brian's interests, behaviors, and probable sexual orientation reflect a successful or failed male sex and gender assignment. Although Brenda's doctors worried that she did not play with dolls, they did not worry that Brian knew more about them and although they were concerned about Brenda's rough play, they did not mind that Brian was mild-mannered. Nor did they even seem to mind that he liked to fight mostly with girls. Money reports an incident in which the twins asked their mother what her breasts were for. When she replied that they were for feeding babies, Brian said that "he wanted to be a mommy."[40] Yet, even this statement seems to have caused no

[40] Ehrhardt, *Man and Woman, Girl and Boy*, p. 120.

concerns about Brian's sex and gender identity. Why the discrepancy? Why was the success of Brenda's sex and gender assignment so closely tied to her capacities, interests, and proclivities when the success of Brian's was not?

How might the alien anthropologists attempt to integrate these asymmetries in their understanding of what men and women are? They might try to resolve the first asymmetry by deciding that on Earth it is one's role in reproductive sexual intercourse that is the most crucial factor in identity as a man or woman. For men, sexual intercourse involves the capacity for penile penetration. Penises are therefore necessary to status as a man because a man must be able to penetrate a vagina. But, for women, reproductive sexual intercourse does not have the same relation to a clitoris. Clitorises are not required to be a woman because, even if they are important for the enjoyment of sexual penetration, they are not needed for the penetration itself. Bruce, then, could not remain a boy because he could not penetrate a vagina without a penis whereas if an infant girl were to suffer a botched clitorodectomy, with doctors taking off more than they meant to, she could nonetheless remain a girl. Our alien anthropologists might resolve the second asymmetry in the sex assignments and gender attributions of Brenda and Brian by supposing that one's identity as a girl or boy allows for some leeway in the closeness of one's identification with gendered activities, behaviors, interests, and sexual orientations as long as no anomalies have entered into one's birth or upbringing. If one was not exposed to too much of the "wrong" hormone *in utero* or if one has a recognizably male or female anatomy and has had it from birth, then, to a certain extent, one can act against sex and gender type. Thus, Brian's failure to take up certain activities and interests was not a worry because he possessed a recognizable and standard male anatomy and had possessed it from birth. Conversely, because Brenda Reimer did not begin life with a standard female anatomy, her failure to develop certain interests and behaviors or a heterosexual orientation raised the fear that she could not really be a girl.

This reading of the status of being a girl or a boy would allow the alien anthropologists to integrate another incident into their analysis, one occurring among members of San Francisco's transgendered community. Matt Califia-Rice was born and brought up as a girl. In his twenties, however, he sought to move from a female assignment to a male one and began to take testosterone. Shortly thereafter he had his breasts removed. He also began to live with a former lover who had also been born and raised as a girl and was now also living as a man, taking testosterone and contemplating chest surgery. Reconstituted as a couple, the two now wanted a baby. Since Califia-Rice's partner had already had a hysterectomy for health reasons, Califia-Rice himself decided to become pregnant. He stopped taking testosterone and had himself impregnated. He and his partner, both living as men, one of whom was now pregnant, resided in San Francisco. Yet, "within that world they were a scandal ... Real men," one transgendered male said, "don't have babies."[41]

The connection of sex and gender with interests and activities means that certain interests and activities pursued by the wrong sex and gender necessarily raise concerns. Hence, if one has changed one's identity from that of a woman to that of a man, one simply ought not to perform certain actions, even if one's body is capable of performing them and even if one wants to perform them. The transgendered community includes those who have had sex reassignment surgery, those who are contemplating some part of it, and those who plan to remain pre-operative. Some in the transgendered community "take hormones to change their secondary sex characteristics; some do not; many dress and live as close to the traditional definition of male and female as possible; others are androgynous."[42] In this community, then, anatomy is of less interest than it was for Bruce Reimer's original doctors. Moreover, differences in life-styles, interests, and activities are met with more tolerance. Nevertheless, even within this

---

[41] Mary McNamara, "Era of the Gender Crosser," *Los Angeles Times*, February 27, 2001, Section A, p. 20.
[42] *Ibid.*, p. 20.

community, tolerance does not always extend to men who have babies. If one intends to bear a child and one has not been a man since birth, then one should not claim to be a man now. The trans-gendered community does not ask for commitment to all the activities or aspects of anatomy of one sex assignment or gender identity: one can evidently decide whether or not to have breasts. Still, if one is to be a man refraining from certain other activities, such as child-bearing, appear to be *de rigueur*.

HOW TO READ SEX AND GENDER IDENTITY

On one reading, status as a girl is more tightly woven with a specific complex of interests and proclivities than status as a boy. Brian Reimer was a quiet, gentle child who disliked fighting except with girls. While he therefore seemed to deviate from some of the activities normative for the male gender, his gender status was not at risk. In contrast, because Brenda was rowdy, assertive, and dominant, her status as a girl was at risk. Men can be men, it seems, however they act. Women can be women only if they act in an appropriate way. But if status as a girl is more tightly woven with interests and proclivities than status as a boy, the latter is more tightly woven with appendages and capacities. Because Bruce could not successfully perform the activities, both sexual and non-sexual, that boys are supposed to be able to perform, he could not be a boy. Indeed, although one can retain one's status as a girl even if one loses one's clitoris, one cannot remain a boy if one loses one's penis. Likewise, one cannot retain one's status as a man if one is pregnant although one can remain a woman if one is not.

How, then, might our alien anthropologists articulate an understanding of sex and gender that takes account of these differences? They might decide that a certain complex of appendages, interests, activities, and proclivities is especially mandatory when it is necessary for heterosexual intercourse and when an anatomy has been re-manufactured after birth. Hence, because a penis is necessary to vaginal penetration whereas a clitoris is not, the lack of a penis has a greater impact on male sex and gender status than the lack of a clitoris does on female sex and gender status. Moreover, because Brian retained the sex and gender assignment he had received at birth, his failure to conform completely to gender norms could escape scrutiny, whereas because Brenda's sex and gender had been reassigned she could not. Similarly, because Matt Califia-Rice was not born with the anatomy of a man, his attention to gender norms had to be especially scrupulous and his waywardness in seeking to bear a child placed his sex reassignment and gender re-identity at risk.

Nevertheless, the anthropologists who offered this account of sex and gender attributions and identities would find themselves stymied by legal decisions in various American states and in a variety of foreign countries. Take two somewhat recent cases. In *Littleton* v. *Prange,* the Fourth Circuit Court of Appeals in Texas ruled against Christie Littleton in her suit against her late husband's physician for the medical treatment that she claimed led to his death.[43] Christie Littleton was once a man but received sex reassignment surgery prior to her marriage. Her husband, Jonathan Littleton, was aware of the surgery. Nor did the lawsuit reveal other troubles within the marriage; it lasted seven years until Jonathan Littleton's death. Christie Littleton was heterosexual according to the standards of her new anatomy and there was no reason to think that she did not embrace the roles, behaviors, and interests linked to it. Yet, the court ruled that she could not recover damages for the wrongful death of her husband because her marriage to him violated the Texas Family Code prohibiting same-sex unions. "Biologically," the court wrote, "a post-operative female transsexual is still a male." The Littleton marriage was thus a marriage between two men and had never been legal.

In a subsequent case, a Kansas court came to the same conclusion. In this instance, another "post-operative female transsexual," J'Noel Ball, tried to defend her right to inherit from the estate of her deceased husband, Marshall Gardiner. The Kansas Supreme Court, however, denied that the marriage was legal because, despite her

---

[43] *Littleton* v. *Prange* 9 SW 3d 223.

sex-reassignment surgery, J'Noel was not a woman. 'The words "sex,' "male" and "female" in everyday understanding do not encompass transsexuals. The plain, ordinary meaning of 'persons of the opposite sex' contemplates a biological man and a biological woman and not persons who are experiencing gender dysphoria."[44]

What are our alien anthropologists to make of these two cases? The difficulty they might have in integrating them into their overall account of sex and gender identities is that both diverge from the ideas that they might have elicited from the David Reimer and Matt Califia-Rice cases. Christie Littleton and J'Noel Ball both had re-manufactured anatomies and therefore, according to the account of male and female status we have constructed, they would have had to adhere carefully to the demands of their new identity. In contrast to David Reimer and Matt Califia-Rice, however, there is no evidence that they did not do so; they both married men and seemed to have helped to make their marriages a success. Nevertheless, neither was accorded the status of women by the courts. Why not? In its presentation of the *Littleton* case, the Texas court asked, "Can a physician change the gender of a person with a scalpel, drugs and counseling, or is a person's gender immutably fixed by our Creator at birth?"[45] The question was rhetorical for the court had no hesitation in picking the second option: one's identity as a man or woman is determined by a person's chromosomes and therefore remains indifferent to the results of any genital reconstructive surgery. Yet, if chromosomes determine gender status, this finding undermines the basis for just the sort of surgery that David Reimer had as an infant. Indeed, if we were to follow the Kansas and Texas courts, the Reimers' attempt to make up for Bruce's circumcision accident would have been legally doomed from the start. He could never have been made into a girl because his chromosomes dictated that legally he would always be a boy.

Operations that medical practitioners often perform on inter-sexed infants also fail to adhere to the logic of the Texas and Kansas

---

[44] *In re Estate of Marshall G. Gardner* 273 Kan. 191; 2002.
[45] *Littleton* v. *Prange*, pp. 230–231.

courts.[46] Instances of intersexuality include Congenital Adrenal Hyperplasia (CAH), in which infants are born with what appear to be either very small penises or large clitorises;[47] Turner Syndrome, in which individuals possess female genitalia but unformed gonads;[48] 5-alpha-reductase deficiency, in which infants are born with what appear to be mostly female characteristics but during adolescence develop male external genitalia, deep voices and hair according to "male" patterns;[49] and Klinefelder Syndrome, in which gonads do not develop "properly."[50] Infants can also be born with hypospadias, in which the urethral opening is not at the tip of the penis.[51] In other cases clitorises may be considered too large (over 0.9 cm) while penises may sometimes be seen as too small (under 2.5 cm). While some pediatricians and intersexuals criticize surgical interventions on infants, in its 2000 report, the American Academy of Pediatrics (AAP) continued to recommend them.[52] The point of such surgeries is to fashion anatomies that would conform to prevailing norms for male and female genital appearances and allow for standard male and female activities. Part of the rationale for this kind of surgery is to help parents: if they are not to be ambivalent in helping their children acquire an appropriate gender identity they need to be comfortable with their genital appearance and the supposition is that they can be comfortable only if that appearance falls within standard parameters. Hence, operations on infants with large clitorises reduce them; operations on infants with hypospadias draw skin from other parts of the body to create tubes so that the children can urinate standing up; and infants with micropenises are sometimes castrated and brought up as

[46] See New York Times, September 19, 2004.
[47] See Anne Fausto-Sterling, Sexing the Body, p. 52.
[48] Fausto-Sterling, Sexing the Body, p. 52.
[49] Fausto-Sterling, Sexing the Body, p. 109.
[50] Fausto-Sterling, Sexing the Body, p. 52.
[51] Domurat Dreger, Hermaphrodites, p. 39. Also, see Geoffrey Cowley, "Gender Limbo," Newsweek, May 19, 1997, pp. 64–67 on the case of Heidi, an infant with one X and one Y chromosome and a small penis with the urethral opening at the base. S/he was castrated and brought up as a girl.
[52] See Committee on Genetics, "Evaluation of the Newborn With Developmental Anomalies of the External Genitalia," Pediatrics, 106, 2000, pp. 138–142.

girls since their original penises are thought too small to allow for vaginal penetration.[53] Since surgeons often assign the sex that is most likely to result in a successful surgery,[54] and since it is easier to create a vagina than a penis, most intersexed infants end up as girls.[55]

On the one hand, these cases seem to re-confirm the standards for sex assignment and gender rearing that we expected our alien anthropologists would infer from Bruce Reimer's reassignment as Brenda. One condition for being a boy is being able to urinate standing up. Accordingly, if one is born with hypospadias either one's urethra must be refashioned so that one can do so or one must be brought up as a girl. Similarly, one condition for being a girl is appropriately delicate genitalia (or, in some cultures, none at all). Consequently, if one is born with a clitoris that is too large, it must be reduced so that one's status as a girl cannot be questioned. Although assessments of the success of operations are mixed, it is clear that they can lead to less than perfect results, as well as to losses of sensation, painful scarring, repeated infections, and the need for new operations or constant vaginal dilations.[56] One study found a failure rate of 64 percent in

---

[53] Suzanne J. Kessler, *Lessons from the Intersexed* (New Brunswick, NJ: Rutgers University Press, 1998), pp. 41–43. Also see Domurat Dreger, *Hermaphrodites*, p. 195 and Julie A. Greenberg, "Defining Male and Female: Intersexuality and the Collision between Law and Biology," *Arizona Law Review*, 41, 1999, p. 272. In one case, a surgeon decided against cutting off a micropenis, despite thinking that it was too small for reproductive purposes, because it was so "well formed" (Fausto-Sterling, *Sexing the Body*, p. 59).

[54] Kessler, *Lessons from the Intersexed*, p. 25.

[55] In Diamond and Sigmunson, "Sex Reassignment at Birth," Web-based version), Milton Diamond cites two pieces of clinical advice. "Because it simpler to construct a vagina than a satisfactory penis, only the infant with a phallus of adequate size should be considered for a male gender assignment" (from J. W. Duckett and L. S. Baskin, "Genitoplasty for Intersex Anomalies," *European Journal of Pediatrics*, 152, 1993 Suppl. 2, p. 580). "It is easier to make a good vagina than a good penis and since ... the absence of an adequate penis would be psychosexually devastating, fashion the perineum into normal looking vulva and vagina and raise the individual as a girl." As at least one surgeon has also remarked, "You can make a hole but you can't build a pole" (Fausto-Sterling, *Sexing the Body*, p. 59).

[56] See Kessler, *Lessons from the Intersexed*, pp. 53–64, for an out-and-out condemnation of the operations. Another assessment is more mixed. See Claude J. Migeon *et al.*, "Ambiguous Genitalia with Perineoscrotal Hypospadias in 46, XY Individuals: Long-Term Medical, Surgical, and Psychosexual Outcome," *Pediatrics*, 110 (3), 2002, www.pediatrics.org/cgi/content/full/110/3/c31.

attempts to repair hypospadias.[57] Nonetheless, because identity as a boy or girl, woman or man depends upon a set of capacities, activities, and proclivities, the AAP continues to see intersexed conditions as "social emergencies"[58] and recommends operations to correct them.

Results of clitoral surgery are mixed. For example, preservation of nerve conduction in the neurovascular bundle of the phallus was reported after excision of the corporeal bodies in infants with ambiguous genitalia, although long-term sexual function remains to be investigated in these patients. A second article reported an excellent cosmetic and functional outcome after clitoral recession; however, an unwanted outcome of clitoral necrosis can occur. When cosmetic outcomes of several types of clitoral surgeries were considered together (recession, reduction, and amputation), the post-surgical appearance of the genitalia were considered to be poor by Creighton et al.: The young age of some of the participants in these studies makes it difficult to interpret the functional significance of the findings. In addition, some of the above-mentioned studies used measures of cosmetic outcome that were determined by the investigators, not by the patients themselves.

Follow-up studies of vaginoplasty are also limited in number. A large study was conducted in women with müllerian agenesis or Mayer–Rokitansky–Küster–Hauser syndrome (also referred to as Rokitansky syndrome) by Rock et al.: In this group of patients, the McIndoe vaginoplasty procedure was rated to be successful in terms of post-surgical vaginal depth for sexual activity by all women. Women who had CAH as a result of 21-hydroxylase deficiency and underwent a McIndoe procedure reported a lower success rate (62 percent) in terms of comfortable penovaginal intercourse. Outcome studies of the McIndoe procedure in women with complete androgen insensitivity syndrome reported satisfactory intercourse postoperatively in 72 percent of patients and orgasm in 78 percent. In a similar group of patients with complete androgen insensitivity syndrome, good sexual function in terms of patients' satisfaction with their genitalia (78 percent), satisfactory libido (71 percent), and orgasm (77 percent) were reported by study participants. Creighton et al. reported the results of several vaginoplasty procedures in girls and young women who were affected by a variety of urogenital abnormalities resulting in ambiguous genitalia. In these patients, the vaginal introitus was absent or small in 82 percent, vaginal length was inadequate in 27 percent, and additional vaginal procedures were required in 75 percent.

Investigations of masculinizing surgeries, like feminizing surgeries, in 46,XY intersex individuals with perineoscrotal hypospadias are limited. The only study to have evaluated exclusively the surgical outcome of the most severe cases of hypospadias reported on nineteen men, approximately half of whom experienced difficulties with micturition, urologic function, and ejaculation. Roughly one-third of patients were affected by marked impairment in quality of life resulting from their ambiguous genitalia, ranging from mild depression to severe psychiatric impairment. Another follow-up assessment of hypospadias repair in adults included eight men with perineoscrotal hypospadias. In all cases, multiple hypospadias repairs were attempted with a post-operative complication rate of 64 percent. Repeated surgical procedures and complications are of particular concern because of scarring and loss of tissue associated with each surgery, as well as the presumed negative impact on sexual function.

[57] See Migeon et al. "Ambiguous Genitalia," p. e31.
[58] Committee on Genetics, "Evaluation of the Newborn," p. 138.

Ironically, however, if we follow the Kansas and Texas courts only those surgeries that align the female sex with two X chromosomes and those that align the male sex with an X and a Y chromosome will pass muster for one's legal identity. In states and countries with rules similar to those of Kansas and Texas, when surgically treated intersexuals become adults, they will be able to select as marriage partners only those individuals whose chromosomes do not match their own, regardless of their reconstructed anatomies or the gender in which they have been raised. In some cases, then, if they are to marry at all, they will have to marry those whose chromosomes differ but whose genitalia and gender identity match their own. Given the Texas and Kansas marriage codes, which explicitly preclude gay and lesbian marriages, this result seems somewhat bizarre. Then again, it is surely a welcome turn of events for those couples who may have been barred from marrying each other because of their anatomies and should now be able to marry because of their chromosomes.[59]

And what of another "condition?" Androgen Insensitivity Syndrome (AIS) is a condition in which individuals possess one X and one Y chromosome but are born with female-like genitalia and at puberty develop breasts because their bodies cannot "read" or process the testosterone in their bodies. According to Natalie Angier, such individuals are often models since their androgen insensitivity gives them a tall stature, large breasts, and beautiful hair and skin. Indeed, she refers to them as *"mama mia"* women.[60] If this is so, a

---

[59] Since the Fourth District's ruling in the *Littleton* case, Bexar County has legitimated at least two such marriages, over public protest. (See John Gutierrez-Mier, "Two More Women Obtain County Marriage License," *San Antonio Express News*, September 21, 2000.) Greenberg notes three more such marriages in Oregon, Ohio and England in which women were allowed to marry male-to-female transsexuals because the latter are still legally men. (Greenberg, "Defining Male and Female," p. 268.)

[60] Natalie Angier, *Woman: An Intimate Geography* (New York: Anchor Books Edn., 2000), p. 34.

chromosomal criterion for status as a woman will not only undermine the legal point of some surgeries on so-called intersexuals; it may also prevent certain Kansas and Texas men from marrying the super-models of their dreams.

When we follow the medical profession through its examination of Brenda Reimer and its operations on intersexed infants, we learn to understand sex and gender assignments in connection with a more or less tightly woven complex of anatomy, roles, behaviors, interests, and sexual orientation. Intersexuality and accidental cas-trations can be corrected by surgeries that align anatomy with rec-ognizably male and female forms together with psychosexual counseling that helps develop the roles and gender identity appropri-ate to one of two strictly delineated kinds of bodies. Something similar holds for "gender dysphoria"; it can be "cured" by creating an anatomy to fit the individual's sense of his or her sex and gender. When we follow Texas and Kansas state law, in contrast, we learn that intersexuality, accidental castrations, and gender dysphoria cannot be cured in this way because one remains what one's chromo-somes are no matter who one thinks one is, what one is capable of, or what one likes to do. Suppose, then, that David Reimer had complied with his surgeons and psychologists in adapting to the female gender roles and behavior they wanted for him. Brenda Reimer would have been unable to marry a man in Kansas, Texas, or a set of other countries and American states. Nor would the ambiguities of her legal status have been limited to marriage. It is not clear that Brenda would have been able to claim sex discrimina-tion in employment in the United States if she were discriminated against as a woman. Instead, courts might have concluded that although she was discriminated against as a woman, since chromo-somally he was a man, Title VII did not apply. And what about certain insurance benefits, the right to be incarcerated with members of one's own sex, and the requirement that men register for the draft? Should AIS supermodels register for the draft? Should they be incar-cerated with men?

The Kansas and Texas decisions on marriage followed similar rulings in New York and Ohio, both of which at least sometimes tie sex to chromosomes at birth. New Jersey, on the other hand, looks to what it terms psychological sex.[61] In the case of *M. T.* v. *J. T*, the New Jersey court ruled that "For marital purposes, if the anatomical or genital features of a genuine transsexual are made to conform to the person's gender, psyche or psychological sex, then identity by sex must be governed by the congruence of these standards."[62] As the Kansas Supreme Court itself conceded, England and Australia have also decided transsexual marriage cases in terms of a harmonization of body sex and psychological gender.

Courts are not only divided on what counts as male and female for the purposes of marriage. They are also divided on the issue with regard to other questions. For instance, Ohio and Oregon deny transsexuals a right to change their sex designation on their birth certificates while for the past twenty-five years New York City has allowed them to do so if they have had sex-reassignment surgery.[63] Likewise, the United States allows transsexuals to change their sex designations on their passports on the condition that they provide proof that they have undergone or are about to undergo sex-reassignment surgery.[64] In 1977, the United States Tennis Association (USTA) sought to prevent Renée Richards, a male-to-female transsexual, from competing in the United States Open Tennis Tournament as a woman. Using the Barr chromosome test, the USTA claimed that Richards remained a man and therefore could not compete in the women's division. Richards sued and the New

---

[61] See Greenberg, "Defining Male and Female," pp. 301–302.

[62] *M. T.* v. *J. T.* 140 NJ Super 77 (1976).

[63] In December 2006, the New York City Board of Health unanimously rejected a recommendation to allow transsexuals to change their sex designation on their birth certificates with or without sex-reassignment surgery. (See Damien Cave, "New York Plans to Make Gender Personal Choice," *New York Times*, November 7, 2006, pp. A1, A21.)

[64] See Greenberg, "Defining Male and Female," p. 315.

York Supreme Court found in her favor, ruling Richards a woman for the purposes of tennis competition. "The requirement," the court said, "that this plaintiff pass the Barr body test in order to be eligible to participate in the women's singles of the United States Open is grossly unfair, discriminatory and inequitable, and violative of her rights under the Human Rights Law of this State."[65] Nevertheless, in the 1988 Olympics, officials from the International Olympics Committee (IOC), conducting similar Barr tests on athletes on the various women's teams, disqualified Maria Martinez Patiño, a member of the Spanish women's hurdling team. Although Martinez Patiño had always considered herself a female, a cotton swab of material from the inside of her cheek found that she possessed XY chromosomes. Further examination found testes hidden by her labia and neither a uterus nor ovaries. Consequently, Olympic officials declared her a man, barred her from the women's competition and stripped her of all her previous medals.[66] Martinez Patiño went to court in Spain and eventually, after two years of inactivity in which she lost her national scholarship, her athletic residence, her coach and her boyfriend, the IOC reinstated her status as a woman, apparently on the basis of her shoulder structure.[67] Shoulder structure does not seem to be a widespread measure of female status but, then again, no measure appears to have general clout. Instead, as this review of cases and decisions indicates, medical and legal professions disagree with one another, the courts of different states and countries disagree, and different parts of the medical profession make different decisions about sex and gender identity. We can chart these disagreements:

[65] *Richards* v. *United States Tennis Association* 93 misc. 2d 713 (1977).
[66] See Susan K. Cahn, *Coming on Strong: Gender and Sexuality in Twentieth Century Women's Sport* (Cambridge, MA: Harvard University Press, 1994), p. 264 and Colette Dowling, *The Frailty Myth: Women Approaching Physical Equality* (New York: Random House, 2000), pp. 176–178.
[67] Fausto-Sterling, *Sexing the Body*, pp. 1–2.

Candidates for female status	XX chromo-somes	Anatomy without a penis	Female interests, behaviors, and roles	Heterosexual orientation as measured by anatomy	Final status
Name					
Bruce	No	Yes	No	No	Woman
Brenda	No	Yes	No	No	Man
Brian	No	No	Yes	Yes	Man
Second Money patient	No	Yes	No	No	Alloyed woman
Littleton	No	Yes	Yes	Yes	Man
Ball	No	Yes	Yes	Yes	Man
Martinez Patiño	No	Yes	No	Unknown	Man (first IOC)
	No	Yes	No	Unknown	Woman (Spanish court and second IOC)
Richards	No	Yes	No	Yes	Woman
AIS model	No	Yes	Yes	Yes	Woman

GENDER IDENTITY AND ALIEN ANTHROPOLOGY

Were alien anthropologists to focus on the operations performed on Bruce Reimer, they might assume that one's identity as a human boy or girl, man or woman depends on one's anatomy. If one has a penis, one is a boy or man and if one does not have one, one is a girl or woman. Since Bruce Reimer did not have a penis he could not be a boy. Yet, were the anthropologists then to look at psychological assessments of Brenda Reimer, they might come to think that one's identity as a girl or boy also involves one's interests and activities. Since Brenda did not have the correct interests and behavior, she could not be a girl. One must have not only the right anatomy but the right interests, desires, and behaviors as well. Since Bruce had the wrong anatomy for his interests and Brenda the wrong interests for her anatomy, alien anthropologists might assume that David eventually corrected the problem by manufacturing a penis. If so, however, they would be confused by the sex and gender identity that courts assigned to J'Noel Ball and Christine Littleton since both also aligned their anatomies with their interests and behavior. While David Reimer was accepted as a man, neither Ball nor Littleton was legally recognized as a woman. The anthropologists might then move on to a chromosomal criterion: David Reimer was a man because of his chromosomes; Ball and Littleton were also men because of their chromosomes. Nevertheless, this conclusion would raise the question of what doctors thought they were doing when they first operated on Bruce Reimer and it would also fly in the face of common perceptions of AIS women.

Alien anthropologists would also remain confused by the differences in the assumptions behind psychological skepticism about Brenda Reimer's femininity, the USTA's decision on Renée Richards, and the IOC's decision on Martinez Patiño. To the extent that the female sex and gender are identified with such activities as cleaning house, we can assume that Olympic athletes will fail to conform. Indeed, Colette Dowling argues that the lack of conformity is the real motivation behind sex testing of female athletes. It is not what it is advertised to be: namely, to prevent genetic males from cheating by joining female sports teams and thereby skewing the competitions in their favor.[68] When a genetic male did try to cheat in this way on behalf of Germany in the 1936 Olympics, three women beat him.[69] When Helene Mayer won the US national fencing title in

[68] Dowling, *The Frailty Myth*, p. 175.
[69] Fausto-Sterling, *Sexing the Body*, p. 2. Hermann Ratgent was bitter about the experience: "For three years I lived the life of a girl. It was most dull," (Dowling, *The Frailty Myth*, p. 178).

1938, the governing body of the sport banned competition between men and women and revoked Mayer's title.[70] When Zhang Shan won a mixed shooting event in 1992, the Olympic committee decided to divide the event into separate male and female competitions for the next Olympics, thereby guaranteeing that no woman could beat a man again.[71] Accordingly, Dowling suggests that the point of the sex testing refers back to conceptions of sex and gender. Because an interest in exercise and competition is considered a male interest, athletic women seem so anomalous that they must prove that they really are women.[72] Genetic testing in sports thus reflects the same assumptions that lead Colapinto to question the gender of a woman who has a blue-collar job. Although Martinez Patiño and Richards ultimately won the right to be labeled as women at least for athletic purposes, Brenda's similar inability to conform to the interests and behaviors of girls meant that she could not really be one.

For his part, Brian Reimer is a boy because he possesses male chromosomes, a male anatomy, and a heterosexual orientation although, like Brenda, he lacks the interests, behaviors, and roles suitable for the status attributed to him. Our anthropologists might think, then, that a heterosexual orientation, as measured by one's anatomy and "confirmed" by one's chromosomes, is the key to sex and gender. In other words, if one lacks a penis, possesses two X chromosomes, and is attracted to those with a penis, one counts as a woman. Yet, this solution excludes Money's unnamed second patient and all lesbians who cannot count as women under the definition. If the anthropologists were to drop the requirement of a heterosexual orientation, they could include lesbians but would still have to exclude Christie Littleton and J'Noel Ball as well as every XY supermodel. If they were to drop the chromosomal requirement, they could

---

[70] See Cahn, *Coming on Strong*, p. 210.   [71] See Dowling, *The Frailty Myth*, p. 193.

[72] *Ibid.*, pp. 179–180, Fausto-Sterling, *Sexing the Body*, p. 3. Dowling quotes Laura Wakwitz: "Sex testing is not an issue of how tall a woman is or what percentage of her mass is composed of muscle; it is an attempt to maintain control over women who challenge the expectations of femininity by entering a stereotypically defined 'male' arena" (*The Frailty Myth*, pp. 179–180).

include Littleton, Ball, and XY supermodels within the female gender, but might have to exclude Brian Reimer from the male one.

To be sure, it may seem more than a little hyperbolic for alien anthropologists to highlight such irregularities in our sex and gender identifications. After all, the irregularities refer to comparatively rare cases of ablated penises, intersexuality, and voluntary changes in sex and gender assignment. We might therefore try to allay the confusions of our anthropologists by assuring them that the cases causing their perplexity are few in number and constitute gray areas in otherwise clear conceptions. Indeed, we could assure them that the gray areas in our sex and gender attributions and identities are really no different than similar gray areas in our other attributions and identities. It may not always be clear, for example, who is to count as a genius. While some investigators may consider a numerical score on an IQ test sufficient for determining whether or not someone is a genius, other observers might want to look at other indices, such as performances and accomplishments, and still others might find IQ tests completely irrelevant. Moreover, those who agree that a certain score on an IQ test indicates status as a genius might disagree about whether to attribute the status of genius to those who score just under it. Yet neither this imprecision in the conception of a genius nor possible disagreements at its edges affects our ability to employ the designation in most cases. Similarly, it is a mistake to think that we need to agree on completely clear standards or a set of necessary and sufficient conditions for identity as a man or a woman. The line between identity as a genius and identity as a non-genius is often vague. Different people will draw it at different points for different purposes and most will allow for ambiguous cases. The same arguably holds for those on the edges of our sex and gender categories. Hence, while our alien anthropologists might be unclear about the boundaries of the set of men and the set of women, we could reassure them to be comfortable with their understanding of its center.

Yet, while our reassurances are surely relevant to the question of sex and gender identities, our anthropologists might not be satisfied.

In the first place, they might wonder how infrequent cases of penis ablation, ambiguous genitalia, or transsexuality really are. It is difficult to calculate cases of intersexuality in part for the reason we have been looking at: namely, what constitutes unambiguous identity as a girl or boy is unclear and medical professionals can therefore differ in what they take intersexuality to be. Indeed, some doctors count only cases in which infants are born with ambiguous genitalia whereas others include cases of odd sorts of hair growth and male pattern baldness in women.[73] All researchers seem to agree, however, that cases of intersexuality are more numerous than those outside the medical profession assume, perhaps as high as 4 percent of the world's population.[74] The same ambiguity surrounds identifications of transsexuality: transsexuals, medical professionals, and legal and political authorities may all define it quite differently, depending on whether they think surgery is necessary to secure status as a man or woman and, if it is, what sort is necessary and to what extent.

In the second place, the anthropologists might point out that identities as geniuses and identities as women or men behave quite differently. Identities and identifications as geniuses do not come with expectations about behaviors, roles, preferences, and sexual interest whereas identities and identifications as men and women do. One does not walk or urinate as a genius. Nor is there a particular set of interests that geniuses are meant to have, activities they are meant to enjoy, or roles they are meant to perform. The failure to have the appropriate sexual interests does not mean that one is not a genius. To be sure, we often presume that geniuses will be less than capable in practical matters and one might argue that their identities therefore do come with expectations. It is because they are geniuses, because they are preoccupied with deeper and more abstruse matters, that we can expect them to forget to put gas in their cars or to leave the coffee pot on, for example. Yet, if a genius does remember to put gas in his or her

---

[73] See Fausto-Sterling, *Sexing the Body*, p. 52–3.
[74] See Greenberg, "Defining Male and Female," p. 267.

car or to turn off the coffee, we do not therefore doubt the validity of his or her attributed identity as a genius. In contrast, because Brenda liked guns and because Money's unnamed second patient had a blue-collar job some observers did doubt the validity of Brenda's attributed identity as a girl and the second patient's attributed identity as a woman, respectively.

Taking their cue from the different ways that identities as men and women and identities as geniuses behave, then, our anthropologists could point out to us that the former are much more rigid than the latter. Indeed, they could point out that we simply do not allow gray areas to remain gray areas in the case of sex and gender. Courts and medical authorities do not take it upon themselves to issue determinative rulings on who is and is not a genius. Instead, our culture allows different institutions and associations to use different criteria for genius status as befits their different functions. Moreover, a person can be "sort of a genius," or a genius in a certain way. One cannot be sort of a woman or a man in a certain way. Conversely, we sometimes say that a certain woman is "like a man" but not that a certain woman is "like a genius."

It might seem remarkable to our alien anthropologists that different courts and different medical establishments differ in which sex and gender identities they attribute to which individuals. Yet, perhaps it would be no more remarkable to them than the circumstance that these institutions make legally or surgically binding sex and gender decisions at all. If our answer to the aliens' perplexity is to be the reference to gray areas, then it would seem to follow that we should give those gray areas the same status they have for other identities. We would think it medically unethical and even insane to break and re-set a child's legs if they had almost but not quite enough turn out to allow him or her to be a ballet dancer. Why is it not equally unethical and insane to castrate a child to if his anatomy almost but not quite allows him or her to be a girl?

In chapters 2 and 3, I want to look at sorts of identities that are perhaps closer in their history and characteristics to men and women than geniuses and ballet dancers are. In the recent past of the United States, racial and ethnic identities had the same relation to law that gender identities possess now. Contemporary debates consider their relation to medicine. We might then look at our racial identities to see if they can offer our anthropologists any clues to our sex and gender identities. In chapter 2, I consider the quandaries that racial identities have caused in the history of the United States. In chapter 3, I propose a way of thinking about racial identities that I hope will transfer to the case of sex and gender identities.

2 Racial identification and identity

Attributions of identities as a man sometimes depend on the presence of a penis; sometimes they depend on the possession of XY chromosomes; in one instance, they required not having a baby. Similarly, attributions of identities as a woman are sometimes contingent upon capacities and proclivities, sometimes they look to sexual orientation, and at least once they were linked to shoulder structure. What remains constant in these various standards for sex and gender identity is their association with some part of some set of behaviors, roles, and preferences, including sexual ones. What is inconstant is that these parts and sets vary. Racial and ethnic status in the United States famously possesses the same sort of variation. I shall therefore begin this chapter with what W. E. B. Du Bois called the "exasperations of race,"[1] to see what help they may be in considering exasperations of sex and gender.

EXASPERATIONS OF RACE IN AMERICA

Americans have been puzzling over their racial attributions for a very long time. In suits for freedom by slaves before the Civil War, in prosecutions for miscegenation between whites and non-whites after the Civil War, and in racial prerequisite cases from 1789 until 1952, states and federal courts had to determine whether particular individuals were black, white, American Indian, or whatever. Until the "one-drop rule" became widespread after the Civil War,[2] different states employed different standards to decide the issue. Some insisted that

---

[1] See W. E. B. Du Bois (1897), "The Conservation of Races", in Robert Bernasconi and Tommy L. Lott, eds., *The Idea of Race* (Indianapolis, IN: Hackett, 2000, pp. 108–117), p. 109.

[2] See Randall Kennedy, *Interracial Intimacies: Sex, Marriage, Identity and Adoption* (New York: Pantheon Books, 2003), p. 223.

3

one was black if one-fourth of one's total "blood"[3] was of African descent while others were satisfied with one-sixteenth of one's blood. In Virginia, one could be white with 24 percent black ancestry until 1910.[4]

Courts also disagreed in how to apply state standards to individual cases. Ian F. Haney López relates the divisions in the Virginia Supreme Court in 1806 when it had to decide whether the Wright family should be freed from slavery on the basis of a misidentification of its race.[5] In 1806, race in Virginia was a matter of maternal descent. The Wrights claimed they were descendants of an American Indian woman, Butterwood Nan, and, as such, after at the very latest 1705 they could not be legally enslaved.[6] Challenging this claim, their owner argued that Butterwood Nan had been a "negro" and that whatever American Indian heritage the Wrights possessed ran through the male line. Hence the family members were legally his slaves. While all the courts agreed with the Wrights, different judges at different judicial levels had different reasons for their conclusions. The Chancellor of the High Court of Chancery used color as the index of race, noting "that the youngest of the appellees was perfectly white and that there were gradual shades of difference in colour between the grand-mother, mother and grand-daughter."[7] Judge Roane of the Virginia Supreme Court cited "the general reputation and opinion of the neighbour-hood"[8] with regard to Butterwood Nan's daughter, Hannah Wright.

[3] See, for example, *Jones* v. *The Commonwealth*, *Gray* v. *Commonwealth* Supreme Court of Virginia 80 Va. 538 (1885). "If his [the accused's] mother was a yellow woman with more than half of her blood derived from the white race, and his father a white man, he is not a negro. If he is a man of mixed blood he is not a negro, unless he has one-fourth at least of negro blood in his veins," p. 544.

[4] Kennedy, *Interracial Intimacies*, p. 223.

[5] *Hudgins* v. *Wrights* Supreme Court of Virginia 11 Va. 134 (1806). See Ian F. Haney López, "The Social Construction of Race: Some Observations on Illusion, Fabrication, and Choice," *Harvard Civil Rights–Civil Liberties Law Review*, 29, 1994.

[6] There was some confusion on this point because Virginia had allowed for the enslavement of American Indians brought into the colony between 1679 and 1691 or 1705. The judges seemed to conclude that the age of the youngest Wright ruled out this possibility. See Counsel in *Hudgins* v. *Wrights*.

[7] *Hudgins* v. *Wrights*, cited in "Prior History".   [8] *Hudgins* v. *Wrights*, p. 142.

Hannah Wright was now also dead but many of her neighbors had thought that she was an Indian and had repeatedly urged her to sue for her freedom. Hence, according to Judge Roane, she probably was an Indian and would have been granted her freedom had the times in which she lived "been as just and liberal on the subject of slavery as the present."[9] Judge Tucker, however, rejected both skin color and reputation and relied instead on hair texture. Indeed, he wrote, "So pointed is this distinction between the natives of Africa and the aborigines of America that a man might as easily mistake the glossy, jetty clothing of an American bear for the wool of a black sheep, as the hair of an American Indian for that of African, or the descendent of an African."[10]

Fortunately for the Wrights the testimony indicated that Hannah had possessed long black hair. Yet, straight hair was not enough for Thomas Gary in Arkansas in 1858. Under Arkansas law of the time one was a "negro" if one had more than one-sixteenth "African blood." When the sixteen-year-old Gary sued for freedom, three doctors testified that he did not. Dr. Brown found no trace of "negro blood" in his eyes, nose, mouth, or jaw, noting in addition that his hair was "smooth and of sandy complexion, perfectly straight and flat with no indication

---

[9] *Hudgins* v. *Wrights*, p. 142.

[10] *Hudgins* v. *Wrights*, p. 140; Haney López, "The Social Construction of Race," p. 2. Regardless of which physical features it took to be dispositive in racial rulings, *Hudgins* v. *Wrights* established the evidence of "inspection" as the foundation of racial ascriptions in Virginia. See *Hook* v. *Nanny Pagee and Her Children* Supreme Court of Virginia 16 Va. 379 (1811) and *Gregory* v. *Baugh* Supreme Court of Virginia 29 Va. 665 (1831). In North Carolina, the Supreme Court considered the question of who was to be qualified to perform such inspections and resolved the issue in *State* v. *Asa Jacobs* Supreme Court of North Carolina, Raleigh 51 NC 284 (1859). It did not require "a distinguished comparative anatomist to detect the admixture of the African or Indian with the pure blood of the white race," the court declared. Instead, just as "persons accustomed to observe the habits of a certain kind of fish have been permitted to give in evidence their opinions as to the ability of the fish to overcome certain obstructions in the rivers ... any person of ordinary intelligence, who, for a sufficient length of time, will devote his attention to the subject, will be able to discover, with almost unerring certainty, the adulteration of the Caucasian with the Negro or Indian blood" (*State* v. *Asa Jacobs*, p. 287).

of the crisp or negro curl."[11] Dr. Wilcox conceded that he could not say that there was "no negro blood" in Gary. Yet, since his eyes were blue, "his hair straight and light, his complexion sandy" no such "blood" was to be discerned "from external appearance."[12] For his part, Dr. Dibbrell thought that Gary might have a "small amount of negro blood, not more than a sixteenth, perhaps not so much" and "would not positively swear that he had any at all, so vague are the signs of the admixture of the negro race, in one so remotely removed from the African blood by crossing with the white." Indeed, he admitted that he had "no definite rule" and knew of no "reliable one" by which to judge cases such as Gary's.

Despite such "expert" opinion, the Arkansas Supreme Court ruled against Gary's suit for freedom. Its justification lay in the race of the woman, Susan, who it determined was his mother. Although she had "a very light complexion" and straight hair, she had never objected to her enslavement; moreover, she was swarthy with "rather thick lips and coarse features."[13] These facts were sufficient "to repel any presumption in freedom in favor of the complainant, even upon the supposition that the evidence, otherwise, left it as a matter of grave doubt, whether he belonged to the white or negro race." Indeed, doubt was "the utmost that could be claimed for him" and more than what the court thought he was "entitled to," for, as it continued, no one could read the evidence and come to the conclusion that it made it appear that "he belongs to the white race, or descended from that race on his mother's side."[14]

For its part, although the Virginia Supreme Court relied on hair texture in the *Wrights* case, it did not always do so. In 1877, a lower court found Rowena McPherson and George Stewart guilty of "illicit intercourse" even though they were husband and wife. According to

---

[11] *Gary* v. *Stevenson* 19 Ark. 580 (1858) p. 583. Also see Jason A. Gilman, "Suing for Freedom: Interracial Sex, Slave Law and Racial Identity in the Post-Revolutionary and Antebellum South," *North Carolina Law Review*, January 2004, p. 538.

[12] *Gary* v. *Stevenson*, p. 583.

[13] *Gary* v. *Stevenson*, p. 585; Gilman, "Suing for Freedom," p. 608.

[14] *Gary* v. *Stevenson*, pp. 586–587.

the court, McPherson was a "negro" and hence her putative marriage to Stewart, a white man, was illegal. By 1877, Virginia's criterion for belonging to the "negro" race no longer lay in the question of maternal or paternal descent. Instead, it lay in the amount of "negro" blood one had. Whether one inherited this blood from one's male or female ancestors, more than one-fourth of it made one a "negro." Using this criterion, the Virginia Supreme Court interpreted the "certificate of facts" in the *McPherson* case to say that McPherson's father was white, that her great-grandfather was white and that her great-grand-mother was "brown." "It was said in the family," the court went on, "that the ... brown skin woman was a half-Indian, a fact which is confirmed by the color of her skin." Indeed, had McPherson's great-grandmother been a full-blooded "negro," her skin would have been black because the skin of full-blooded "Negroes" "is black and never brown." The court concluded that McPherson had "certainly derived at least three-fourths of her blood from the white race." Moreover, of that fourth that was not derived from the white race some "residue" must have been American Indian and "if any part of the said residue of her blood, however, small, was derived from any other source than the African or negro race, then Rowena McPherson cannot be a negro."[15]

In Arkansas, then, blackness lay in the possession of more than one-sixteenth "negro blood" while in Virginia it lay in a "negro" female ancestor in a case in the beginning of the nineteenth century and in more than one-fourth negro blood in a case at the end. The evidence of "blood," for its part, lay in coarse features and failure to pursue one's

[15] *McPherson* v. *The Commonwealth* 69 Va. 939 (1877), p. 940: "It appears from [the certificate of facts] 'that her father was a white man; that her mother was also by a white man, out of a brown skin woman; that Washington Goode, the half-uncle of the said Rowena McPherson, testified that the said brown skin woman, who was his grandmother and the great grandmother of said Rowena McPherson, told him that she was a half-Indian; and that his mother, her daughter also told him the same.' It thus appears that less than one-fourth of her blood is negro blood ... Besides having certainly derived at least three-fourths of her blood from the white race, she derived a portion of the residue from her great-grandmother, who was a brown skin woman, and of course, not a full-blooded African or negro, whose skin is black, and never brown." Also see Kennedy, *Interracial Intimacies*, p. 224.

freedom in Arkansas while in Virginia it lay in hair texture in the beginning of the nineteenth century and in skin color towards the end. An 1835 ruling in South Carolina took up Judge Roane's idea in the *Wrights* case and insisted that the evidence of one's race lay in "the general reputation and opinion of the neighbourhood." Here, the South Carolina Supreme Court declared that, "The condition of the individual is not to be determined solely by a distinct and visible mixture of Negro blood, but by reputation, by his reception into society and [by] his having commonly exercised the privileges of a white man."[16]

Over a hundred years later, the 1940s case of *Bennett* v. *Bennett* took the same position. The facts of this case mirror those of *In re Estate of Marshall G. Gardiner*. In the *Gardiner* case, a nephew sued to prevent his uncle's estate from going to his wife, J'Noel Ball, because she was really a man. In *Bennett* v. *Bennett*, Franklin Bennett's daughter sued to prevent her father's estate from going to his second wife, Louetta Chassereau Bennett, because she was really a "Negro." Louetta Bennett fared better than J'Noel Ball, however, for while the court in the *Gardiner* case looked to J'Noel's chromosomes rather than what it might have seen as her feminine and wifely behavior, the *Bennett* court looked at Louetta's behavior and the behavior of others with regard to her. Hence, although the daughter alleged that "she had more than an eighth of negro blood in her veins,"[17] the court noted that:

> Upon the death of the defendant's father and mother she was first taken into the home of white people, then she was placed in a church orphanage for white children, she was confirmed ... as a communicant of the Holy Communion Church of Charleston, a white church; she was taken from the orphanage and placed in a white home as a member of the family, and from there into another white home as a member of that family; she married a white man ... she votes in the democratic primaries, both City and State,

---

[16] Kennedy, *Interracial Intimacies*, pp. 227–228.
[17] *Bennett* v. *Bennett* 10 S.E. 2d (SC 1940), p. 2. See also Kennedy, *Interracial Intimacies*, pp. 226–227.

whose rules bar negroes from voting; her children attend the white public schools of Walterboro of which one of the plaintiff's attorneys is a trustee.[18]

Randall Kennedy remarks on what might have been a sufficient rationale for appealing to reputation in the *Bennett* case: "In the aftermath of a contrary holding, any white South Carolinian might have felt compelled to peer into the mirror with a new intensity and ask nervously, 'Where will it end?'"[19] Judge Roane and the 1935 South Carolina court may have had the same thought. Anyone's family history could be scoured for evidence of "Negro" blood and, moreover, given the conditions of slavery, it might be quite easy to find it. Hence, it would be far safer to rely on reputation.

Nevertheless, it is not clear what to make of the differences and even contradictions in different courts' assessments of the criteria and evidence of race. One might think that the Southern states resolved their differences after the Civil War with the one-drop rule that counted as a black person anyone with one African ancestor. Yet, the *McPherson* and *Bennett* cases both used different criteria of identity. Moreover, since the solution requires deciding who has African ancestry, it raises complexities of its own, as the *Wrights* and *Gary* cases might have predicted,[20] and it requires stipulating how far back in a particular family tree to go in looking for evidence of African ancestry.[21] In addition, the solution simply shifts the problem of racial

---

[18] *Bennett* v. *Bennett*, p. 5. [19] Kennedy, *Interracial Intimacies*, p. 228.
[20] See *Hudgins* v. *Wrights* and *Gary* v. *Stevenson*.
[21] See *State* v. *William Chavers* 50 N.C. 11 (1857). Chavers was charged with carrying a shot-gun in violation of the prohibition against free blacks doing so. His lawyer tried to argue that Chavers was a white man, and hence entitled to his gun, because he was five generations removed from a pure African ancestor. Instead, the court agreed with the Brunswick Superior Court:

> Take ... two families, the father of one family a white person and the mother a negro, and the father of the other family a negro and the mother a white woman; the members of these families are of the half blood, and in the first generation from a negro, let them intermarry, and their descendants intermarry, until by generation, they are removed beyond the fourth generation from the pure negro ancestors, the father of the one, and the mother of the other, from whom they are

determinations from the question of who is black to the question of
who is white.

From 1790 until 1952, the United States restricted naturalized
citizenship to "whites," amending the law in 1870 to include "persons
of African nativity and African descent." Consequently in petitions for
citizenship brought by natives of different countries, federal and state
courts had to decide which foreign-born applicants could count as
white or black and which, in contrast, were excluded from possible
citizenship on the basis of being neither. In his documentation of
these cases, Haney López shows that courts failed to agree with one
another on what they meant by a white person and that they sometimes failed even to agree with their own recent rulings.[22] In 1922, for
instance, in the case of *Takao Osawa* v. *United States,* a native of
Japan, Takao Osawa, argued for his eligibility for citizenship on the
basis of the white color of his skin. As he put the point: "The Japanese
are of lighter color than other Eastern Asiatics, not rarely showing the
transparent pink tint which whites assume as their own privilege."[23]
Nevertheless, the US Supreme Court rejected his petition and denied
that the words "white person" referred to color:

> descended, are they any the less free negroes in the fifth than they were in the
> first generation from their negro ancestors? They still have half negro blood in
> their veins, and that is all they had in the first generation. In the fourth gener-
> ation they were unquestionably free negroes, but they certainly had no more
> negro blood than their children ... Can it be that a remove by one generation has
> the effect, in law, of turning a half negro into free white man in spite of the color
> of his skin or the kinking of his hair? It seems to me both unreasonable and
> absurd ... No person in the fifth generation from a negro ancestor becomes a
> free white person, unless one ancestor in each generation was a white person ...
> and unless there is such purification it makes no difference how many gener-
> ations you should have to go back to find a pure negro ancestor; even though it
> should be a hundred, still the person is a free negro. (*State* v. *William Chavers,*
> pp. 12–13)

In Germany, Himmler decided on 1650 as the stopping point for prospective SS
members. If research showed their family trees to be free of Jews back to that time,
they were declared Aryan. See Berl Lang, "Metaphysical Racism (Or: Biological
Racism by Other Means)," in *Race/Sex: Their Sameness, Difference, and
Interplay,* Naomi Zack, ed. (New York: Routledge, 1997), p. 19.

[22] Ian F. Haney López, *White by Law: The Legal Construction of Race* (New York: New
York University Press, 1996).

[23] *Ibid.,* p. 81.

Manifestly the test afforded by the mere color of the skin of each individual is impracticable as that differs greatly among persons of the same race, even among Anglo-Saxons, ranging by imperceptible gradations from the fair blond to the swarthy brunette, the latter being darker than many of the lighter hued persons of the brown or yellow races. Hence to adopt the color test alone would result in a confused overlapping of races and a gradual merging of one into the other, without any practical line of separation.[24]

Scientifically more legitimate, the court decided, was an equation of the meaning of white with Caucasian. While Osawa might be light in complexion, he remained Japanese and since the Japanese were not Caucasian, Ozawa was not white. The same court decided *United States* v. *Bhagat Singh Thind* three months later. Relying on *Takao Osawa*, Bhagat Singh Thind argued that he was a high-class Hindu of the Aryan race and noted that experts from Johann Friedrich Blumenbach on had identified Aryans with Caucasians.[25] Since the *Takao Osawa* decision defined whites as Caucasians, Thind argued that he was indisputably white. Nevertheless, shortly after rejecting Osawa for naturalization as a non-Caucasian, the Supreme Court said that "The Aryan theory as a racial basis seems to be discredited by most" and that "the word Caucasian [the word the court had itself used three months earlier] is in scarcely better repute."[26] "Mere ability on the part of an applicant ... to establish a line of descent from a Caucasian ancestor will not *ipso facto* and necessarily conclude the inquiry," the court ruled, for "'Caucasian' is a conventional word of much flexibility." Indeed, rejecting all "scientific classification" the court based its decision on the immigrants from the "British Isles and Northwestern Europe" whom the framers "must have had affirmatively in mind" along with the "immigrants from Eastern, Southern

---

[24] *Takao Osawa* v. *United States* 260 US 178 (1922). See Haney López, *White by Law*, Appendix B, p. 220.

[25] Counsel in *United States* v. *Bhagat Singh Thind* 261 US 204 (1923).

[26] *United States* v. *Bhagat Singh Thind*. See Haney López, *White By Law*, Appendix B, p. 223.

and Middle Europe" who "were received as unquestionably akin to those already here."[27]

In these racial prerequisite cases, then, white sometimes refers to skin color, sometimes it means Caucasian, and sometimes it means European. In trying to determine whether a person was black, courts sometimes relied on inspection,[28] sometimes on ancestry, and sometimes on reputation. Similarly, in trying to determine whether a person was white, courts sometimes appealed to science, sometimes to common sense, and sometimes to the intentions of the framers. Nor did the courts become clearer about their criteria for racial ascription after 1927. In twelve cases between 1923 and 1942, numerous ethnicities were dubbed "not white," including Japanese, "Asian Indians," Armenians, Punjabis, Filipinos, Afghanis, and "Arabians." In 1944, however, Arabians became "white." The rationale for the federal court in Michigan calling them not white in 1942 referred to both common knowledge and legal precedent. So too did the rationale for the federal court in Massachusetts that in 1944 called them white.[29]

THE CONSTRUCTION OF RACIAL IDENTITIES

A quick survey of court cases in the nineteenth and first half of the twentieth century indicates just how much time federal and particularly state courts had to spend defining and policing racial lines. For this reason, it is even less plausible in the case of inconsistencies in racial attributions than in the case of inconsistencies in sex and gender attributions to suppose that the irregularities represent gray areas in mostly stable conceptions. Given the extent of the variations in the racial attributions different authorities made at different times, and even in the racial attributions that the same authorities made at almost the same time, our alien anthropologists might well be amazed at our stubbornness in continuing to insist on racial identities. Indeed,

---

[27] *United States* v. *Bhagat Singh Thind*. See Haney López, *White By Law*, Appendix B, p. 224.

[28] And also dealt with the question of who had the authority to do inspections.

[29] See Haney López, *White by Law*, Appendix A, p. 208.

witches!

one can imagine that the anthropologists would be at least as exasperated about identity in American society as a black or white as Evans-Prichard was about identity in Zande society as a witch.[30] The Azande, he noted, thought witchcraft was inherited through the male line and they also believed that it could be detected through a post mortem examination of a person's intestines. Given the Zande clan system, however, just a few post mortem examinations performed on just a few individuals of different clans would show either that every Azande was a witch or that none was. Yet, to Evans-Prichard's chagrin, the Azande did not push their beliefs to this logical conclusion and therefore did not consider their claims about witchcraft to be problematic. We might make the same point about our notions of race. On the one hand, the one-drop rule says that a person who has one African ancestor is a black. On the other hand, a few checks of a few family trees would reveal just how many of those who function as whites, conceive of themselves as whites, and are considered by reputation to be white are, on this criterion, black. Indeed, a 1958 study already found that "approximately 21 percent of those classified as white have an African element in their inherited biological background" and that most of those with an African element were living as whites.[31] Either, then, many more people than we tend to think are "black," or far fewer are. In fact, the number of people who were "really" white or "really" black might be, depending on the criteria used, either everyone or no one, just as in the case of Zande witches.[32]

Of course, from the point of view of a more culturally sensitive anthropology, Evans-Prichard was simply a British imperialist, unwilling to immerse himself in the Zande conceptual universe. Peter Winch famously thought it important that the Azande do *not* push their beliefs to their logical conclusion because it shows that

---

[30] See E. E. Evans-Prichard, *Witchcraft, Oracles and Magic among the Azande* (Oxford: Oxford University Press, 1937).

[31] See Robert P. Stuckert, "African Ancestry of the White American Population," *Ohio Journal of Science*, 58(3), p. 158. K. Anthony Appiah cites this article in his *The Ethics of Identity* (Princeton, NJ: Princeton University Press, 2005), p. 324, n. 48.

[32] Appiah, *The Ethics of Identity*, esp. pp. 184–186.

their witchcraft conceptions have a different function. Whereas the European anthropologist conceives of witchcraft as a theoretical system offering a pseudo-scientific understanding of the world, the Azande do not.[33] We could likewise say that the question of whether our racial ideas are coherent does not arise for us – or, at least, does not require us to abandon them – because they are part of our practices, not of our science. We can debate the scientific question of how many elements in our inherited biological background and which elements make one a member of a certain population group, but the question of racial identity is different: it is a question of identities that are constituted for us by a universe of action and practice.[34] Outside of our practices and activities, blacks and whites as well as Latinos, Latinas, and Asians have no more reality than witches. Within it, they have the same amount.

Another way of putting this point is to say that the identification of racial identities is a matter of knowing how rather than knowing that. It may be that we cannot articulate a set of rules and criteria by which to place particular people in particular racial categories. Nor can we teach someone how to play basketball by giving them a book of rules. Rather, someone learns basketball by coming to understand how to play it and in the United States we know, at least roughly, how to play our game of race. One tells a beginning basketball player to pass only to a player who is not being effectively guarded but if the beginner is constantly stripped of the ball by holding on to it for too long, it becomes clear to him or her that learning the game is less a question of reviewing a set of rules in his or her head than understanding how to play it.[35] Similarly, if a group of alien anthropologists

---

[33] Peter Winch, "Understanding a Primitive Society," in Fred R. Dallmayr and Thomas A. McCarthy, *Understanding and Social Inquiry* (Notre Dame: University of Notre Dame Press, 1977), p. 172.

[34] This point seems to be the gist of Lionel McPherson's and Tommie Shelby's criticism of Appiah, in "Blackness and Blood: Interpreting African American Identity," *Philosophy and Public Affairs* 32 (2), 2004.

[35] For this example, see Stanley Fish, "Fish v. Fiss," *Stanford Law Review*, 36, 1981, pp. 1331–1334.

are trying to learn how to identify blacks and whites in the United States, it would presumably become clear to them that racial identification and self-identification is less a question of memorizing specific criteria than a question of knowing how to engage in a certain racial practice.

Yet, basketball is coherent as a game. Are racial identification and identity? While the Azande may be unconcerned about the contradictions in their practice of witchcraft, they cannot expect outsiders to be similarly unconcerned. Winch thinks that anthropologists must find that standpoint from within their own culture from which they can begin to make sense of the practices and beliefs of another.[36] In the case of Zande witchcraft, he thinks the problem with Evans-Prichard's account lies in its Western assumptions linking witchcraft to a primitive form of science or even pseudo-science. Witchcraft, he argues, becomes much more intelligible once it is linked to Western practices of prayer and religion. But can the same be said about our racial practices? From what point of view should we be unconcerned about their contradictions?

Contemporary social theorists offer us one answer: the perspective of power. Racial identities may be practical identities. Nevertheless, more salient to dissecting them is an appreciation of the benefits those with social, political, and legal authority accrue from making use of the contradictions they involve. On an Evans-Prichard-type reading of the judicial rulings we have surveyed, they are exasperating because they fail to sort out consistent or plausible criteria for determining a person's race and because they fail to recognize that they have failed. On what we can call a social constructionist reading, however, unacknowledged contradictions are a boon for those in power precisely because they open up multiple possibilities for imposing their own agendas.[37]

---

[36] Winch, "Understanding a Primitive Society," p. 171.

[37] Daniel Sharfstein argues that Southern courts were well aware that the lines they were creating between races were arbitrary. See Daniel Sharfstein, "The Secret History of Race in the United States," *Yale Law Journal*, April 2003.

Michael Omi's and Howard Winant's account of racial formation is the classic social constructionist account of race.[38] What Omi
and Winant term the macro-level of formation involves the social,
historical, and political practices, events, and actions that established
the United States' particular racial typology. Although early English
encounters with Africans say little about race and more about labor,
gold, and the Portuguese,[39] racial forms of identification emerged with
the African slave trade. Slave traders collected people of diverse cultures and dubbed them indiscriminately as black Africans. Slave owners reinforced this form of identification by consciously mixing slaves
of different ethnicities in their individual forces and refusing to recognize bonds of kinship between spouses, parents, or children.
Individual colonies further entrenched racial identifications by establishing legal distinctions between African and non-African servants,
establishing African servitude for life and consciously setting black
and white laborers against one another. Virginia's reaction to Bacon's
Rebellion is a particularly good example of the last tactic. Recognizing
the threat to the gentry posed by a coalition of African and European
servants and non-landowners, it set out to re-center the conflict from
non-landowner against landowner to white against black. To this end,
it repealed all penalties imposed on Europeans for their participation
in the rebellion but enforced them on African participants; it
employed the European rebels to help quash slave revolts; and it sold
the livestock formerly owned by the African participants to poor
Europeans. The colony also prohibited African slaves from assembling
and moving freely and, in 1691, it passed a series of even more restrictive laws prohibiting the manumission of slaves unless their master
paid to remove them from the colony, levying fines on free white

---

[38] Michael Omi and Howard Winant, *Racial Formation in the United States from the
1960s to the 1980s* (New York: Routledge, 1986), p. 66.

[39] See Kathleen M. Brown, *Good Wives, Nasty Wenches and Anxious Patriarchs:
Gender, Race and Power in Colonial Virginia* (Chapel Hill, NC: University of
North Carolina Press, 1996), pp. 37–40.

women who gave birth to racially mixed children, and denying free blacks the right to vote, hold office, or testify in court.[40]

While actions such as these helped to construct racial identifications on the macro-level, the internalization of the identifications constructs what Omi and Winant call the micro-level. Individuals introject or appropriate their macro-level racial identification and make it a part of their self-identity. The separation of slaves from their original ethnic and linguistic consociates as well as from their families is part of this process since it forced displaced Africans to forge new systems of solidarity based on their new circumstances as well as new customs and hybrid forms of religion to overcome their cultural distance from one another.[41] Frederick Douglass writes about his ties on the plantation where he was enslaved that the slaves "were as true as steel, and no band of brothers could have been more loving ... We never undertook to do anything of importance, which was likely to affect each other, without mutual consultation. We were generally a unit, and we moved together."[42] Of course, white consciousness of a separate identity followed a similar trajectory insofar as whites consciously distinguished themselves from blacks and other "non-whites." After the Civil War, this racial consciousness flourished in racial ideologies and Jim Crow laws while black racial consciousness grew in the efforts of blacks to lead successful lives in a society legally and politically armed against them.

Ian Hacking emphasizes another element of social construction in what he calls "looping effects,"[43] which, in the case of racial constructions, we can see as the reciprocal influences of macro- and micro-levels on one another. Individuals take up their external racial

[40] See Ronald Takaki, *A Different Mirror: A History of Multicultural America* (Boston: Little, Brown & Co., 1993), pp. 63–67.

[41] Stephen Cornell and Douglas Hartmann, *Ethnicity and Race: Making Identities in a Changing World* (Thousand Oaks, CA: Pine Forge Press, 1998) pp. 104–106.

[42] Frederick Douglass, *My Bondage and My Freedom*, William Andrews, ed. (Urbana: University of Illinois Press, 1987), pp. 164–165.

[43] Ian Hacking, *The Social Construction of What?* (Cambridge, MA: Harvard University Press, 1999), p. 34.

identification as part of who they are; indeed, the racial identities they adopt become fundamental to them insofar as they shape prospects and life-plans, determine who is part of which "unit," and offer reasons for action. At the same time, lives lived in terms of particular racial designations "loop" back to develop and change the meaning of the designations themselves. "Looping effects are everywhere," Hacking says:

> Think what the category of genius did to those Romantics who saw themselves as geniuses, and what their behavior did in turn to the category of genius itself. Think about the transformations effected by the notions of fat, overweight, anorexia. If someone talks about the social construction of genius or anorexia, they are likely talking about the idea, the individuals falling under the idea, the interaction between the idea and the people, and the manifold of social practices and institutions that these interactions involve.[44]

Being identified by others as a genius or an anorexic has consequences for the way one thinks about oneself, the goals one sets for oneself, and the expectations one has. One's external identification thus affects and helps to construct an internal identity. In turn, the goals and expectations that individuals have as geniuses and anorexics feed back into the designations. Institutions, practices, and medical, educational, and perhaps even legal discourses develop to deal with the identities; these discourses then feed back into the way those designated as geniuses and anorexics think about their prospects and identify themselves and these feed back into the social and institutional level, and so on. The same holds for identifications as black, white, Asian, and Hispanic. The ascription establishes the circumstances of one's life, one's sense of how one fits into one's society, and the life trajectory one foresees and establishes for oneself. One's racial identification thus arranges the list of possibilities one draws from in

[44] *Ibid.*, p. 34.

planning one's life and it shapes the way one reacts both to others and to events. In turn, the sense that individuals have of their prospects and their expectations loops back to develop the meaning of racial classifications. Institutions, practices, and a series of medical and legal discourses develop around the identities. Indeed, societies change to fit and regulate the racialized individuals they have created. Think, then, of "the manifold of social practices and institutions" created by the interactions between notions of race, particular racial attributions, and social and political life in the United States.

In place of a Whiggish exasperation with racial identifications and identities as well as with interpretive efforts to make sense out of them, then, social constructionists offer a causal account, the virtue of which is that it explains not only the identities but their durability in the face of their own contradictions. Racial identities are the contingent effect of a series of different events, different concerns, and different agendas. These last include such different aims as the attempt of wealthy landowners to keep their extensive property holdings, the urge of non-landowners to acquire property at whomever's expense, and the efforts of displaced, imprisoned individuals to survive in a strange country. Because of the different aims that racial identities reflect they are cobbled together and likely to be inconsistent. Different parts of the construction coexist in different sorts of tension with one another and issue in the contradictory decisions we have canvassed issued by different legal and political authorities at different times. Why do these differences not raise suspicions about the racial categories? There are at least two reasons. First, as long as the criteria of race can change over different times and different states, authorities can make and justify whatever racial identifications they want. Depending on the circumstances, black identity can refer to skin color, hair texture, ancestry, or reputation, and white identity can refer to status as a Caucasian, status as a European, or status as a group the founders must have had "affirmatively in mind." Second, the micro-level of racial identification means that individuals adopt and demand recognition for the identities they have internalized. Racial construction is both a top-down and a bottom-up process in which macro- and micro-levels loop into and reinforce one another.

THE POLITICS OF IDENTITY

A social constructionist answer to Evans-Prichard-type worries about racial identity would be to wonder not at their Whiggishness but at their naïveté. "Ask all you want about the apparent incoherence of our racial conceptions," social constructionists might say to our alien anthropologists:

> Identity is a question of power and of the introjection of power. The inconsistencies and incoherencies to which you point not only do not undermine power but rather give it room to maneuver.
>
> Moreover, the appropriation of racial identifications by individuals means that the attempt to question race comes too late.

On this view, what is required to deal with exasperations of race is not the abolition of race but an acknowledgment of the contributions of racial diversity. All individuals have already become racialized; race is thus a fait accompli. The project now is to see what race can achieve. Or so Du Bois argues after cataloguing his own exasperations. It may be, he complains, that individuals cannot be coherently grouped together on the basis of color, hair, cranial size, or morphology, since these features do not line up with one another to provide for separable groups. Instead, people with dark skin may have straight hair like the Chinese and those with white skin curly hair like the Bushman. "Nor does color agree with the breadth of the head, for the yellow Tartar has a broader head than the German."[45] Still, Du Bois insists that different races stand for different ideals and, moreover, that the promise of the "Negro" race means that blacks must work against assimilation. "We are Americans, not only by birth and by citizenship, but by our political ideals, our language, our religion," he

---

[45] Du Bois, "The Conservation of Races," p. 109.

writes. "Farther than that our Americanism does not go. At that point we are Negroes ... the first fruits of this new nation, the harbinger of that black to-morrow which is yet destined to soften the whiteness of the Teutonic today."[46] The contemporary philosopher, Lucius Outlaw echoes this claim: "Both the struggle against racism and invidious ethnocentrism and the struggles on the part of persons of various races and ethnicities to create, preserve, refine, and, of particular importance, share their 'messages' that is to say, their cultural meanings with human civilization at large, require that the constantly evolving groups we refer to as races ... be 'conserved' in democratic politics."[47]

What Charles Taylor calls the politics of recognition takes up this demand for racial conservation.[48] The politics of recognition differs from older struggles for civil and political rights by replacing demands for the equal treatment of minority groups with demands that social and political institutions acknowledge and accommodate difference. Women and ethnic, racial, and sexual minorities are not to try to reshape their distinct identities to fit a standard that the politics of recognition claims is modeled on the majority culture or white Western European men. Instead, women and minorities are to demand a form of participation in social and political institutions that sufficiently respects who they are.[49] Taylor traces such demands back to the influence of Jean-Jacques Rousseau and Johann Gottfried von Herder, who both reject the ideas of honor associated with social hierarchies in favor of the ideas of dignity associated with demands to be true to oneself and to one's *Volk*.[50] Yet, the demand also derives

---

[46] *Ibid.*, p. 114.
[47] Lucius Outlaw, "On W. E. B. Du Bois's 'The Conservation of Races'," in *Overcoming Racism and Sexism*, Linda A. Bell and David Blumenfeld, eds. (Lanham, MD: Rowman & Littlefield, 1995), pp. 79–102.
[48] See Charles Taylor, "The Politics of Recognition," in *Multiculturalism: Examining the Politics of Recognition*, in Amy Gutmann, ed. (Princeton, NJ: Princeton University Press, 1994), pp. 25–73.
[49] See, for example, Will Kymlicka, *Liberalism, Community and Culture* (Oxford: Oxford University Press, 1989).
[50] Taylor, "The Politics of Recognition," pp. 27–31.

from principles of equality. Individuals are arguably not equal participants in civic and political life if the institutions and practices that
compose this life privilege certain identities over others or require
minority identities to become more like majority ones. Nor are individuals arguably equal participants if allegedly neutral laws have a
greater impact on the ability of certain identities to sustain themselves than they do on others. For this reason, theorists such as Will
Kymlicka insist on the necessity of forms of group rights that can
protect minority cultures from external decisions of the larger society
that threaten their existence and hence the identities of those who
belong to them.[51]

On the one hand, then, the account of race as a social construction
leads to the politics of identity. The idea here is that since we are already
racially constructed, we should live with that fact and demand recognition for our racial identities. On the other hand, to the extent that
racial identities are the result of arbitrary and contradictory decisions
and of contemptible actions, policies, and events, they are difficult to
square with Rousseau's and Herder's ideas of being true to oneself. Racial
identities are the product of racializing actions and events; they were
imposed on individuals as sources of negative and demeaning expectations and impoverishing life-conditions. Why then, we might ask,
should we be true to precisely these identities? To be sure, racial identities have not only been imposed on us from above, we have also created
them from below as a result of the bonds of solidarity and opposition to
power forged between individuals along the lines that Douglass stresses.
Still, it is unclear why we should demand continuing recognition for the
identities just because they were once crucial to our survival. Why
should we take up just those identities and identifications that history
has imposed on us? Why should we demand recognition in their terms?

We might argue that we should do so because we are not free to
choose or reject these identities. Insofar as our history and traditions

[51] Will Kymlicka, *Multicultural Citizenship: A Liberal Theory of Minority Rights*
(Oxford: Oxford University Press, 1995), p. 35.

have bequeathed them to us, they are simply part of who we are. At the very least, then, we should insure that they are respected. Yet, we fail to choose many of our identities and identifications, those as widows and cancer patients, for example. Must we demand recognition for these identities or should we not rather try to prevent or to overcome them? We identify people as racists, bigots, and sexists, as well. Should we recognize them? Bigots are surely socially constructed through events, controversies, and actions. They can also introject and take pride in their identifications. Yet, if they organize around the politics of recognition, should we applaud their efforts as expressions of being true to themselves?

We tend to think, instead, that individuals ought to make a normative decision about their identities. They ought to endorse them as good and valuable identities or reject their value and try to develop other identities. To be sure, trying to become a different sort of person from the sort one is already can be difficult. Moreover, it may not be possible to revise all of one's identities at once. Still, we often try to revise some of them, to stop being pushovers, alcoholics, and insensitive brutes, for example. Why should the same not hold for our other identities, including our racial ones? History, institutional authority, and social power may have made me white. Yet, why should I endorse that identity if I cannot justify it as a good one?[52] The same question could be asked about our identities as blacks, Hispanics, and Asians.

Nor does a concern with collective self-esteem provide a clear case for the politics of recognition. The politics of recognition tries to mobilize groups to combat the negative evaluations their identities once involved. Individuals are to wear what Du Bois calls the "badge of color"[53] as a badge of victory rather than defeat. Nevertheless, it is unclear that we should expect to reverse evaluations in this way.

[52] See Harry Frankfurt's distinction between first-order and second-order desires in "Freedom of the Will and the Concept of the Person," in Harry Frankfurt, *The Importance of What We Care About* (Cambridge: Cambridge University Press, 1988), pp. 11–25.

[53] W. E. B. Du Bois, *Dusk of Dawn: An Essay Toward an Autobiography of a Race Concept* (New York: Schocken Books, 1968), p. 117.

Eighteenth-century libertines tried to treat adulterous identities and identifications as sources of value. Rather than shunning the label of "adulterers" they embraced it as who they were and tried to assert the equal value of being adulterers with respect to less sexually adventuresome identities.[54] Yet, the identity of being an adulterer does not easily admit of this sort of revaluation – in part, it seems, because the ascription brings its history and its disvalue with it. Why suppose that the transformation of the identities of black or white has any more potential? Suppose we were to try to achieve equal recognition for "savages?" We might value the art, literature, philosophy, and culture produced by those labeled as savages. Indeed, we might conclude that the poignancy, beauty, or profundity of their art and thought stemmed at least in part from their being labeled as savages. Nevertheless, what we seek equal recognition for in these cases is the art and thought, not the identity that the label constructs. Indeed, to the extent that we emphasize the identity at all it is to marvel at the potential for human creativity in the face of how humans brand and treat one another. We could object that we would not have the art without the identity but that fact does not provide a reason to seek equal recognition for the identity, any more than the art of refugees or cancer patients should lead us to devote our energies to their equal recognition. Instead, surely, we ought to eliminate the causes of refugees and cancer patients.

Instead of looking to eighteenth-century libertines, then, we might look to Hester Prynne, whose identity as an adulterer in Nathaniel Hawthorne's novel is marked by the scarlet letter she is forced to wear.[55] While she herself becomes a respected member of the community, she does not do so by transforming the meaning or value of an adulterous identity. Instead, she transcends it so that the scarlet letter no longer carries that meaning. Were we to follow Hester Prynne's model instead of that of the politics of recognition, we

[54] See George E. Haggerty, *Men in Love* (New York: Columbia University Press, 1999), pp. 10–15.
[55] The citation is *The Scarlet Letter* (1850) (New York: Penguin Books, 2003).

would not struggle to transform the value of racialized identities. Instead, we would work to strip various marks of their racial implications. Just as the scarlet letter no longer carries the meaning of adultery at the end of Hawthorne's novel, physical characteristics, ancestry, or whatever other "badge" we looked to would no longer carry the meaning of race.

This solution raises other questions, however. Hester Prynne transcends her identity as an adulterer and the scarlet letter becomes the sign of a healer. Yet, towards what would we transcend our racial identities? What could we aspire to be? What if we were to embrace identifications as Yoruba, Xhosa, Roman, or Celt rather than black or white? Yoruba, Xhosa, Roman, and Celt are no less constructed and introjected identities than black or white. Like the latter, they were forged through macro-level events, practices, histories of exclusions and inclusions, through micro-level appropriations, and through the looping of these constructions into one another.[56] It is questionable whether tracing our identities beyond black and white to "prior" identities resolves the questions that race raises since we have no reason to suppose that identity as a Celt is better or worse than identity as a white, or that identity as a Xhosa trumps identification as a black.

More importantly for issues of equality, it is not clear that we could continue to monitor the deleterious effects of racism if certain badges no longer carried the meaning of race. If we were to transcend our racial identities and identifications, would we not risk losing the ability to trace the racism in our history or to tend to its on-going effects? A 2004 study found that whites were one-and-a-half times more likely than blacks to come from families with assets. Further, among those families who were able to pass financial wealth on to their families, the amount white families were able to pass on was four

---

[56] See K. Anthony Appiah, In *My Father's House: Africa in the Philosophy of Culture* (New York: Oxford University Press, 1992), esp. chapter 9.

times that of blacks.[57] This discrepancy is not an accident. One need only look at twentieth-century housing policy to see part of its cause and to trace it to the wave of white violence against blacks. In reaction to the wave of black migration from the south to the north between 1900 and 1920, whites burned black homes in what were once integrated neighborhoods and shot, beat, and lynched blacks found in white neighborhoods.[58] Subsequently, communities employed restrictive covenants to preserve certain areas for white-only residential expansion and threatened sellers or their agents who tried to violate this color line.[59] The federal government provided low-interest loans to white homeowners who lost their homes in foreclosure actions while intentionally diverting funds from black neighborhoods and from neighborhoods that looked as if they might become black. When they were established the Federal Housing Authority and the Veterans Administration in housing followed suit.[60]

The consequences are clear. On threat of death, blacks of all economic classes were forced into black ghettoes. Funds were not available to rehabilitate housing in these areas or to encourage home-ownership. The neighborhoods therefore acquired outside, "slum" landlords and were seen by private and public institutions as poor credit risks. While housing in white neighborhoods increased in value, housing in black neighborhoods did not. While the wealth that whites invested in their real estate increased, that of blacks did not. While whites passed on their wealth to their children and continue to do so, blacks could and can pass on much less. How can we trace progress toward eliminating this discrepancy unless we continue to categorize people as black and white?

On the one hand, then, in taking up identities as blacks and whites we take up dubious identifications, identifications that are,

---

[57] See Thomas M. Shapiro, *The Hidden Cost of Being African American: How Wealth Perpetuates Inequality* (New York: Oxford University Press, 2004), p. 62.

[58] See Douglas S. Massey and Nancy A. Denton, *American Apartheid: Segregation and the Making of the Underclass* (Cambridge, MA: Harvard University Press, 1993), p. 30.

[59] *Ibid.*, pp. 36–7.   [60] *Ibid.*, pp. 50–53.

at least in part, the results of coercion and violence and, moreover, that are riven with internal contradictions. On the other hand, in not taking them up, we threaten our capacity to assess progress towards and retreat from equality. What, then, should we do about our racial identities? In order to answer this question, we need, I think, to return to the question of what our racial identities are. Calling them the consequences of power, solidarity, and opposition to power does not answer the question of what they are. In order to do so, I want to look at the phenomenon of passing.

PASSING AND AUTHENTICITY

K. Anthony Appiah attempts to get clear on what race is (and is not) by turning to Hacking's account of Sartre's description of the garçon de café. Hacking employs this description to illuminate the contextual character of identity: like a witch, the garçon de café, whose movements are "quick and forward, a little too precise, a little too rapid,"[61] is possible only within a certain set of social practices, institutions, and linguistic formulations. One can no more possess the identity of a garçon de café in the United States of the early twenty-first century than one can possess the identity of a witch or a serf in 1940s Paris. Yet, while the identity of a garçon de café requires a specific institutional, linguistic, and practical context, Appiah insists that racial identities require more: "The ideal of the garçon de café lacks," he says, "the sort of theoretical commitments that are trailed by the idea of the black and the white."[62]

What theoretical commitments does the idea of black and white trail? Examining the phenomenon of passing sheds some light. There is no difference between being a garçon de café and passing as one in a Parisian café in the 1940s. If one functioned as a waiter in the

[61] Cited in K. Anthony Appiah, "Race, Culture Identity: Misunderstood Connections," in K. Anthony Appiah and Amy Gutmann, *Color Conscious: The Political Morality of Race* (Princeton, NJ: Princeton University Press, 1996), p. 78. Also see Appiah, *The Ethics of Identity*, p. 66.

[62] Appiah and Gutmann, "Race, Culture Identity," p. 79. Also see Appiah, *The Ethics of Identity*, p. 66.

appropriate context and if one has mastered the appropriate movements and sensibility, one simply is a garçon de café. In contrast,
there is a difference between being a white and passing as one in the
United States. Suppose one functioned as a white undergraduate in a
1940s American university and suppose one mastered the appropriate
movements and sensibility of a white American undergraduate. One
might still have been "passing." If we want to know what the source
for this difference is – that is, the source of the difference between, on
the one hand, being a garçon de café and passing as one and, on the
other hand, being a white and passing as one – we should ask, first,
what the source is for the difference between being a white and passing
as one. When certain nineteenth-century courts appealed to the
behavior and the exercising of the privileges of whites in as criteria
for being white, they did not do so because they thought that passing
as white was the same as being white. Rather, they feared the consequences of looking much beyond behavior and privileges. To have
been brought up as a white person sometimes counted as being a white
person but not because the courts thought there was no difference
between passing as and being white. Rather, at least according to
Randall Kennedy, given the intermixing of populations, courts could
not guarantee that they would not find skeletons in the wrong closets.

So, if there is a difference between being white and passing as
white, what is it? It cannot rest on physical characteristics since the
condition of passing is that there are none of the physical features that
might signal membership in the "wrong race." Nor can the difference
rest on genetic characteristics. To be sure, if suspicious university
administrators had had the technology in the 1940s, they might have
swabbed the insides of prospective students' cheeks in order to
retrieve DNA samples, just as Olympic officials currently do in trying
to determine the sex of athletes. Of course, given that 21 percent of
whites had black ancestry in 1958 and that most "blacks" were then
living as whites, 1940s university administrators might have had to
sustain a serious deficit in eligible students if they had looked to DNA.
Nor is it clear that the DNA samples would have done them any more

good than they do Olympics officials. Just as one can be a woman with XY chromosomes, one can be a white with a very different genetic make up than another white.[63] Indeed, although some recent research correlates certain short segments of DNA known as markers with broad geographical groups that sometimes correspond with the groups that count socially as races, they do not always do so. Furthermore, the long history of population mixing between people from different continents (for both conquest and other reasons) means that we would need to select a necessarily arbitrary date for linking markers with groups to have any correlation between genes and social races. Among others, Armand Marie Leroi tries to defend distinctions between races (without considering them "very fundamental") by insisting that "people of European descent have a set of genetic variants in common that are collectively rare in everyone else."[64] The problem for the university administrators, however, would be to decide, first, whether by white they meant European and, second, whether a prospective student who possessed the set of genetic variants was a European or someone belonging to the group in which the genetic variants were rare.

The difference between being a white and passing as a white cannot be attributed to physical or genetic features. So to what can it be attributed? Appiah's claim that our ideas of black and white trail "theoretical commitments" suggests that the difference lies only in these "theoretical commitments." That is, it lies only in our commitment to the belief that there is a difference. Holding firm to this commitment, we admit that we may not yet possess plausible or consistent grounds for making racial ascriptions. Nevertheless, we remain faithful to three ideas: first, it is possible that there is a racial difference between whites and blacks as well as between whites,

---

[63] See Cornell and Hartmann, *Ethnicity and Race*, pp. 22–23; Amy Gutmann, "Responding to Racial Injustice," Appiah and Gutmann, *Color Conscious*, p. 115; and Lawrence Blum, *I'm Not a Racist, But: The Moral Quandary of Race* (Ithaca, NY: Cornell University Press, 2002), pp. 138–140.

[64] Armand Marie Leroi, "A Family Tree in Every Gene," *New York Times*, March 14, 2005, p. A23.

blacks, and other races; second, in the future science will tell us what this difference is; and, third, one can therefore pass as a white without really being one.

Appiah's reference to theoretical commitments thus suggests that the basis of the distinction between being white and passing as white is a commitment to the idea that there is a fact of the matter as to whether someone is white or not. One need not know, or even want to know, what that fact of the matter is, but one assumes that it exists. To return to the question of the difference between passing as a white and passing as a garçon de café, then, the difference here is that the identity of a garçon de café "trails" no such theoretical commitments. Being white is more than performing as a white in a way, then, that being a garçon de café is not more than the performance. One is a garçon de café as long as one acts as one.

The comparison of racial identities with identities as geniuses and anorexics reveals an additional feature of our theoretical commitments. On the one hand, it is hard to see how there could be a difference between being an anorexic and passing as one. Even if one began by only passing as an anorexic, sooner or later the effect of not eating would be enough to make one an anorexic. Similarly if one pretends to be a genius by secretly working harder than anyone else, the quality of one's ideas and progress could turn out to be such as to make one a genius in the eyes of the world. On the other hand, doctors and educators can stipulate very precise standards for status as an anorexic or genius. Doctors can define an anorexic as someone who eats less than a certain number of calories a day and educators can define a genius as someone who scores above a certain level on an IQ test. These stipulative definitions mean that, in a certain sense, one can pass for an anorexic or a genius in one's daily life without actually being one, at least if being one means meeting the stipulated criteria. Yet, these criteria are useful only for carefully delimited purposes in medical care and education. Moreover, they reflect just the kind of professional agreement that stipulations of racial identity lack. Instead, in the nineteenth century, one court's definition of being black or being white was on another court's rejection list. Even after the one-drop rule became widely employed, courts such as the *Bennett* court continued to look elsewhere and the rule was of no use in deciding who was white. Some American Indian tribes have stipulated ancestral requirements for membership. Yet, these requirements stipulate membership in the tribe, not status as an American Indian. Instead, American Indians are another racialized group to whose separate identity we have theoretical commitments. Indeed, the difference between stipulated criteria for being a genius or an anorexic and our ideas about racial identities makes the difference between being white and "passing as white" all the more a merely theoretical commitment. The difference depends both on supposing there is a difference and on supposing that, even though "experts" do not agree now on what the difference is, someday they will.

Yet, if the difference between being white and passing as white rests only on theoretical commitments, we should rethink the difference between racial identity and identity as a garçon de café. Our commitments are theoretical in the pejorative sense. We are committed to the idea that there is a difference between being a white and passing as a white, whereas we are not at all committed to the idea that there is a difference between being a garçon de café and passing as one. Of course, social constructionists have taught us that our thinking and behaving as if there were a difference functions simply and efficiently to create one. Yet, this analysis of the creation of racial identities leads to a question similar to the one I asked about a de-essentialized politics of recognition. If our racial identities and identifications differ from other sorts of identities and identifications only on the basis of merely theoretical commitments, we might ask whether we should uphold these commitments and continue to act as if there were a difference. Indeed, given the horrors and confusions to which our commitments have given rise, we might ask why we should not de-commit from them and work against racial identities and identifications. This option is one that Appiah has also considered so I want to conclude this chapter by considering his proposal.

RACE AND RECREATION

Appiah asks us to remember that:

> We are not simply black or white or yellow or brown, gay or straight
> or bisexual, Jewish, Christian, Moslem, Buddhist or Confucian ...
> we are also brothers and sisters; parents and children, liberals,
> conservative, and leftists; teachers and lawyers and auto-makers
> and gardeners; fans of the Padres and the Bruins; amateurs of grunge
> rock and lovers of Wagner; movie buffs; MTV-holics, mystery
> readers; surfers and singers; poets and pet-lovers; students and
> teachers; friends and lovers ... even as we struggle against racism ...
> let us not let our racial identities subject us to new tyrannies.[65]

Appiah makes a two-pronged plea here. On the one hand, he asks us
to continue to struggle for racial justice and even to do so under the aegis
of a politics of recognition. On the other hand, he asks us not to suppose
that the racial, religious, and national identities we currently possess are
ones that we ought unthinkingly to project into the future. Instead, he
thinks that we ought to work against their tendency to "go imperial"[66]
and to remember, instead, the power of cross-cutting and interlocking
affiliations. The effect of this emphasis, he suggests, would be to move
our racial and national identities in more "recreational"[67] directions.

It is not entirely clear what Appiah means by "recreational"
directions, but he does point to Irish American identity as an example.
Calling an Irish American identity a recreational one is not to deny
that it is the result of various social, historical, and political processes.
Nor is it to deny that this identification once possessed social and
political meaning, or that it was introjected by individuals who therefore identified as Irish. Finally, it is not to overlook the possible
psychological importance and meaning that an Irish American identity can have. For some, the identity is a source of self-esteem and

[65] Appiah and Gutmann, "Race, Culture, Identity," pp. 103–104. Also see Amartya
Sen, *Identity and Violence: The Illusion of Destiny* (New York: W.W. Norton,
2006), esp. chapters 1–5.

[66] Appiah and Gutmann, "Race, Culture, Identity," p. 103.   [67] *Ibid.*, p. 103.

value in their lives.[68] Yet, Appiah's point is surely that Americans with some amount of Irish ancestry have options. They can seek identification as Irish Americans and they can appropriate and endorse their Irish American identities. Nevertheless, they can also elect not to. Furthermore, even if they do insist on recognition as Irish Americans, the identity no longer has clout as a source of possible life-plans or possibilities. Although the identity can be individually meaningful, social practices and institutions simply no longer serve to construct the Irish American as a socially meaningful type. In reflecting on their Irish heritage, then, Irish Americans can look to a feature of their history that remains purely incidental in as much as it simply possesses no influence on what they can or decide to do. Being Irish American is an entirely personal feature of identity, a feature of heritage that one might to refer to in casual conversation, celebrate on certain holidays, and use as a reference point in naming one's children. On most other occasions, it has no purchase.

These considerations may not be the ones Appiah intends to highlight in citing Irish American identities. Nevertheless, developments in Irish American identities and attributions serve as good examples of what we might call the privatization of a public identity. Indeed, Irish American identities have moved from what the nineteenth century understood as racial identities to non-racial, ethnic, and, indeed, ornamentally ethnic ones. In the 1840s, American Anglo-Saxons defined the "race" of new Irish immigrants in terms of dark skin, big hands and feet, broad teeth, and pug noses. The Irish were "pot-bellied, bow-legged, and abortively featured ... especially remarkable for open, projecting mouths, with prominent teeth and exposed gums, their advancing cheekbones and depressed noses bearing barbarism on the very front."[69] In addition, they were ignorant and

[68] See David Copp, "Social Unity and the Identity of Persons," *Journal of Political Philosophy*, 10 (4), 2002.

[69] Cited in Matthew Frye Jacobson, *Whiteness of a Different Color: European Immigrants and the Alchemy of Race* (Cambridge, MA: Harvard University Press, 1998), p. 46.

possessed of genetic propensities to violence and other riotous forms of behavior that emphasized their intrinsic difference from the civilized races. The nineteenth-century Irish themselves acknowledged and introjected their racial status. In an early form of the politics of identity, they simply reversed the value of being Irish and demanded recognition for it. Nevertheless, in the course of American history, Irish American identities became optional, identities worthy of only occasional and ceremonial comment.

If an African American identity were to follow the Irish American trajectory, it would involve two steps: a move from a racial identity to an ethnic one and a move from African ethnicity as a socially important identification to African ethnicity as an entirely personal option. While it might influence the artifacts one chose to help decorate one's home or the names one gave one's children, it would have no bearing on one's life-plans, opportunities, public roles, or public identity. Nevertheless, this second step highlights the difference between Irish American identities and an African American one. Arguably, the transition of an Irish American identity from a socially important racial ascription to an optional ethnic self-identification itself contributed to reinforcing the non-optional character of a black racial identity. During the course of the nineteenth century, various immigrant groups, including the Irish, were integrated and even assimilated as parts of American society, at least in part, as an element in the justification of slavery. Because slavery had to be shown to be legitimate, other so-deemed racial differences had to be distinguished from the African racial difference. Hence, one strategy for viewing the Irish immigrants was to understand them as simply a diseased stock of whites, a stock that over time could be restored to health. "It is wonderful," one observer wrote, "how rapidly the lower class of Irish ... do improve in America when they are well fed and comfortably lodged."[70] The same could not be said for the Africans. They were,

---

[70] Josiah Nott, *Two Lectures on the Connection Between the Biblical and the Physical History of Man* (1849). Cited in Jacobson, *Whiteness of a Different Color*, p. 46.

in the words of a pro-slavery advocate, "as absolutely and specifically unlike the American as when the race first touched the soil and first breathed the air of the New World."[71]

Differences between Anglo-Saxons and Irish became matters of health and environment while differences between Anglo-Saxons and Africans became matters of nature. This development suggests a disturbing relation between racial identities and Appiah's recreational identities. Attribution and self-attribution as an Irish American can be recreational and largely private because attribution and self-attribution as a white becomes or remains non-recreational and public. In contrast, it is not possible to identify oneself or to be identified as an African American in a recreational or private way. In fact, neither identification as an African American nor identification as a black is recreational. One remains publicly African American because and insofar as one remains publicly black. The same holds for Asian and Hispanic identities. One cannot either self-identify or be identified as Chinese American or Japanese American in a recreational way. Instead, one remains publicly Asian and, indeed, foreign. Nor can one identify oneself or be identified as Mexican American or Columbian American in a recreational way. Rather, one remains publicly Hispanic or Latino/a. The move in which some racial identities become ethnic identities and then recreational ethnic identities thus entrenches the move in which other racial identities are reinforced.

In chapter 3, I want to see if shifting focus can help to rethink racial identities in the way that Appiah favors. Rather than focusing on the mechanics of social construction as a means of doing so, however, I want to turn to the interpretation of meaning.

---

[71] J. H. Van Evrie, *The Negro and Negro Slavery* (1863). Cited in Jacobson, *Whiteness of a Different Color*, p. 44.

3   Race and interpretation

Some of our identities are clearly only occasional and, moreover, recreational since they are defined by occasional and recreational activities. We are BBC lovers and baseball fans, for example, because and to the extent that we watch the BBC and baseball games. These identities are "constructed" to the extent that they depend on events, activities, and amusements specific to the histories and societies of which we are a part. We could not be baseball fans unless there were a game of baseball and we could not be BBC lovers in the USA before the advent of cable television. The identities also have looping effects, as we saw in chapter 2. They are not only made possible by the availability of these activities and amusements in the society of which we are a part but also loop back to develop the activities and amusements that make them possible. Someone invents the game of baseball, for example, and people begin to enjoy playing and watching it. Professional teams appear and individuals become fans of specific ones. This team identification feeds back into the public institution of baseball and changes the place and status it has in the society of which it is a part. In turn, the public institution of baseball changes and restructures what it means to be a baseball fan.

The dependence of this sort of occasional identification and identity on activities that are regarded as entertainments means that the identifications and identities are optional and their scope is only partial. We must consciously adopt the activities that contribute to them and the identity never goes "imperial," invading all or even most contexts of identification. Even if one is an inveterate Red Sox fan, for example, and even if one advises others of one's preference, talks constantly about the Red Sox, wears Red Sox paraphernalia, and so on, one does not receive medical treatment as a Red Sox fan nor is the baseball team one roots for a question on the US census. Identities that we possess other than those as fans take precedence in different situations. Moreover, one can give up being a Red Sox fan simply on one's own initiative and simply by ceasing to "perform" as one. Even if it is not clear that a Red Sox fan can ever become a Yankees fan, he or she can stop identifying as or being identified by others as the former.

We possess other identities and make other sorts of identifications that seem to be less partial and optional. We are siblings, for example, if we have a brother or sister and we are not the ones with options in this matter. As part of the institution of the family, this identity and identification possesses its own feedback loop in which the identity strengthens the institution of the family and the institution strengthens the identity. At the same time, our identities as siblings remain occasional ones. Few people identify themselves as siblings in most aspects of their lives; similarly, we identify others as siblings usually only if they are our own or if we come to know them through their siblings. Furthermore, if identity as a sibling is not optional, the psychological place the identity has in our life is optional. We can choose to take up the burdens and benefits of the identity or, at least as adults, refuse to have any contact at all with our brothers or sisters. Our status as Americans is similar. If we are born and raised in the United States, being an American is initially beyond our control. Yet, we can decide that we no longer want to be Americans; we can emigrate to other countries and apply for citizenship elsewhere. Although some of the citizens in our adopted country may continue to see us as Americans, if we shed or downplay all of our American characteristics, affiliations, and so on – if, in other words, we cease to behave as Americans – it is also possible that this identification will fade and that we will come to be identified in other terms.

Racial identities and identifications appear to be different. On the one hand, just as in the case of our identities and identifications as baseball fans or Americans, we cannot be blacks and whites unless the identity and identification are available. Just as we cannot be garçons de café in Medieval France, we cannot be blacks or whites until and unless our society makes use of racial categories. Moreover, race involves the same sort of looping effect that baseball or American citizenship does. Certain individuals come to be identified as black on the basis of a series of actions, institutions, legal decisions, and so on, and this identification loops back into the way these individuals come to think of themselves and to react to their environment. The internal identification then reacts back upon the external one: in order to survive and flourish Africans create new institutions, religions, and forms of solidarity that emphasize their identities as blacks and reinforce their distinction from whites. The religious institutions and civil rights organizations that blacks establish loop back onto the society to change both it and the significance of various identifications. The feedback loop continues.

Nevertheless, our racial identities and identifications go "imperial" in a way that neither our status as baseball fans nor even our status as Americans or brothers and sisters does. We must opt in to being baseball fans; we can opt out of being Americans and can have so little to do with our siblings that any identification of who we are as a brother or sister will be confined to the most narrow of contexts. We have none of these options with regard to our racial identities and identifications. We cannot opt in to being a black, a white, an Asian, or a Hispanic in the way that we can opt in to being a baseball fan; instead we are always already "in." Nor can we opt out of these designations even to the degree that we can opt out of being Americans. To be sure, we can move to a country with a different racial typology where we might not be black, for example. Yet, when ex-Americans return to the United States to visit, they arguably remain ex-Americans or at the very least can intelligibly insist that they are. When ex-blacks return, they become blacks and they cannot intelligibly insist that they are not. Those of "mixed" heritage may define themselves in many ways. The 2000 US census allowed individuals to select up to six races and ethnicities as descriptions of who or what they were and the result was fifty-seven possibilities and combinations.[1] It is not clear, however, that these combinations have dislodged our basic racial categories or restricted the contexts in which people possess them. We self-identify and others identify us as Irish Americans only in special situations. The same does not hold of identifications as whites or blacks, Latinolas, or Asians. We cannot become an ex-white in the same way that we can become an ex-patriot. If we shed or downplay our white characteristics and affiliations – if we cease to act as whites – we remain whites trying to pretend that we are not. The same inability to shed one's racial identity holds of being black. Indeed, in this case, shedding or downplaying one's black characteristics – ceasing to live and act as a black – is seen as a form of inauthenticity or "passing." The conditions of racial identities and identifications deviate from the conditions of other identities and identifications because, in Appiah's words, we are theoretically committed to them in a way that we are not theoretically committed to other identities we possess.[2]

We may not want to erase our racialized identities entirely. Indeed, in moral – psychological terms, we may find a great deal of value in them. That is, it may be important to us that we are Irish American or African American and we may even find this identity to be the source of what is best about us. Nevertheless, recognizing the moral – psychological value of some identities, including racial ones, is consistent with worrying about the basis for our theoretical commitments. The worth of an identity is its worth for our private flourishing, not its worth for purposes of public identification. Our racial commitments are as fraught with difficulties as they are difficult to dislodge. How might we make a start?

---

[1] "Census' Multiracial Option Overturns Traditional Views," *Los Angeles Times*, March 5, 2001, p. 1.

[2] K. Anthony Appiah, "Race, Culture, Identity: Misunderstood Connections," in K. Anthony Appiah and Amy Gutmann, *Color consciousness: The Political Morality of Race* (Princeton, NJ: Princeton University Press, 1996), p. 78.

Social constructionist accounts of racial identities do not allow us to discriminate between public and private identities, or even between good and bad identities. All identities are similarly constructions and similarly bound up with power. Yet, suppose we focus not on the causes of racial constructions but, instead, on the structure of racial understandings. That is, suppose we ask not why or how individuals become raced but what being a particular race is. In this chapter, I want to suggest that to identify oneself or someone else as a black, white, Asian, Latino, or Latina is to understand oneself or the other person in a certain way. In this regard, our racial identities and identifications are no different from our identities and identifications as baseball fans, siblings, and Americans. They are ways of understanding individuals within a certain context, from a particular point of view, and in light of certain relations. In order to clarify this suggestion, I shall start with literature and the arts, where questions of understanding have their principal home.

UNDERSTANDING TEXTS AND WORKS OF ART

Just as we want to know what or who we and others are, we want to know what particular texts and paintings are, and just as we understand individuals in certain ways as blacks, whites, Asians, or Latinas, or Latinos, we understand texts in certain ways: as arguments for theories of justice, as life-stories, and so on. How do we come to these understandings and how do we determine their validity? In what follows, I want to try to skirt debates over literary theory as much as possible and simply to describe the process of what we might call ordinary understanding in our reading of texts and works of art. The description of this process relies, in part, on the German hermeneutic tradition of Schleiermacher, Heidegger, and Gadamer.[3] Nevertheless, to the extent

---

[3] See, in particular, Friedrich Schleiermacher, *Hermeneutics and Criticism and Other Writings* , trans. David Bowie (Cambridge: Cambridge University Press, 1998), esp. pp. 24, 27–29; Martin Heidegger, *Being and Time*, trans. John Macquarrie and Edward Robinson (New York: Harper & Row, 1962), esp. sections 31, 32; Hans-Georg Gadamer, *Truth and Method*, 2nd rev. edn., trans. Joel Weinsheimer and Donald G. Marshall (New York: Continuum, 1994), esp., pp. 265–380.

that it does so, it tries not to offer a competing theory to deconstruction, reception theory, queer theory, or the like but to try to get at the aspects of reading and understanding central to all of them.

In approaching a text or work of art, we anticipate the meaning the work has as a whole as an orientation to deciphering its initial parts. We then use the way we understand the initial parts to reconsider and possibly revise our anticipation of the meaning of subsequent parts and the whole, and we do the same with each new part of the text we read. We suppose that a particular text is a piece of philosophy and we there-fore approach its first sentences as the specification of a problem or the first steps in an argument. We suppose that another text is a love story and so we read its first pages as the setting up of an emotional tension or personal issue that will later be resolved. Our subsequent reading of the texts tries to work out these assumptions. Coming to understand the text is a circular process of projecting and revising in which we try to fit our readings of part and whole together so that the text emerges for us as a self-consistent unity of meaning. Of course, this attempt can fail. Our initial assumptions about the text may make it impossible for us to understand its beginning parts or our understanding of its beginning parts may make it impossible to understand its later parts. If so, we can revise our initial understandings and projections in light of our under-standing of the later parts and continue attempting to fit the parts of the text together until we reach an understanding that succeeds in integrat-ing the parts with the whole.

To be sure, this description of the so-called hermeneutic circle seems right at the start to involve itself in literary debates. Deconstructive approaches to texts insist that the attempt to integrate the text as a self-consistent whole not only can fail, but must fail. Rather than "totalizing" the text, a close reading illuminates its fis-sures – or, in other words, the points in the text in which what is not said undermines what is said.[4] On this view, the procedure described

---

[4] See Jeffrey T. Nealon, "The Discipline of Deconstruction," *PMLA*, 107 (5), 1992, pp. 1266–1279.

above is not a neutral description of the process of coming to understand a text. Instead, it is a particular prescription for how we ought to
try to understand a text – a prescription, moreover, that fails to question conventional and traditional assumptions. In contrast, following
Jacques Derrida, deconstructive critics promote readings that try to
challenge the "binary oppositions" a particular text assumes. The first
point of a deconstructive reading is to show that these oppositions
involve hierarchies: speech over writing, serious over non-serious,
philosophy over literature, inside over outside, literal over figurative,
for example.[5] The second point is to dismantle the hierarchy and
restructure the oppositions in a new and revealing way.[6] Yet, it is
difficult to see how we can avoid totalizing in our understanding
of texts. Deconstruction of oppositions requires that we first recognize them. If we want to show that the "privileged term" in an opposition depends upon the unprivileged one, or that presence depends
upon absence, we must first understand that presence or the privileged term and the way it is defined by its opposite. Derrida, at least,
seems to conceive of this understanding as a contextual one in which a
term derives its meaning from the whole of which it is a part. He
writes:

> The word "deconstruction" like all other words acquires its value
> only from its inscription in a chain of possible substitutions, in
> what is too blithely called a "context." For me, for what I have tried
> and still try to write, the word only has an interest within a certain
> context where it replaces and lets itself be determined by such other
> words as "écriture," "trace," "supplement," "hymen," "pharmakon,"
> "margin."[7]

---

[5] See Jonathon Culler *et al.*, "The Discipline of Deconstruction," *PMLA*, 8, 1993,
p. 534.

[6] J. Douglas Neale, "Deconstruction," Michael Groden and Martin Kreiswirth, *The
Johns Hopkins Guide to Literary Theory and Criticism* (Baltimore, MD: Johns
Hopkins University Press, 1994), pp. 186–187.

[7] Jacques Derrida, "Letter to a Japanese Friend," in Robert Bernasconi and David
Woods, eds., *Derrida and Difference* (Coventry, UK: Parousia, 1985), p. 7.

The circular process of understanding the part in terms of the whole and the whole in terms of the part, however "blithely" understood, remains necessary to reading even if our primary concern is to show that the way the meaning the text might be taken to possess is altered by the meanings it excludes. What is excluded can be as much a part of our totalized understanding as what is included insofar as it contributes to the whole in terms of which we understand the parts.

The description of understanding in terms of the hermeneutic circle raises another question, however: namely, can texts and works of art be understood in only one way? Deconstruction takes as part of the holistic content of a text that which it excludes or refuses to privilege. Does this strategy not suggest that there are many different ways in which we might try to understand a text or work of art, even if all of them attempt to integrate parts and whole? If so, how do we determine which integration best illuminates the text at issue? Take two views of Jane Austen's novel, *Sense and Sensibility*. One reading of it contrasts Elinor's virtues of self-restraint to Marianne's excesses of emotion. What *Sense and Sensibility* shows on this reading is that the communication of hopes, fears, joys, and disappointments that we contemporary Americans often take to be constitutive of intimate relationships is, instead, a kind of vice. Real consideration for those we love demands that we forgo burdening them with the particular circumstances of our life, especially if they can do little or nothing about them. But compare this understanding to Eve Sedgwick's in "Jane Austen and the Masturbating Girl," which focuses not on the contrast between Elinor and Marianne but instead on the homoerotic character of their relation.[8] Elinor, in Sedgwick's view, is obsessed with Marianne while Marianne is obsessed with herself. Marianne is masturbatory and Elinor is codependent in a way that undermines the self-restraint that the first reading attributes to her. "Elinor's pupils, those less tractable sphincters of the soul, won't close against the

---

[8] Eve Sedgwick, "Jane Austen and the Masturbating Girl," in Eve Sedgwick, *Tendencies* (Durham, MD: Duke University Press, 1993).

hapless hemorrhaging of her visual attention flow toward Marianne."[9] Which reading of the novel is better or correct? One reading takes the whole of the novel to involve an illustration of a particular virtue and reads the parts of the novel in these terms, understanding Elinor's attraction to Edward Ferrars, for example, as an attraction to someone similar to her in his restrained propriety. In contrast, Sedgwick's reading takes the whole to be the specification of a forbidden emotion and reads the rest of the novel in these terms. Thus, Elinor's attraction to Edward Ferrars involves his similarity, not to herself, but to Marianne in that both suffer from what Sedgwick calls *"mauvaise honte."* Are these readings competitive with one another? Might they both be valid?

Intentionalism in literary theory has always tried to avoid an affirmative answer to this question by insisting that the context or whole necessary to understanding a part is the one the author intended.[10] Schleiermacher saw the point of the hermeneutic circle as that of ensuring a correct apprehension of what an author meant to say, and E. D. Hirsch argued that the task of understanding the meaning of a literary or artistic work remained that of determining the meanings that its author or creator was trying to express. Hirsch and other intentionalists were willing to concede that such efforts often diminished the work by engaging in a kind of biographical excess. Nevertheless, they also rejected the suggestion of W. K. Wimsatt, Jr. and Monroe C. Beardsley's famous 1946 article, "The Intentional Fallacy."[11] If texts were to be understood in their own terms rather

---

[9] Sedgwick, "Jane Austen and the Masturbating Girl," p. 124.

[10] See, for example, E. D. Hirsch, *Validity in Interpretation* (New Haven, CT, Yale University Press, 1967, 6th edn., 1975); Stephen Knapp and Walter Benn Michaels, "Against Theory," in W. J. T. Mitchell, ed., *Against Theory: Literary Studies and the New Pragmatism* (Chicago, IL: University of Chicago Press, 1985); Stephen Knapp and Walter Benn Michaels, "Against Theory 2: Hermeneutics and Deconstruction," *Critical Inquiry*, 14, 1987; Noël Carroll, "Art, Intention and Conversation," in Gary Iseminger, ed., *Intention and Interpretation* (Philadelphia, PA: Temple University Press, 1992).

[11] In W. K. Wimsatt, Jr., *The Verbal Icon: Studies in the Meaning of Poetry* (Lexington, KT: University of Kentucky Press, 1954).

than their biographical context, those terms remained the author's. Any particular sequence of words could have many meanings, E. D. Hirsch pointed out. Hence, attaching a particular or "determinate" meaning to a sequence required that readers identify it with a particular author's "act of will." Otherwise, "there would be no distinction between what an author does mean by a word sequence and what he could mean by it."[12]

Some contemporary intentionalists have pointed to the oddness of the conception of intentions involved in the original controversy over Wimsatt and Beardsley's article.[13] Wimsatt, Beardsley, and Hirsch all refer to intentions as if they were mental events and to texts and works of art as if they were public events, related to intentions as effects to causes. Following Wittgenstein, however, Noël Carroll re-positions intentions within a text or work of art. Intentions are linguistic rather than mental phenomena and, as such, they are already parts of the sequences of words that Hirsch wants to define in reference to them. Hence, while Hirsch claims that "meaning is an affair of consciousness not of words,"[14] a neo-Wittgensteinian view insists that the attempt to determine what the intentions of the author of a text are does not require looking outside of the text itself. Instead, they are part of its "purposive structure." As Carroll puts the point:

> Searching for authorial intention is ... not a matter of ... looking for some independent, private, mental episode or cause that is logically remote from the meaning ... of the work. The intention is evident in the work itself, and, insofar as the intention is identified as the purposive structure of the work, the intention is the focus of our interest in and attention to the artwork.[15]

[12] Hirsch, *Validity in Interpretation*, p. 47.
[13] See Carroll, "Art, Intention and Conversation" and Colin Lyas, "Wittgensteinian Intentions," in Gary Iseminger, ed., *Intention and Interpretation* (Philadelphia, PA: Temple University Press, 1992).
[14] Hirsch, *Validity in Interpretation*, p. 4.
[15] Carroll, "Art, Intention and Conversation," p. 101.

Carroll uses this point to argue against Beardsley's anti-intentionalism. In an example that is supposed to show the irrelevance of an
author's intention, Beardsley writes that "if a sculptor tells us that his
statue was intended to be smooth and blue, but our senses tell us it is
rough and pink, we go by our senses."[16] Yet, in this case, Carroll
claims, we do not dismiss the sculptor's remarks because we think
that an artist's intentions are irrelevant to the meaning of a work.
Rather, we dismiss them because we suspect that this particular artist
is being insincere. Carroll thinks that the same holds for the note with
which Andrew Greeley prefaces his novel 1983, Ascent into Hell, a
novel that Carroll calls "soft-core pornography, spiced with religious
taboos."[17] In his note, however, Greeley implies that the novel is an
allegory of Passover. Should we not therefore understand it in the way
that Greeley, its author, advises? Carroll rejects this idea but denies
that doing so implies any anti-intentionalism. Instead, "The inten-
tionalist can reject the "Passover interpretations of Ascent into Hell in
the face of Greeley's implied intentions by denying that it is plausible
to accept the authenticity of Greeley's ostensible intent."[18]

But what is the basis on which we deny the authenticity of the
"ostensible intent?" It has to be our understanding of how the parts –
in this case, the novel and the note – fit together as a coherent whole.
We can understand Greeley's note as an attempt "to reassure his
Catholic readership that his book was not irreligious."[19] If we do so,
however, it is because we are trying to integrate our understanding of
the note with our understanding of the text. If the text is soft-core
pornography, as Carroll thinks, then the note must be an attempt to
placate Greeley's readers. In contrast, if we understand the text as an
allegory, we might understand Greeley's intentions in the note as
guiding us to that recognition. The same need to integrate part and
whole holds for the way we understand the sculptor's intentions.

[16] Monroe C. Beardsley, Aesthetics (New York: Harcourt, Brace & World, 1958) p. 20;
cited in Carroll, "Art, Intention and Conversation," p. 98.
[17] Carroll, "Art, Intention and Conversation," p. 99.
[18] Ibid., p. 99.   [19] Ibid., p. 99.

Because we understand the statue to be rough and pink, we understand the sculptor's expression of an intention to make something smooth and blue to be either ironic or an attempt to achieve notoriety. In both cases, the meaning we ascribe to the text or sculpture conditions the meaning we ascribe to the author's or artist's intentions. Despite his defense of intentionalism, Carroll makes the same point, "The artwork is criterial to attributions of intention."[20] We decide what an author's or artist's intentions are, not by asking him or her, but by reading or looking at the work itself. Indeed, when we do ask an author or artist what he or she meant to do, as in the case of Beardsley's sculptor, we understand their answer only in terms of our understanding of the work.

So how are we to understand the work? Consider our understanding of actions. In acting, we intend to do one thing rather than another. Yet, what we actually do is rarely a perfect expression of our intentions. Instead, we often act upon intentions we did not know we had, or we do more than or something different from what we intended to do. We are also obliged to react to the actions of others and to modify our plans to respond to unforeseen circumstances. Indeed, even where we are able to execute our own plans without modification, they become part of a sequence of reactions and events over which we can have no intentional control. We intend to supply water to a village by pumping water to it from a well. Yet, because, unbeknownst to us, someone has poisoned the well, we kill the villagers.[21] We understand the beginning events of the Six-Day War as the beginning events of the Six-Day War even though no one intended them as the beginning events of the Six-Day War and even though we can understand them in this way only in conjunction with the subsequent events that continued and ended the war in six days.[22] For these reasons, it is misleading to read actions as expressions of their actors' original

[20] *Ibid.*, p. 101.
[21] See G. E. M. Anscombe, *Intentions* (Oxford: Basil Blackwell, 1957), p. 39.
[22] See Arthur Danto, *Analytical Philosophy of History* (Cambridge: Cambridge University Press, 1965).

intentions. We may have intended to pump water to a village but it is still possible to describe the action as poisoning its inhabitants. Firing shots at Fort Sumter can be understood as the start of the Civil War even though the shooters may have themselves intended only to proclaim their independence. Thus, the understanding that we and others have of our actions normally includes accounts that float free of our or anyone's intentions because actions become parts of a history that goes beyond these intentions. How we understand the action depends upon the subsequent history in terms of which we understand it.

The same holds of texts and works of art. They enter into an interpretive history by connecting up with other texts that had not yet been written when they first appeared as well as with criticisms not yet made and with actions and events that had not yet occurred. When we understand them, then, what we understand includes a history that neither their authors not their original audiences could possess. Terence Hawkes writes of Shakespeare's *Hamlet*, "At one time, this must obviously have been an interesting play written by a promising Elizabethan playwright. However, equally obviously, this is no longer the case."[23] *Hamlet* can no more be simply an interesting play for even the most unsophisticated high-school student than, for him or her, the First World War can be The Great War. Just as we understand the meanings of actions as parts of particular histories, we understand texts in terms of what Gadamer calls "effective history."[24] The meaning *Hamlet* has for us contains its afterlife. When we read it or see it performed, we read and see a different text than the one Shakespeare may have thought he was writing or than his original audience may have seen. We read and see a play that includes connections and intersections with texts written after it and ideas that post-date it. We understand *Hamlet* in terms of *Oedipus Rex*, whether or not Shakespeare meant us to because Freud taught us to; we understand

---

[23] Terence Hawkes, *Meaning by Shakespeare* (New York: Routledge, 1992), p. 4.
[24] Gadamer, *Truth and Method*, esp. pp. 300–302.

it in terms of existentialism because writers after the Second World War illuminated it in this way; we might even understand it in terms of Disney's "The Lion King," as a recent essay "The Lion King and Hamlet: A Homecoming for the Exiled Child" did. Disney, too, conditions our frame of reference.[25]

We need not be experts in the work of Freud, Sartre, or Disney for this work to be a possible part of the text for us. When we read the texts of our history, we do so from a historical perspective that goes beyond them. Yet, this perspective is one to which they have also already contributed. If we can read *Hamlet* in terms of *The Lion King*, we can do so because *Hamlet* has already influenced the world in which *The Lion King* is written and the world for which *Hamlet*'s story is iconographic. *Hamlet* is thus not only an object of interpretation for us but also a framework for understanding other texts, our lives, and our world. For Hawkes, this framing is the most important aspect of *Hamlet*'s legacy, for not only do we understand it from the perspective of historical experiences that go beyond it, we understand those historical experiences from the perspective it shapes:

> As an aspect of the works of "Shakespeare," the play helps to shape large categories of thought, particularly those which inform political and moral stances, modes and types of relationship, our ideas of how men and women, fathers and mothers, husbands and wives, uncles and nephews, sons and daughters ought respectively to behave and interact. It becomes a means of first formulating and then validating important power relationships, say between politicians and intellectuals, soldiers and students, the world of action and that of contemplation. Perhaps its probing of the relation between art and social life, role-playing on stage and role-playing in society, appears so powerfully to offer an adequate account of important aspects of our own experience that it ends by constructing them. In other words, *Hamlet* crucially helps to determine how

---

[25] Rosemarie Gavin, "The Lion King and Hamlet: A Homecoming for the Exiled Child," *The English Journal*, 85 (3), pp. 55–57.

we perceive and respond to the world in which we live. You can even name a cigar after it.[26]

If you can even name a cigar after it, you can also write a Disney movie in its terms and then understand *Hamlet* through this movie. The hermeneutic circle involved in understanding the meaning of the parts of a text in terms of our understanding of the meaning of the whole and understanding the meaning of the whole in terms of our understanding of the parts is thus a historical circle. In reading *Hamlet*, we bring a whole comprising our historical and textual experience to bear on it and in reading our historical and textual experience we bring *Hamlet* to bear on it. Hawkes limits his implicit reference to this historical hermeneutical loop to Shakespeare's work, but we can extend it to include all the texts that remain part of our interpretive traditions. We both try to understand these works and understand through them.

To be sure, in the course of trying to decide which of two readings of *Sense and Sensibility* to accept we seem to have arrived at a bizarre conclusion. We have found that we cannot pick between the two readings by identifying Austen's intention because we understand that intention only in terms of our understanding of the text. We have also found that our understanding of a text is influenced by our participation in an on-going history and that our participation in this on-going history is influenced and oriented by our understanding of the text. But how, then, do radically new readings of a text emerge? How is understanding it anything but the reflection of a vicious circle in which we understand a text in the way the history or tradition of understanding that text bequeaths to us? How do we arrive at two different understandings such as the two we looked at of the meaning of *Sense and Sensibility*? Moreover, insofar as any understanding of textual meaning involves the whole of our history, will the understanding not participate in whatever power relations that history

[26] Hawkes, *Meaning by Shakespeare*, p. 4.

involves? If *"Hamlet* crucially helps to determine how we perceive and respond to the world in which we live," how can we offer what we might call autonomous accounts of meaning or understandings that do not bring with them all the failures, ideologies, and biases of that *Hamlet*-produced world?

In trying to make sense of *Sense and Sensibility*, Sedgwick writes that she has "most before" her two books that discuss Emily Dickinson's "heteroerotic and her homoerotic poetics."[27] She also says that "reading the bedroom scenes [in *Sense and Sensibility*] ... I find I have lodged in my mind a bedroom scene from another document, a narrative structured as a case history of 'Onanism and Nervous Disorders in Two Little Girls' and dated '1881.'"[28] These self-references suggest that it is misleading to think of the whole or the context that history offers us for understanding our texts as a monolithic one. Rather, we should speak of the different wholes that different historical strands, sequences, and relations offer us. Sedgwick places *Sense and Sensibility* in a history that includes studies of Emily Dickinson's poetry and nineteenth-century science. Contrast this placement not only with one that connects the text to a consideration of virtue but with one that understands Austen's works from the perspective of the history of the Islamic Republic of Iran. Taking issue with Charlotte Brontë's criticisms of the novels as narrowly conventional, what strikes Azar Nafisi instead is: "the individual, her happiness, her ordeals and her rights." For Nafisi, Austen's women:

> Put at the center of our attention ... not the importance of marriage but the importance of heart and understanding in marriage; not the primacy of conventions but the breaking of conventions. These women ... are the rebels who say no to the choices made by silly mothers, incompetent fathers ... and the rigidly orthodox society. They risk ostracism and poverty to gain love and companionship,

---

[27] Sedgwick, "Jane Austen and the Masturbating Girl," p. 115. [28] *Ibid.*, p. 118.

and to embrace that elusive goal at the heart of democracy: the right to choose.[29]

Nafisi's students provide new takes on the famous opening line of *Pride and Prejudice*: "It is a truth universally acknowledged that a Muslim man, regardless of his fortune, must be in want of a nine-year-old virgin wife" and it is "a truth universally acknowledged that a Muslim man must be in want of many wives."[30] The importance of the meaning that Austen's work has for Nafisi and her students is thus that it both reflects an orientation made possible by their world and provides a way of making sense out of this world. If Hawkes shows that we understand with Shakespeare, we also understand with Austen. Moreover, the contrast between Sedgwick's and Nafisi's interpretation indicates that textual understanding as well as our understanding with texts are pluralistic. Texts are intelligible in terms of more than one set of historical relations and they shed more than one light on these relations. Sedgwick understands *Sense and Sensibility* from the perspective of one set and Nafisi from another, but the continuing nature of historical developments and relations guarantees that the different perspectives we can bring to our understanding of and with texts will be infinite. They will always illuminate and be capable of illumination in different terms within different contexts of interpretation.

The consequence of this pluralism is two-fold. First, the answer to the initial question provoked by deconstructive readings of texts is affirmative: there are many perspectives from which we can understand a text or work of art. Second, because understanding is pluralistic, no dogmatic understanding can escape alternatives forever. Human beings try to make sense of their world, their history, and their heritage and they draw on various historical strands and resources in order to do so. Nafisi and her students make sense of Austen in

---

[29] Azar Nafisi, *Reading Lolita in Tehran: A Memoir in Books* (New York: Random House, 2004), p. 307.

[30] Nafisi, *Reading Lolita in Tehran*, p. 257.

part through the historical actions and events in which they are participants and they make sense out of the strain of Islam that governs them in part through Austen. Sedgwick makes sense out of Austen in terms of queer theory and contributes to queer theory through her understanding of Austen. As it turns out, then, far from being limited by history, the engagement of our understanding in the multiplicity of interpretive lines and sequences that various histories make available means that we possess many different ways to understand both our texts in terms of our world and our world in terms of our texts.

This pluralism may seem to conflict not only with Hirsch's claim that the meaning of a text is determinate and can therefore be understood in only one way but also with our own sense that when we understand a text we understand it "correctly." Indeed, we might ask what the point of articulating any understanding of a book is unless we think it is the right one. The answer here, of course, is that a reading of a text can be correct without being exclusively so. Sedgwick is quite uncomplimentary about what she considers to be moralizing understandings of *Sense and Sensibility*. Nevertheless, what she says about her own reading is only that she wants "to make available the sense of an alternative, passionate sexual ecology."[31] Making an alternative available is not at all the same as assuming that one's reading is the only possible one. Of course, we might insist that although other readings are possible, our account gets at the text's most fundamental or basic meaning. This strategy seems to be the one that Hirsch adopts in trying to distinguish between the meaning of a text and its significance.[32] Yet, it is hard to see how we could argue that *Hamlet* is fundamentally Freudian and only secondarily existentialist, or that it is less about Renaissance politics than it is about, say, the unreliability of signs.[33] Instead, *Hamlet* has been and continues to be intelligible from a variety of perspectives. *Othello* cannot be said to be

---

[31] Sedgwick, "Jane Austen and the Masturbating Girl," p. 126.

[32] See Hirsch, *Validity in Interpretation*, p. 61.

[33] See Jonathan Culler, *Literary Theory* (Oxford: Oxford University Press, 1997), p. 65.

most fundamentally a play about race and only in a peripheral way a play about jealousy, nor can *King Lear* be said to be primarily a story of filial relations and only secondarily a story of fools. Indeed, King Lear's tragedy is precisely that he insists on a solitary and exclusive definition of filial love. Just as love comes in many forms so, too, does the understanding of meaning.

But just how many forms does understanding come in? Is no understanding better or worse than any other? Is one of the points of *King Lear* not precisely that however many forms love comes in, it does not arrive in the sort of speeches that Goneril and Regan offer? In distinguishing between plausible and implausible understandings, we can only refer again to the standard that the hermeneutic circle supplies in the unification of part and whole. What makes a particular interpretation of a particular text illuminative of its meaning is the way that the interpretation is able to fit the text's parts into an interlocking whole. Doing so requires interpretive decisions about which parts are crucial to the overall meaning and which are less important. It may be that no interpretation of a particular text is able to give equal weight to all of its facets. Instead, different interpretations cast light and shadow on different aspects. Sedgwick's interpretation of *Sense and Sensibility* highlights the bedroom scene in which Marianne writes to Willoughby with Elinor by her side. Noting that bedroom scenes are somewhat rare in Austen's novels,[34] Sedgwick illuminates the importance this bedroom scene has for understanding the novel and helps us to see the whole of the novel in its terms. A different interpretation might highlight the scene in which Elinor finally lashes out at Marianne who has attributed her stoicism in the face of Edward's impending marriage to her lack of real depth in her feeling for him. While Sedgwick's interpretation has little to say about this outburst, we might use it to advance a virtue-based interpretation of the novel in as much as Elinor's response stresses the importance of a fidelity to the promises one has made over an easy emotionalism. The

---

[34] Sedgwick, "Jane Austen and the Masturbating Girl," p. 113.

two different readings thus take different scenes to be more and less important to the meaning of the novel as a whole. In doing so, each highlights different elements and relegates others to the comparative shadows.

Nevertheless, giving different weights to different parts of a text because these parts figure in different understandings of the whole is not the same as failing to make sense out of the parts at all because the whole in terms of which one tries to understand them does not allow one to integrate them. Contrast the two interpretations of *Sense and Sensibility* to Graham L. Hammill's interpretation of Caravaggio's second "Sacrifice of Isaac," for example.[35] In Hammill's view, the painting presents an alternative to the "Pauline historiography that would have us understand the origin of Christianity in a conversion from Jewish carnality to Christian brotherhood."[36] Hammill thinks that Caravaggio also offers us another conversion to Christianity, one from "an erotic homosexual, pederastic, and anal carnality."[37] For Hammill, the "strikingly erect knife" that Abraham is holding is the key to this meaning; in preventing Abraham from bringing the knife down on Isaac, he thinks that the angel is pointing to a substitution of European civilization for anal sex between Abraham and Isaac. "This scene of pederastic anal sex is the social fantasy that Caravaggio's aesthetic assumes."[38] However, this interpretation fails to integrate its understanding of the "strikingly erect knife" with other elements of the painting. For Hammill, civilization is represented by a building in the background of the painting, behind the figures of Abraham, Isaac, and the angel, that Hammil sees as the beginnings of a modern city. Yet, why the standard interpretation of the building as either a villa or a monastery is not more plausible he never makes clear. More to the point, perhaps, it is difficult to see how the angel can be pointing to it insofar as he directs his finger across Abraham's body not behind him and is presumably pointing towards

[35] Graham L. Hammill, *Sexuality and Form: Caravaggio, Marlowe and Bacon* (Chicago, IL: University of Chicago Press, 2000), pp. 87–89.
[36] *Ibid.*, p. 88. [37] *Ibid.*, p. 88. [38] *Ibid.*, p. 89.

the ram that he wants Abraham to substitute for Isaac. Finally, given the positioning of Abraham with respect to Isaac in the painting it is hard to see how anal sex should be part of the interpretation. Instead, we must either re-think the physical possibilities for pederasty or rethink the meaning of the knife. Hammill's interpretation does more than simply de-emphasize some parts of the painting in favor of others. Sedgwick's interpretation of *Sense and Sensibility* can ignore Elinor's outburst without making it unintelligible. Indeed, if we take up Sedgwick's interpretation of the point of the novel, we can see this part of it as a depiction of the intensity of Elinor's reaction to being criticized by the one she loves. In contrast, Hammill cannot make any sense of elements in Caravaggio's painting, and this inability counts against the plausibility of his interpretation of it.

RACIAL IDENTITIES AND IDENTIFICATIONS
How does thinking about textual interpretation help in thinking about racial identities and identifications? Social constructionist accounts of racial identities are interested in tracing the multiple events, institutions, interactions, and introjections that make people blacks, whites, and the like. Suppose we look, instead, at the conditions for racial understandings. That is, suppose we ask not why or how individuals become who or what they are, but instead simply who or what they are. Instead of looking at mechanisms of racialization, in other words, suppose we look at interpretations of racial meanings. Interpretations of texts are interested in illuminating what they mean. Interpretations of individuals are similarly interested in understanding meaning.

If we can depend upon the conclusions we have reached in examining textual interpretations, then our attempts to understand who or what we or others are are always understandings within frameworks and from particular perspectives. Who or what individuals are depends upon the parts of which they are wholes, while the wholes of which they are parts are composed of them and other parts. Understandings of who we are thus move in circles. We understand each other within wholes and understand the wholes in terms of how we understand one another. Moreover, these circles are historically rooted. In our attempts to understand one another we make use of the particular frameworks for understanding people that are bequeathed to us by the histories and traditions to which we belong. For us, these include those frameworks that comprise the afterlife of the European encounter with Africans and subsequent ideas for cheap labor. Our heritage is therefore one that includes the Atlantic slave trade, the institutions of slavery and segregation, the development and demise of biologistic notions of race, and the civil rights movement and its aftermath. Given this heritage, we cannot go back before the point at which racial understandings of individuals became available to us any more than we can go back before the point at which Freudian interpretations of *Hamlet* became available. Instead, certain historical interactions and entanglements allow for Freudian interpretations of *Hamlet* and other historical interactions and entanglements allow for racial interpretations of individuals.

These interpretations are no more limited by the intentions of those we are trying to understand than our interpretations of texts are by their authors' intentions. An author writes a book to express certain themes and ideas. Critics interpret the book and if their interpretations are compelling, they become part of the text that subsequent readers read – *Hamlet* as, in part, the depiction of Oedipal relations between son and mother, for example – whether or not these themes and ideas were part of the original author's intentions. The same holds of people. A person may act so as to express membership in a certain cultural group and yet find him or herself on a slave ship stacked up with people from different cultures and understood by the slave traders as indiscriminately African or black. Those Ashanti, Beruba, and so on who survived the Middle Passage became slaves and came to possess the identity as African and black, first, against their original self-interpretation but eventually as part of it. After the Civil War, Du Bois wrote of his own somewhat similar experience:

> In a wee wooden schoolhouse, something put it into the boys' and
> girls' heads to buy gorgeous visiting cards ... and exchange. The
> exchange was merry, till one girl, a tall newcomer refused my card, –
> refused it peremptorily, with a glance. Then it dawned upon me
> with a suddenness that I was different.[39]

It was not part of Du Bois' intention or original self-understanding to be different. Nevertheless, the understanding the newcomer had
of him reconfigured the understanding he had of himself, just as new
approaches and new texts can reconfigure our understanding of
Hamlet. Moreover, just as *Hamlet*, with all the meanings it comes
to contain, offers us an interpretive framework for understanding and
thereby living in and creating our world so, too, do our understandings
of one another and ourselves. The little girl's understanding of who Du
Bois was supplied him with an interpretive framework for understanding and living his life. Not only did a racial interpretation of who he
was become available to him; as a psychological matter, he made this
identity fundamental to who he understood himself to be. He began to
live his life as a black and from the time of the visiting cards incident
on, he wrote, a veil shut him out from the white world of his classmates. So he held that world "in common contempt," seeking only to
beat those classmates whenever he could:

> At examination-time, or ... in a foot-race, or even beat their stringy
> heads ... The worlds I longed for ... were theirs not mine. But they
> should not keep these prizes, I said; some, all, I would wrest from
> them. Just how I would do it I could never decide: by reading law, by
> healing the sick, by telling the wonderful tales that swam in my
> head – some way.[40]

---

[39] W. E. B. Du Bois, *The Souls of Black Folk*, ed. with an introduction by David W.
Blight and Robert Gooding-Williams (Boston and New York: *Bedford Books*, 1997),
p. 38. Also see Robert Gooding-Williams, "Race, Multiculturalism and Democracy,"
Constellations, 5 (1) 1998, p. 23.

[40] Du Bois, *The Souls of Black Folk*, p. 38.

When we understand *Hamlet*, we understand a different text from the one that either Shakespeare or his original audience understood. Similarly, what Du Bois understood when he looked at himself after the visiting cards incident was a different "text" from the one with which he began. And as it did for the person on the slave ship, this new understanding helped to orient his future and was revised in light of it. Lives move in hermeneutic circles in which we anticipate our future in terms we take from our past and revise our understanding of our past in light of the future we anticipate for ourselves. Moreover, Du Bois' story and countless others like it became part of the history of race. In reading each other and ourselves as black, white, Asian, Latino, or Latina, we are part of a historical tradition in which we understand each other in terms of the history of which we are a part and develop the historical tradition of racial interpretations in the on-going interactions and entanglements in which our racial understanding of one another participates.

To be sure, this historical hermeneutic circle raises the same issue for racial identity that it raises for literature. For, if we understand *Hamlet* in terms of its interpretive history and if this interpretive history is already the afterlife of *Hamlet* itself, why is that historical hermeneutic circle not a vicious one? Why do we not simply understand *Hamlet* the way it has always been understood? This question is of obvious importance for our racial understandings. We want to know how we should understand ourselves and others but if we cannot escape a historically "effected" answer to this question, an answer the terms of which are dictated by our history, then what have we achieved by looking at textual understanding? Do our understandings of who or what we are not bring with them the failures, ideologies, and biases of our racially produced world? If so, the move from questions of identity and social construction to an account of understanding will have been of little help. Just as it is difficult to see how we could unravel our constructions as raced individuals to move to non-racialized constructions of identity, we will have to admit that we retain racial meanings as part of a vicious hermeneutic circle.

The answer that we gave to this worry in the case of literary interpretation stressed the multiple histories in terms of which *Hamlet* is intelligible. There is not just one set of historical relations or interpretive traditions from the point of view of which the play is uniquely intelligible, just as there is not just one frame of reference from which to understand the American Civil War. Instead, there are countless historical sequences and contexts of concerns, events, and issues in terms of which we can illuminate meaning. Different understandings of *Hamlet* develop by taking up different strands of thought as their point of reference. The same holds for the identification of who or what we and others are. We are not uniquely intelligible from only one perspective or within one context of concerns, events, and issues. If the meaning of *Hamlet* is not exhausted by a Freudian interpretation and the meaning of *Sense and Sensibility* is not exhausted by a queer interpretation, nor is the question of who or what individuals are exhausted by a racial interpretation. Appiah's worry about the way in which identities can "go imperial" speaks to this point.[41] We can add to it the recognition that the multiple interpretations we develop are valuable because and to the extent that they illuminate the texts and people as parts of wholes. Just as *Sense and Sensibility* is, in turn, a novel about virtue, onanism, and individual rights, depending upon the context of concern, individuals are in turns blacks, Red Sox fans, mothers, and Americans, once again depending on the context of concern.

Of course, a critic might say that *Hamlet* is fundamentally a play and that *Sense and Sensibility* is fundamentally a novel, no matter how we understand what they are about. Similarly, one might say that an individual is basically a black, white, Asian, or Hispanic, no matter what else he or she is. She is a black Red Sox fan or a white parent. Yet, we typically decide whether we need to attend to a text's theatrical or novelistic elements or whether we are interested in its themes, as we understand them, apart from these elements. A critic might contend

[41] Appiah and Gutmann, "Race, Culture, Identity," p. 103.

that one cannot understand *Hamlet* unless one understands it in its theatrical dimensions. Critics have likewise argued that we need to attend to the theatrical dimensions of Plato's dialogs. Nevertheless, these arguments remain ways of approaching Shakespeare and Plato among a myriad of ways, none of which can plausibly claim to be exclusive or exhaustive. Indeed, the usual response to a claim that we can understand a text only as a play or as a novel is to show just the way in which we need not, in which we can understand it as a philosophical argument or a tableau. Furthermore, since we often understand what a play or a novel is differently as well, it is unclear that insisting that *Hamlet* is a play tells against pluralism in understanding.

Similar conclusions hold for understandings of individuals. Take the parallel with the plurality of ways in which we can understand what a play is. It may be that, for historical reasons, we can intelligibly understand ourselves and others as blacks, Latinos, Latinas, Asians, and whites. Yet, if insisting that *Hamlet* is a play does not tell against pluralism in understanding, nor does insisting that someone is a black or African American. One might be a black from the perspective of a focus on one's heritage or from the perspective of a focus on one's color. Moreover, if one is understood as black from the perspective of one's heritage it may be either because all of one's ancestors can trace their lineage to sub-Saharan Africa, or because only one can. Of course, it is precisely this pluralism in understanding racial identity that allowed courts to prevent various kinds of immigrants from becoming naturalized citizens of the United States. Immigrants could be denied citizenship rights for being non-whites on a variety of understandings of whiteness: skin color, being Caucasian, being European, or being what the founders must have had "affirmatively in mind." Nevertheless, the racist use of principles of interpretive pluralism does not make the principles themselves any less valid. Moreover, each of the understandings of whiteness that the court used has problems of its own. It may be possible to understand Elinor's concern for Marianne as either sisterly virtue or illicit passion. In contrast, very few individuals actually have skin that is pearly white; the court itself admitted that Caucasian is a word "discredited by most"; being European is an odd criterion for whiteness since Europe surely includes people the court would not consider white; finally, determining what the founders had "affirmatively in mind" raises all the issues surrounding intentionalism in interpretation.

Moreover, if individuals can be blacks or African Americans in different ways, they are not always either black or African American. *Sense and Sensibility* has a different meaning within the context of works on onanism than it does within the context of virtue ethics or political changes in Iran, and the same holds for who we are. We have different meanings or identities within different contexts as well and are only white or non-white within particular contexts. Again, of course, a particular nation can try to argue that citizenship forms a whole of which questions of racial identity form coherent parts. Yet, we can also use the variations to make a point: if individuals can be understood in different ways from different perspectives, then the insistence that they are "really" black or really white is both arbitrary and dogmatic. Moreover, if that insistence leads to enslavement, segregation, or a host of other actions, then those actions are themselves nothing more than the arbitrary use of state power. Of course, we do not need to refer to the interpretive character of racial identities to show that slavery and segregation reflect the arbitrary imposition of state power. Nonetheless, if social constructionists emphasize the extent to which the contradictions of construction give license to state institutions to impose whatever agendas they want, we can also emphasize the extent to which acknowledging differences in interpretation undermines any patina of legitimacy such state power may pretend it has.

Dimensions of meaning come variously into light and darkness in both textual understanding and in accounts of what and who we are. Racial understandings of ourselves and others, then, are problematic where they claim to be exhaustive of who we are, "go imperial" or claim a necessary pre-eminence. Even if racial understandings are sometimes legitimate accounts of who we are, their legitimacy is limited to restricted contexts with restricted purposes. Nafisi illuminates the drive for freedom in Austen's novels but she does not illuminate all the meanings they possess nor does she exhaust the different interpretive contexts in which the novels' different meanings arise. Similarly, even if we can often legitimately understand people as "black" given the history of which we are a part, this understanding does not exhaust either their identities or the different contexts in which different identities emerge. Hence, to the extent that racial understandings do attempt to monopolize who or what individuals are they violate the conditions of understanding in general. They obscure the equal status of other identities and identifications and appear in contexts in which they make no sense because they cannot be integrated with the particular context or whole in play. Racial understandings are possible only on a non-dogmatic basis, one that recognizes that the equal status of other identities as understandings of who and what we are and that links racial identities not only to particular histories but also, within those histories, to specific contexts of interpretation.

If the tendency of racial identities to "go imperial" is a misconception of the conditions of understanding in general, how do we know precisely when they must cede ground to other identities? How do we know when a particular interpretation of a text should cede ground? In this latter case, we refer back to the hermeneutic circle and to the capacity of an interpretation to integrate the parts of a text into a unity of meaning. While many different interpretations may succeed in integrating the parts in this way, interpretations that fail to do so also fail as interpretations. Thus, while we may try to understand the Abraham of Caravaggio's "Sacrifice of Isaac" as an about-to-be-reformed pederast, it not clear how we can integrate this understanding with the rest of the painting. We can assess interpretations of identities in the same way insofar as identities form part of a larger text-analog. Take the practice of racial profiling. The justification for this practice is the claim that identifying individuals as blacks and Hispanics enhances the ability of law enforcement officials to discover criminal activity. But these identifications as often, if not more often, lead officials to violate the rights of law-abiding citizens, to humiliate them at best, and to prosecute or kill them for no reason at worst. Moreover, the identifications often lead officials to overlook actual criminals who, because they are identified as white, move below law enforcement radars. Placing racial identities within a crime-fighting context thus issues in the same kind of contradiction as placing a pederastic Abraham within Caravaggio's painting. Viewing the painting as a whole as an illustration of the Pauline substitution of Christian brotherhood for carnality and understanding Abraham's position in the painting as an immediate threat to Isaac allows for the integration of part and whole. In contrast, in order to see the painting as an illustration of the substitution of civilization for "homosexual, pederastic, and anal carnality," we must overlook or distort the position that Abraham has in it. Likewise, take the "whole" or context of fighting crime. If we view individuals within this context as either engaged in suspicious activities or not, then part and whole cohere. In contrast, if we understand individuals as blacks and Hispanics within the same context it is difficult to see how whole and part possibly can. The quip about "driving while black" aptly captures just this incoherence.

Similar problems issue from understanding people as raced individuals in the context of fighting disease. Some medical scientists have argued for the importance of racial identifications in this context and have seen using them as a benevolent form of racial profiling.[42] "Blacks" or African Americans have been found to have higher rates of heart disease, to respond differently than "whites" and other groups to certain drugs, and to be susceptible to certain diseases to which whites are not susceptible. Smoking in African Americans, for example, has

---

[42] See, for example, Edwin J. C. G. Van Den Oord and David C. Rowe, "Racial Differences in Birth Health Risk: A Quantitative Genetic Approach," *Demography*, 37 (3), 2000, pp. 285–298.

been linked to a higher incidence of lung cancer than smoking has for other groups and it has been linked to cardiovascular disease, low birth weight, and infant mortality, as well. One study associated these higher risks of smoking with genetically lower capacities for metabolizing nicotine.[43] Yet, suppose in doing so the study misunderstands who the individuals are, seeing a phallic symbol, as Hammill does, where this meaning conflicts with the meaning of the whole? Tobacco companies target poor people for sales of cigarettes high in tar and nicotine. Moreover, doctors refer some patients with early-stage lung disease for surgery and not others while in the United States many people live in the sorts of degraded environments that may influence metabolism.[44] Hence, to claim that patients are black in the context of lung disease is to overlook other possibilities: for instance, that in the context of lung disease, patients are simply poor. Moreover, if the identity that has lung disease is different, if it is poor people as opposed to blacks, then the explanation may change as well. Indeed, since biological variations do not flow along the patterns established by sociocultural conceptions of race, a better explanation for the increased health risks of smoking for some people might look to impoverished living conditions and different levels of stress. The insistence on racial identities is equally if not more dangerous for medicine than it is for law enforcement since it can impede investigation into more salient causes of disease such as behavior, degraded environments, and poverty.

The history of research on asthma in the United States is a good example of this danger. In a study undertaken in the mid-1960s, researchers uncovered a two-and-a-half- to eight-fold increase between 1952 and 1962 in the number of visits for asthma presentations to four

---

[43] Lynne E. Wagenknecht *et al.*, "Racial Differences in Serum Cotinine Levels Among Smokers in the Coronary Artery Risk Development in (Young) Adults Study," *American Journal of Public Health*, 80, 1990, p. 1053. Cited in "The Meanings of 'Race' in the New Genomics: Implications for Health Disparities Research," *Yale Journal of Health Policy, Law and Ethics* Spring 2001, p. 55.

[44] See "The Meanings of 'Race'," pp. 55–56.

hospitals in New York City.[45] Two of these hospitals served primarily minorities, African Americans at Harlem Hospital and Puerto Ricans at Metropolitan Hospital. Excluding visits for trauma and childbirth, one out of every four visits at Harlem Hospital was for asthma-related problems while at Metropolitan Hospital one out of seven visits dealt with asthma. All of the causes of asthma are still not known, but in the 1960s many psychiatrists attributed it to deep-seated emotional insecurities. They also thought that self-hatred was a common trait of "the black personality." Putting the two together, researchers explained the increase in asthma at the two hospitals as the effect of the psychic damage induced by centuries of racial discrimination. Moreover, they thought that the civil rights movement simply exacerbated the problem, creating conflicts between what John Osmudson of the *New York Times* called "hostile feelings and dependent needs." Because asthma was a reaction to psychological stress, it was easy to see why it would "arise among members of racial minority groups on whom civil rights activists focus."[46]

Yet, suppose the researchers had not assumed that asthma patients should or could be identified by race as well as by illness? A separate study examined the sensitivity of a group of New Yorkers to the newly discovered cockroach allergen. The study found that many more African Americans and Puerto Ricans tested positive to the allergen than did members of other groups. Further, positive reactions to the allergen corresponded to the severity of cockroach infestations in housing. Some commentators promptly pointed to the sanitary habits of poor, ethnic minorities as an explanation of these infestations. Nevertheless, a study of cockroach allergies in the Dominican Republic found that they were far more prevalent in wealthy children. Poor children lived in drafty wood frame homes with outdoor toilets

[45] The information in this paragraph and the next comes from Greg Mitman's, *Breathing Space: How Allergies Shape our Lives and Landscapes* (New Haven, CT: Yale University Press, 2007). The author was kind enough to let me read the manuscript before the book was published.

[46] John Osmudson, "Asthma Linked to Emotions," *New York Times*, August 1, 1965, p. 25, cited in Mitman, *Breathing Space*.

and sinks. Rich children lived in well-built homes with tight masonry construction, indoor plumbing, humidity, and an absence of air exchanges, precisely the conditions in which cockroaches thrive. These were also the conditions prevalent in the deteriorating housing of Harlem. Leaky pipes, falling plaster, and rotting garbage left by non-resident landlords in stairwells supplied the food, water, and humidity that cockroaches needed. As it turned out, 63 percent of the people in the cockroach study were also asthmatic. It is now known that some asthmatic reactions are tied to allergies and, in particular, to allergies to cockroaches, rather than race.

To be sure, one might argue that racial identities serve as useful proxies for other identities for medical purposes. In other words, doctors and medical researchers can identify individuals by race as rough indices of possible susceptibilities while conceding that these susceptibilities may stem from the fact that a higher percentage of the group in question are the victims of degraded environments. Nevertheless, even this "soft" application of racial understandings in medicine is problematic. Not only can it reinforce "the 'hard' [biological] conceptualization of race,"[47] as on-going genetic approaches to asthma make clear. In addition, a "soft" application can be disastrously misleading. Asians, for instance, have been found to be one of the healthiest groups in the United States. Nevertheless, individuals with Vietnamese ancestry are five times as likely to contract cervical cancer as other individuals.[48] In this case, assigning racial identities to individuals can serve to obscure health risks. "Soft" racial understandings can also result in dangerous assumptions about who will or will not respond to a certain drug, and why they do or do not do so. Researchers have found that the glaucoma drug, Travatan, for example, works better for blacks than it does for whites.[49] Yet, if it does so because the etiology of the disease differs for environmental reasons then directing the drug to black populations mistakes the identities for whom the drug is

---

[47] Reanne Frank, "The Misuse of Biology in Demographic Research on Racial/Ethnic Differences: A Reply to Van den Oord and Rowe," *Demography*, 38 (4), 2001 p. 565.

[48] "The Meanings of 'Race'," p. 44. [49] *Ibid.*, p. 57.

helpful. The identity that is part of the curative whole is that belonging to people living under stress or in degraded environments, for
example, not that belonging to a certain race. Even the diagnosis of
diseases that are linked to heredity is risky when it proceeds by way of
racial identities since the ancestries relevant to a particular disease do
not always follow the lines we associate with these identities. Sickle
cell anemia, for example, is badly described as a black disease since it
is rare in the Xhosa of South Africa but found in southern India and the
Arab peninsula.[50]

In what contexts, then, do individuals intelligibly possess racial
identities? We might understand someone as a sports fan when sports
form the context of concern, when we want to discuss a game or go to
one, for instance. Similarly, we might understand individuals as
African American in the context of a discussion of plans for Kwanza
or as Irish American in the context of St. Patrick's Day. One might
understand oneself and certain others as siblings with regard to family
gatherings or in discussion of issues such as nepotism. Likewise, one
might understand others and oneself as Africans, Europeans, or Asians
when discussing or emphasizing certain parts of one's heredity or
upbringing. These contexts are personal or festive ones, limited to
certain sorts of conversation and certain occasions. Just as one might
be a left-hander in the context of learning to play golf, one might be an
African American or American black in the context of planning a trip
to Africa.

Another context in which racial identities and racial understandings of individuals remain intelligible, however, speaks to the
continuing difference, say, between St. Patrick's Day and Martin
Luther King, Jr. Day. The historical consequences of understanding
individuals as African American in non-occasional and non-festive
contexts remain whereas the historical effects of understanding individuals as Irish American in non-occasional and non-festive contexts

---

[50] See Amy Gutmann, "Responding to Racial Injustice," K. Anthony Appiah and Amy
Gutmann, *Color Conscious: The Political Morality of Race* (Princeton, NJ:
Princeton University Press, 1996), p. 117.

do not. The move to an incidentally Irish American identity required only the dismantling of legal barriers in employment, education, and the like. Because African Americans came to the United States as slaves, because their segregation was wholesale, and because slavery and segregation have on-going consequences for African American wealth, income, education and opportunity, the move to an incidentally African American identity requires extra steps. For this reason, black or African American identities have an excuse for appearing in contexts that would appear to have no interpretive room for them. We arguably still need to target these identities within some interpretively inappropriate contexts in order to analyze and to correct the continuing disparities that issue from the ways they have historically appeared in interpretively inappropriate contexts. The same arguably holds for Asian, Latino, and Latina identities.

This conclusion leads to a thin form of a black politics of recognition and a limited defense of racially targeted governmental policies such as affirmative action. Tommie Shelby defends the former on the basis of what he calls a thin black identity. Such an identity does not depend on "thick" commonalities of "race," ethnicity, culture, or nationality. Instead, Shelby sees black identity as "a vague and socially imposed category," one that identifies people as blacks under two conditions: either they "have 'certain easily identifiable inherited physical traits ... and ... are descendents of peoples from sub-Saharan Africa' or, although they do not possess or only ambiguously possess these physical traits, they 'are descendents of Africans who are widely presumed to have had' them."[51] If one acknowledges that human beings vary considerably in their physical traits and that the family tree of any individual contains countless upper branches and countless ways of tracing ancestry back to a putative beginning, then a thin black identity becomes very thin indeed. Moreover, Shelby does not think that black solidarity requires that one endorse even this

[51] Tommie Shelby, *We Who Are Dark: The Philosophical Foundations of Black Solidarity* (Cambridge, MA: Harvard University Press, 2005), p. 207.

thin black identity or have any attachment to it at all. Instead, he claims, black solidarity depends only on a "shared experience with anti-black racism and [a] mutual commitment to ending it."[52] Hence, it might be that with regard to governmentally initiated policies such as affirmative action in employment and education, a hermeneutic integrity would suggest policies of strict racial neutrality: racial under-standings of individuals can be no more easily integrated with educa-tional and employment contexts than they can with crime-fighting ones. Nevertheless, following Shelby, we can also acknowledge that dogmatic and imperial uses of racial understandings led to the system-atic exclusion of certain groups from important social institutions and practices and that this exclusion was total, endured for centuries, and had devastating consequences that still continue. Further, since racial understandings were introjected or looped into self-understandings, they resulted in demeaning and self-limiting life plans or "scripts" that have themselves not yet entirely disappeared.

For these reasons, it is at least arguable that the legacy of histor-ical discrimination cannot be corrected by restricting racial under-standings to festive or ceremonial contexts alone. The French experience would seem to support this point in as much as the race-neutral path France has pursued has not resolved the problem of racial discrimination and has, instead, led to violence, bitterness, and dis-may. Taking France as a cautionary tale, we can defend Shelby's thin politics of recognition along with his important proviso that "the physical and genealogical characteristics that constitute ... thin blackness, apart from the unjust treatment that they engender [need] have no intrinsic significance for the members of the united oppressed group."[53]

We can also defend minority preferences in college admissions and employment with similar reservations. Minority preferences reflect an interest in looking for eligible candidates beyond the boun-daries that dogmatically racial understandings of individuals

---

[52] *Ibid.*, p. 237.   [53] *Ibid.*, p. 237.

established. Moreover, even where candidates have not themselves been the victims of exclusion or have managed to overcome its consequences on their own, such preferences provide new scripts and new life-models for those who have been victims or have not been able to overcome the legacies of discrimination on their own. Nevertheless, given how uneasily racial identities fit within educational and employment contexts, care is required here. It is surely appropriate to ask whether affirmative action programs in employment and in university admissions are the most efficient means for overcoming racial discrimination. Given the small number of individuals they help directly, and given the bitterness and consternation they elicit, we might argue that we should look for other ways to equalize benefits and burdens, such as improving public schools and equalizing the funding for them.

We might also ask whether the context of university admissions is the proper venue for redressing the consequences of racial identification. Diversity in college classrooms advances educational purposes since students and faculty learn from one another and learn from their differences. Yet, students differ along many lines: they are violinists, basketball players, Iowans, and Cambodians, conceivably all at once. Moreover, all of these differences contribute to student and faculty learning. Increasing or maintaining diversity reflects an educational purpose while correcting for historical injustice reflects a quite different one. Social institutions that are interested in the diversity of people who have access to them should be interested in diversity across the wide spectrum of who and what we are. Social institutions properly tasked with creating a more equal society should look at those understandings of who and what we are, including racial understandings, that have contributed to our inequality.

Furthermore, even if our history renders it excusable to understand people in terms of racial identities for purposes of employment and college admissions, it does not follow that it is also excusable to understand people in terms of these identities on the job or in college classrooms. Where racial identifications lead educators to treat certain students differently than others and to expect less of them than they do of others, as some opponents of affirmative action suspect,[54] then the identities of these students have been misunderstood. Once in the classroom, students are students not races, and they must be educated equally. To the extent that understanding people as races is excusable in contexts where doing so militates against the possibility of integrating part and whole, this excuse is limited to the purpose of struggling against and redressing the inequalities that were caused by dogmatic and monopolistic racial understandings in the first place. Insofar as the crucial factor for black solidarity is experience with anti-black racism where "black" refers to a presumption about ancestry, strictly speaking, the identity at issue here is not a black identity but identity as a victim of oppression due to theoretical assumptions about race. As Shelby puts it, "Once a racially just social order is achieved, thin blackness may in fact lose all social and political significance."[55]

CONCLUSION

Racial identifications and identities are ways of understanding who and what we and others are. There are many such ways. Our understanding of *Hamlet* or *Sense and Sensibility* is historically informed, non-dogmatic, and non-exhaustive. It contains within it various entanglements of the text with other texts and different concerns. Even when we think that our understanding is illuminating and important, we do not think that it is the only possible way of illuminating the text or showing its importance. Instead, we think it illuminates the text from within a specific horizon. In addition, we look forward to other interpretations and other views of the text. We want to know what they understand in the text that we might have overlooked and we want to see it illuminated from various different vantage points. Our understandings of others or ourselves as Red Sox fans

---

[54] See, for example, Charles Murray, "Affirmative Racism," in Nicolaus Mills, ed., *Debating Affirmative Action: Race, Gender, Ethnicity and the Politics of Inclusion* (New York: Delta Books, 1994).

[55] Shelby, *We Who Are Dark*, p. 238.

and siblings follow in these paths: they contain all the historical trials, tribulations, and triumphs entwined with the identities; they take themselves to be partial understandings of who certain individuals are and they leave room for other understandings and other vantage points. We do not assume that understanding someone as a Red Sox fan or an Irish American will help to solve a crime or assess qualifications for a job. Nor is it an identity we mark on the US census or our drivers' licenses.

These conditions of understanding require the same recognition of the limits of our understandings of one another in racial terms. We must acknowledge the conditions of their possibility in a particular history; we must take them to be no less partial and no more fundamental accounts of who people are than accounts of people as Red Sox fans or siblings, and we must allow for numerous other possibilities of identity and identification. If the question of whether someone is Irish comes up only infrequently, with reference only to certain concerns or activities, the same must hold of our understanding of one another as black, white, Hispanic, or Asian. Like the former, the latter is only an occasional understanding, one that is illuminating only within limited contexts. While these contexts currently include the remediation of past injustices and do so only with some violation to the integrity of part and whole, by recalling the conditions of understanding we can work towards the time at which these contexts will include only celebrations and personal settings. In chapters 4 and 5, I want to argue that the same holds of our understandings of one another in sex and gender terms.

4   Sex and science

As coherent ways of understanding who we are, our racial identities are historically rooted and situationally limited. Yet, the analogous idea for our identities as women and men seems to be quite implausible. We have seen that the features that determine which sex one is can be as arbitrary as the features that determine which race one is. Nevertheless, since the division of human beings into two sexes is at the root of our form of sexual reproduction, that division would seem to be less arbitrary than the division of human beings into a set of races. Indeed, insofar as human history has the reproduction of the species as its prerequisite, sex identities would seem to be quite different from identities and identifications that result *from* history, such as racial or national identities. Instead, sex identities would seem to form the condition for our having a history at all.

Furthermore, if evolutionary psychology, one branch of behavioral ecology that studies human beings, is correct, the role that sexual reproduction plays in human evolution means that the characteristic traits and proclivities of the two different sexes just follow. Hence, gender as well as sex is arguably less situational than other identities. Race cannot be found in our genes even if, as Armand Marie Leroi insists, groups can be distinguished from one another insofar as they each possess a set of genetic variants in common that "are collectively rare" in the other groups.[1] For the problem for any given individual or set of individuals is to decide whether they are rarities. Yet, our identities and identifications as men and women or males and females would seem to be quite different. As Naomi Zack puts the point: "The

---

[1] Armand Marie Leroi, "A Family Tree in Every Gene," *New York Times*, March 14, 2005, p. A23.

sexual identification paradigm is objective or real in a scientific way while the racial parts of clusters of racial traits are solely 'in the head.'"[2]

Lines of research other than evolutionary psychology appear to confirm this view. Studies of intelligence and the brain examine the differences that follow from our evolutionary development with regard to the structure and functioning of male and female brains, while endocrinology looks at hormonal differences. Such differences seem to indicate that sex and gender are not simply theoretical commitments. Instead, they pervade our bodies in precisely the way that race does not. Consequently, in contrast to identifications and identities of individuals in racial terms, identifications and identities of individuals in sex and gender terms would seem to be non-historical, non-perspectival, and non-incidental to who we are. We are sexes and genders in a global and non-contextual way that we are not races.

Certain versions of psychoanalytic theory may seem to present a further challenge to any attempt to "de-center" identifications and identities as men and women. If Juliet Mitchell is correct, "No human being can become a subject outside of the division into two sexes."[3] As a Lacanian, Mitchell claims that psychoanalysis cannot make a distinction between what she calls "biological gender" and "socially defined sex." Yet, if we must be socially defined sexes (more usually called genders) and if socially defined sex cannot be stripped of biological gender (more usually called sex), then no way of parsing psychoanalytic theory would allow us to curtail or incidentalize our identities as men, women, males, or females. If we are to be subjects at all, we must be sexed and gendered ones, and if we are not subjects, what are we?

---

[2] Naomi Zack, "Race and Philosophical Meaning," in Naomi Zack, ed., *Race/Sex: Their Sameness, Difference and Interplay* (New York: Routledge, 1997), p. 37.

[3] Juliet Mitchell, "Introduction – I," in Juliet Mitchell and Jacqueline Rose, eds., *Feminine Sexuality: Jacques Lacan and the école freudienne*, trans. Jacqueline Rose (New York: Pantheon Books, 1985), p. 6.

Nevertheless, Lacanian psychoanalytic theory presents less of a challenge to a pluralistic and interpretive account of identity than the "harder" sciences of evolutionary biology, endocrinology, and the brain. As Mitchell construes it, Lacanian theory stresses the extent to which "subjectification" is also sex and gender construction and, in Lacanian terms, therefore involves the imposition of power in the form of the "castration complex."[4] At the same time, Lacanians also emphasize the extent to which identity as a man or a woman (and, therefore, a subject) is precarious because of its origins in fantasies having to do with the child's relation to its mother, father, and language itself. This emphasis provides theoretical room for a more protean account of identity, for it leaves open the possibility that who we are depends upon the context in which we are trying to function. Moreover, psychoanalytic theories typically understand the elements of the fantasies it explores as constructs that have their point in the clinical situation. The notions of the castration complex, repression, and incestuous desire have their utility only in the capacity to provide a structure for illuminating individual life-histories.[5] While sex and gender identities and identifications may be important modes of "subjectification" for purposes of coming to terms with our life-history within a therapeutic situation, it is not self-evident that they are always important outside of it. For both reasons, then, Mitchell's view is compatible with an interpretive and pluralist view of our identities and identifications as men and women.

In contrast, sciences such as evolutionary psychology, endocrinology, and neuroscience make more essentialist claims. Evolutionary psychology claims that the two human sexes serve as bedrock explanations for a series of human characters and behaviors linked to evolutionary success. Sciences of the brain declare that differences in the brains and intelligences of men and women are equally explanatory. Indeed, some maintain that they condition

---

[4] Mitchell, "Introduction – I," p. 14.
[5] See, Jürgen Habermas, *Knowledge and Human Interests* (Boston, MA: Beacon Press, 1971), p. 260.

many of the social differences that many feminists would like to overcome. Finally, some endocrinologists arguably make even more out of male and female differences. In this chapter, I do not intend to dispute differences between men and women or, at least, between males and females. Rather, I am interested in what meaning they have, and from what point of view. In specific terms, I want to ask whether we need to put males and females at the crux of our evolutionary history and what is behind the interest in male and female differences. My goal here is to clear the brush, as it were, for the pluralist account I shall offer in chapter 5. I shall begin by quickly reviewing the standard evolutionary account, or at least the one that has captured the popular imagination.

SEX, GENDER, AND EVOLUTION

Behavioral ecology famously begins with the idea of "selfish genes" or, in other words, with the idea that the genes that "get themselves copied into more and more individuals will be the genes that prevail and persist through time."[6] Since "those of us alive today are the descendants of those who successfully survived and reproduced in past environments,"[7] whatever genes proved to be successful in the evolutionary situation will be the ones we continue to possess today. To be sure, in species that reproduce sexually only a part of an individual's genetic material can be duplicated in his or her offspring. Nevertheless, sexual reproduction is more efficient for genetic survival than is non-sexual reproduction because it produces variable offspring that have a better chance of surviving in changing environments. Moreover, while sexual reproduction does not always involve just two different sexes in all species, behavioral ecologists argue that a division into two is optimally efficient because it allows for just the right division of labor. Bobbi S. Low explains, "Reproducing in sexual species requires two quite different sorts of effort: getting a mate

---

[6] See, for example, Bobbi S. Low, *Why Sex Matters: A Darwinian Look at Human Behavior* (Princeton, NJ: Princeton University Press, 2000), p. 19.

[7] *Ibid.*, p. 21.

(mating effort: striving to gain resources or status, getting mates), and raising healthy offspring (parental effort such as feeding, protecting, and teaching offspring)."[8]

In order to explain this bifurcated division of labor in at least a relatively perspicacious way, Low tells a story that begins with a floating population of "something like jellyfish ... reproducing by releasing into the sea haploid gametes, each carrying half the adult number of chromosomes."[9] These gametes are of different sizes, ranging from very small to very large, but each must unite with another gamete in order to form a zygote. The smaller gametes will need to expend less effort to move than the larger ones and will therefore move fastest and farthest in the ocean currents. The larger gametes will have the resources to live longer and to contribute to better-endowed zygotes. Over time, then, mid-sized gametes will be likely to die out. The smaller gametes, who can travel further more quickly, will come into contact with more additional gametes and will therefore be better favored for contributing to a greater number of zygotes while the larger gametes will be better favored to contribute to well-endowed ones. Moreover, natural selection will favor any behavior by the gamete carrier that enhances the advantages of its gametes. Hence, because the tasks of "seeking" and "nurturing" are so different, carriers will specialize in producing either small or large gametes but not both:

> The only advantages to a small gamete are that it gets there faster and is energetically cheap ... The only advantage to a large gamete is its contribution to a healthy well-endowed competitive zygote. So typically it is more profitable for a single individual to make – and promote the success of – only one of the two gamete types. This pattern ... is so ubiquitous that, without thinking about it, we tend to call small gametes "sperm" and small-gamete-makers "males," and to call large gametes "eggs," and large-gamete-makers "females."[10]

---

[8] *Ibid.*, p. 38.   [9] *Ibid.*, p. 38. What follows is distilled from chapter 3.
[10] *Ibid.*, p. 39.

Males can produce large numbers of sperm countless times over. For them, therefore, the task of inserting their genes into the next generation favors mating as often as possible. However, because in mammals gestation takes place within the body of the female, mating many times over when already pregnant will have no effect on genetic survival. Thus, while sperm-producing males are interested in mating with as many egg producers as possible, egg-producing females look for quality in mating opportunities rather than their quantity.[11] It follows that females will be coy and choosy and males relatively indiscriminate. In human beings, these differences are universal, Robert Wright insists, ranging from Western cultures to the Trobriand Islands. He summarizes:

> If we accept even the three meager assertions made so far – (1) that the theory of natural selection straightforwardly implies the "fitness" of women who are choosy about sexual partners and of men who often aren't; (2) that this choosiness and unchoosiness, respectively, is observed worldwide; and (3) that this universality can't be explained with equal simplicity by a competing, purely cultural theory – if we accept these things, and if we're playing by the rules of science, we have to endorse the Darwinian explanation: male license and (relative) female reserve are to some extent innate.[12]

Additional male and female dichotomies follow according to the standard evolutionary account. Because each male increases the chances of his genetic survival by mating with as many females as possible, each is forced to compete with other males who are trying to increase the chances of their genetic survival in the same way. Hence, the males of a species will develop those features that allow success both in competition against other males and in winning the favors of the choosier females. Males will thus tend to develop showy displays

---

[11] See Robert Wright, *The Moral Animal: Evolutionary Psychology and Everyday Life* (New York: Vintage Books Edn., 1995), p. 36.
[12] *Ibid.*, p. 46.

such as decorative tail feathers, to grow larger than the females, and to produce weapons such as antlers to use against other males. They can also make themselves attractive to females by offering resources. Wright connects resource provision in apes and human beings to the relatively high parental investment that the males of these species have in their children. Since the biology of female mammals limits the number of times they can reproduce, not only are they less interested in greater numbers of mating opportunities, they also possess a relatively high degree of parental investment in each offspring both before and after birth. The parental investment of males before birth is nil since the production of sperm is so easy. Yet, after birth, the relative helplessness of their infants means that the males of human and ape species have a higher parental investment than males of other species. If those children are going to survive at all, human and ape males have to help provide for them.[13] Male parental investment still tends to lag behind that of females because males retain greater opportunities for insuring their genetic survival. Still, a male's ability and willingness to provide resources to his offspring both accounts for female choices in selecting partners and leads to characteristic traits: females select males for mating who can provide and are willing to share resources; males therefore try to show that they can provide more resources than others, by showcasing their wealth, status, or power.

While females want resource providers, males want females who are healthy, young and not currently pregnant, although capable of becoming pregnant.[14] In human beings, health is indicated by lustrous hair and clear skin; youth is indicated by a lack of wrinkles and sags; and the state of being both not-pregnant but young enough to become pregnant is signaled by a narrow waist or a low waist-to-hip ratio. Since possession of these attributes facilitates getting a mate, women strive to attain and manufacture them artificially, through clothing, cosmetics, adornments, and even operations.[15] Low thus argues that traditional differences in male and female preferences

[13] Ibid., pp. 57–60.   [14] Low, Why Sex Matters, p. 80.   [15] Ibid., pp. 83–87.

continue to hold into the present: "Women rank men's ability to get resources high, and men rank women's youth and health high."[16]

What are we to make of this standard story? Wright insists that we play "by the rules of science" and Low claims that behavioral ecologists begin at the beginning: with "simple conditions that are conducive to analysis."[17] Nevertheless, it is worth noting, although certainly not for the first time, how closely the standard account tracks obvious stereotypes.[18] Indeed, Low's account of the sedentary character of large egg producers largely reproduces the demand that nineteenth-century medicine made of women. Its view seemed to be that sitting was a good idea for women, at least during their childbearing years since they needed to preserve their energy for menstruation, pregnancy, and lactation. Physicians therefore advised women to perform no strenuous activity lest they jeopardize their ability to bear and nurture healthy children. Climbing more than two flights of stairs during menstrual periods was dangerous; long walks could produce unhealthy degrees of fatigue; and any form of higher education risked depriving the reproductive organs of the necessary "flow of power,"[19] no doubt issuing in sickly, sallow children. In 1877 the

---

[16] *Ibid.*, p. 79. See also Wright, *The Moral Animal*, p. 60 and Deborah Blum, *Sex on the Brain: The Biological Differences between Men and Women* (New York: Penguin Books, 1998), p. 122. In some species, males develop decorations such as brightly colored feathers to attract females. Many evolutionary theorists argue that the presence of frivolous ornaments signals honesty in genetic contribution: if a male can survive with ornamentations that seem to reduce his swiftness or ability to compete, the fact that he can survive at all indicates the superiority of his genes and makes him attractive to females.

[17] Low, *Why Sex Matters*, pp. xiii–xiv.

[18] See, for example, Marlene Zuk, *Sexual Selections: What We Can and Can't Learn about Sex from Animals* (Berkeley, CA: University of California Press, 2002, http://ark.edlib.org/13030/kt0v19q0bp/) pp. 9–10.

[19] See Colette Dowling, *The Frailty Myth: Women Approaching Physical Equality* (New York: Random House, 2000), pp. 15–20. Recent textbooks have reversed the nineteenth century's view of the processes of sperm and egg production. Whereas the nineteenth century thought menstruation, pregnancy and childbirth required that women reserve all their minimal strength for these tasks, more recently it is the production of sperm that seems more onerous while menstruation is debris and the production of eggs is all over at birth. "Far from being produced, as sperm are, they merely sit on the shelf, slowly degenerating and aging like overstocked inventory" (Emily Martin, "The Egg and the Sperm: How Science has Constructed a Romance

Regents of the University of Wisconsin therefore supported a lighter course load for women:

> Every physiologist is well aware that at stated times, nature makes a great demand upon the energies of early womanhood and that at these times great caution must be exercised lest injury be done .... Education is greatly to be desired but it is better that the future matrons of the state should be without a University training than that it should be produced at the fearful expense of ruined health; better that the future mothers of the state should be robust, hearty, healthy women, than that by over study, they entail upon their descendants the germs of disease."[20]

Yet, while Low's account of egg producers echoes nineteenth-century medical views of women, her account of sperm producers seems to come straight from a country and western song. Small gamete producers are rootless, iterant and promiscuous, leaving a pregnant girl in every town. Perhaps these similarities confirm Low's analysis: nineteenth-century physicians and twentieth-century songwriters accurately express our evolutionary heritage. Yet, given developments in medical ideas since the nineteenth century and given the parochial nature of country and western songs, it seems at least as likely that evolutionary psychologists have written historical ideas about sex and gender into their accounts of elementary conditions. We might wonder if there are not other vantage points to take on our evolutionary history. Are there ways to conceive of sexual selection that do not involve coy women and promiscuous men?

As Marlene Zuk points out, even biologists who continue to accept female choice as a crucial part of sexual selection mostly reject

based on Stereotypical Male-Female Roles," in *Feminist Theory and the Body*, Janet Price and Margrit Shildrick, eds. (New York: Routledge, 1999), p. 180.

[20] Quoted in Carol Smith-Rosenberg and Charles Rosenberg, "The Female Animal: Medical and Biological Views of Woman and Her Role in Nineteenth-Century America," in *Woman and Health in America*, Judith Walzer Leavitt, ed. (Madison, WI: University of Wisconsin Press, 1984), p. 16. Smith-Rosenberg and Rosenberg note that female physicians tended, not surprisingly, to disagree with this assessment.

the idea that females are therefore coy. Instead, "evidence from insects, birds, primates and other organisms ... suggests that females often mate many times, with many different males."[21] The primatologist, Sarah Blaffer Hrdy agrees. Chimpanzees, for example, live in relatively separate groups policed by bands of related males. Despite the fact that females cannot increase their reproductive success through promiscuity a female chimpanzee, according to Hrdy "mates on average 138 times with some thirteen different males for every infant she gives birth to."[22] In one group of chimpanzees studied, over half of the infants had fathers who did not belong to the group, supporting the view that female chimpanzees – and female baboons and Barbary macaques as well – are every bit as promiscuous as their male counterparts are meant to be. On the other hand, the biologist and evolutionary theorist, Joan Roughgarden suggests that males may not be as promiscuous as advertised. Male rhesus monkeys, baboons, and lion tail macaques reject the females of their respective species on a regular basis and Roughgarden hypothesizes that they do so because sex has implications. "Mating is a public symbol. Animal 'gossip' ensures that everyone knows who's sleeping with whom. Therefore mate choice, including male mate choice, manages and publicizes relationships."[23] Men, then, are as choosy as women. Sexual intercourse is not any "cheaper" for them than it is for females.

If we must rethink the standard story of promiscuous males and coy females, we might also rethink the story about resource provision. In the account that evolutionary psychology offers, the biology and physics of gamete production is supposed to encourage specialization in either producing off-spring or providing for them. Conversely, it is simply inefficient for one gamete producer to try to do both. Hence, Low minces no words in declaring different male and female

[21] Zuk, *Sexual Selections*, pp. 9–10.

[22] Sarah Blaffer Hrdy, *Mother Nature: Maternal Instincts and How They Shape the Human Species* (New York: Ballantine Books, 1999), p. 85.

[23] Joan Roughgarden, *Evolution's Rainbow: Diversity, Gender and Sexuality in Nature and People* (Berkeley, CA: University of California Press, 2004), p. 170.

preferences in a mate: what men want is "virtually universal" and it is women who are "healthy, young, not-pregnant"; what women look for in men, on the other hand, are "signals of resource control."[24] Nevertheless, alternative evolutionary accounts give a more active and important role than Low does to the resource-securing capacities of the women of the evolutionary period. Some suggest that women provided up to 70 percent of their families' nutrition, in part through their "gathering" activities but also in hunting and trapping both small and large game.[25] While men apparently did most of the large-game hunting, the nutrition they supplied by doing so was unreliable, dependent on the hunt's success and widely dispersed to the community at large rather than to their own families.

Take the Hazda of Northern Tanzania. The research team of Kristin Hawkes, James F. O'Connell, and Nicholas G. Blurton Jones found that "mean time allocation to most activities is similar for childbearing-aged women and adult men, the only significant difference being that women do more food processing."[26] They also found that individual male hunters failed 97 percent of the time. Indeed, by tracking large game only, "the hunter routinely forgoes opportunities to supply a steady stream of small prey to his household." In contrast, "If he gathered plant foods, he could provide even more calories to his own family."[27] Hawkes, O'Connell, and Blurton Jones conclude that women's foraging rather than male hunting "differentially affects their own families' nutritional welfare."[28] Even if this conclusion fails to give enough credit to large-game hunters, it hardly constitutes a reason to minimize female contributions in the evolutionary

[24] Low, Why Sex Matters, p. 83.
[25] See Heather Pringle, "New Women of the Ice Age," Discover, April 1998, pp. 62–66. Also see Natalie Angier, Women: An Intimate Geography (New York: Anchor Books Edn., 2000), p. 244.
[26] K. Hakes, J. F. O'Connell, and N. G. Blurton Jones, "Hadza Women's Time Allocation, Offspring Provisioning and the Evolution of Long Postmenopausal Life Spans," Current Anthropology, 38 (4), 1997, p. 557.
[27] Ibid., p. 573.   [28] Ibid., p. 573.

situation. Women were no worse providers than men. In fact, they may very well have been better.

Hawkes, O'Connell, and Blurton Jones did find that while a Hazda mother's foraging is the most important factor in determining her children's nutritional welfare, when she has a very young newborn, the time she can spend foraging and, further, the efficiency with which she forages, decreases.[29] The people who step in to help with the nutrition of the older children, however, are typically not men but grandmothers. If grandmothers are not available, then it is older aunts and cousins who step in. Hawkes, O'Connell, and Blurton Jones argue for an evolutionary explanation for this help. The assistance that grandmothers and older women without young children offer means that their daughters and younger relatives can wean their babies earlier, produce more babies more quickly, and thereby increase the probability of some of the older women's genes surviving into subsequent generations. In her work, Hrdy adds a further thought. Because of the help that those she calls "allomothers" offered, recently weaned children in the evolutionary period did not have to be independent. And because their grandmothers and older aunts continued to provide for them, they could enjoy a longer childhood and period of dependency than most animals, one that allowed human brains to continue to grow and develop. Hrdy does not think long human childhoods can be fully explained by the opportunity they allow for this brain development: "The reproductive benefits of being a little bit smarter would have had to be tremendous in order to offset the obvious costs of taking a long time to mature."[30] If, however, the resource provisions of post-menopausal women already allowed for long childhoods, then the costs of developing brains could be initially much smaller.[31] According to this story, then, grandmothers are the evolutionary motor behind human intelligence.

If Hrdy and Hawkes, O'Connell, and Blurton Jones are correct, we need not look at mating proclivities and resource provision in

[29] *Ibid.*, p. 559.   [30] Hrdy, *Mother Nature*, p. 287.   [31] *Ibid.*, pp. 284–287.

either sex or gender terms. Individuals of many species are circumspect about sexual intercourse and parents and older relatives together provide for their young. Indeed, it might be more illuminating to focus on those who are not producing children than on those who are, since the former arguably provide for human intelligence, healthy children, and genetic survival. Moreover, updating the "grandmother hypothesis" (which Hrdy calls the "grandmother's clock hypothesis"[32]) does more than merely provide an evolutionary explanation for menopause and human intelligence. It provokes a second set of questions. Until recently, medical science pathologized menopause and advocated hormone replacement therapy as a means of coaxing women's bodies to function as if they remained childbearers. Hawkes, O'Connell, and Blurton Jones point out, however, that human beings are fertile on average for as long as other primates are: namely, for about thirty years. What needs to be explained, then, is not the early termination of fertility in human beings but the longer life spans that human beings possess. But then the question arises as to whether individuals or evolution itself are adequately understood in terms of a division between egg carriers and sperm carriers. Is it not because certain human beings are conceived of primarily as egg carriers and in terms of their parental effort that the question arises as to why they live on when they no longer bear or rear children? Would anyone ever have thought such individuals needed dangerous hormone replacement therapy after menopause if they had not been defined fundamentally and primarily as egg carriers?

Perhaps we should throw out the entire theory of sexual selection. Roughgarden thinks that we should because it cannot account for the amount of same-sex sexuality in fish, birds, animals, and even some species that reproduce asexually. Yet even if we draw back from abandoning the theory of sexual selection entirely (since it follows from the theory of natural selection) we can admit that mating has purposes in addition to reproduction. Indeed, accounts of

[32] Ibid., p. 285.

homosexuality seen in animal kingdom

homosexuality in primates go back to the 1970s.[33] Scientists have offered ninety-four descriptions of homosexual behavior in bird species, over one hundred accounts in mammalian species, and substantial evidence of same-sex matings in dolphins, whales, and manatees. Roughgarden draws two theoretical consequences from these accounts. First, we must allow for the possibility that secondary sex characteristics such as showy tail feathers are as much about attractiveness to the same sex as they are as attractiveness to the opposite sex. Here she cites Zuk, who notes in passing that the bonobo clitoris may be in the front of its body "because selection favored a position maximizing stimulation during the genital–genital rubbing common among females."[34] Second, we must admit that mating has a wider function than simply conjoining sperm and egg. Rather than being directly connected only to the production of offspring, both homosexual and heterosexual mating contributes to what Roughgarden calls "social inclusion."[35]

theory as to why

ex *bonobo sex as social activity*

The contribution is clear in bonobo activities where a day consists in many brief sexual encounters with both same-sex and opposite-sex partners. Bonobos trade sex for what Roughgarden calls "candy," bundles of branches and leaves or sugarcane. Yet, sex also facilitates sharing. Bonobos invite each other for sex in various same- and opposite-sex pairings before they eat, apparently so that they are more likely to share their food instead of fighting over it. In addition, sexual encounters provide a means of reconciliation after disputes and a means of integration: "When females migrate to a new group, the new arrivals establish relationships with the established matriarch through frequent GG [genital–genital] rubbing and grooming."[36] Finally, sexual activities between females help in the formation of coalitions. The upshot of these encounters is, in general, an increased ability to

sex as trade; peace before food (share), reconciliation, & formation of coalition amongst females

[33] Roughgarden, *Evolution's Rainbow*, pp. 128–129, 132–136, 140–142, 164.
[34] *Ibid.*, p. 157; Zuk, *Sexual Selections*, p. 143.
[35] More often, she talks of "social inclusionary traits." See Roughgarden, *Evolution's Rainbow*, p. 6.
[36] Roughgarden, *Evolution's Rainbow*, p. 149.

establish and maintain relationships necessary to both survival and the ability to reproduce. Roughgarden hypothesizes that female–female sex, in particular, allows for increased control over food and protection from males. In turn, this control and protection allows females to start reproducing at a relatively early age and hence to have greater reproductive success. "A female who doesn't participate in this social system, including its same-sex sexuality, will not share in these group benefits," Roughgarden writes. "For a female bonobo, not being lesbian is hazardous to your health."[37]

If Roughgarden is correct, then it is mistaken to begin an account of evolutionary history with heterosexual sex for the purposes of reproduction. We should begin, instead, with object-unspecified sex for the purposes of social inclusion. Moreover, once we do so, we can tell an evolutionary story that focuses on the genes selected for enhancing these latter capacities rather than those more narrowly tailored to reproduction. We might put the point as Zuk does:

> The lesson is that even in nonhumans, sex can be about more than reproduction. People find this surprising, and in a way it is not quite accurate, because of course ultimately everything is "about" reproduction; any trait that is not passed on will disappear. Thus foraging is about reproduction, keeping warm is about reproduction, maintaining blood pressure is about reproduction. Doing these things correctly means that the animal doing them has offspring that do them too, which is what life is all about. But if keeping warm is about sex, none of us expects to get pregnant every time we put on a sweater. It stands to reason, then, that even sex is not always about sex, at least in the short term ... Sexual behavior ... broadly contributes to fitness but does not have to result in offspring every time.[38]

What does this broader view of sex suggest for mate choice in human beings? It may be that men want young, healthy women

---

[37] Ibid., p. 150.   [38] Zuk, Sexual Selections, p. 181.

*seeking more than suitable mate for
children — sense of humor, too (among other things)*

capable of having children, as Low claims, and that women "rank
men's ability to get resources high." Nevertheless, Low also admits
that the contemporary surveys that cite such differences in gender
preferences indicate similarities as well, in as much as all individuals
are interested in mates with senses of humor.[39] Robin Goodwin's
studies confirm that for both men and women "the kind-considerate-
honest-humorous mate" is "the most highly prized potential partner."[40] Another study indicates that at the very top of both
American men's and American women's lists of what they want in a
mate are a dependable character, emotional stability, and a pleasing
disposition[41] while a study of Serbians finds the most desirable traits
for both men and women to be "faithfulness, tenderness, passion,
reliability, maturity, and intelligence."[42] Rather than focusing only
on differences, then, might we not stress the similarities in human
preferences? What is the basis for singling out the divergences towards
the middle or end of the preference lists?[43] If we refrain from doing so,
might we not be led to look for evolutionary explanations of our similarities, for our common desires for honesty and reliability, for example, rather than our differences? And might we take these similarities as
evidence of something other than sex and gender – for example, an
interest in compensating for a general *human* vulnerability?

Our evolutionary history is open to more than one interpretation. The popular story that Wright and Low repeat begins with the
elementary conditions necessary to sexual reproduction. This story

[39] Low, *Why Sex Matters*, pp. 79, 83.

[40] Robin Goodwin, "Sex Differences among Partner Preferences: Are the Sexes Really
Very Similar?," *Sex Roles*, 23 (9/10), 1990, p. 510.

[41] See David M. Buss *et al.*, "A Half Century of Mate Preferences: The Cultural
Evolution of Value," *Journal of Marriage and the Family*, 63, 2001, p. 499.

[42] Bojan Todosijevic *et al.*, "Mate Selection Criteria: A Trait Desirability Study of Sex
Differences in Serbia," *Evolutionary Psychology*, 1, 2003, p. 119.

[43] According to Buss' research, women's interest in a mate's financial prospects ranked
between eleventh and thirteenth out of eighteen characteristics. For men, a mate's
"good looks" ranked eighth and fifteenth out of eighteen characteristics. See "A Half
Century of Mate Preferences," p. 499. Todosijevic notes that "there is not a single
trait referring to physical appearance in the upper third of the list." See "Mate
Selection Criteria," p. 122.

features resource-providing, promiscuous men and sedentary, cautious women who bear and nurture children. Men look for young, healthy mates and women look for signs of resource control. Men and women are not only necessary to our evolutionary history in this story, but its stars. In contrast, a story that we might write, relying on Hrdy, Roughgarden, Zuk, Hawkes, and others begins with the traits and behaviors necessary to social inclusion. This story features individuals who are interested in sex for the social integration it fosters – and hence for the ultimate reproduction it allows – but who are also wary of its costs. Individuals cannot reproduce unless they are part of the crowd, so to speak, and membership in the crowd requires all sorts of couplings as well as the practical knowledge of when to mate and when not to. The revised story also features resource-providers whose specific sex and gender identities are important parts of the evolutionary plot-line only when their childbearing years are over. And here the story gives allomothers a starring role because of the contributions they make to human intelligence in providing resources to weaned children and allowing them to remain children. Finally, the story highlights the importance of humor, kindness, and integrity in compensating for human vulnerability. The characters in this story, in short, are not men and women but members of communities.

If we adopt the view of textual interpretation I laid out in chapter 3, this second story is at least as compelling as the first in integrating the parts of our evolutionary history into a unified whole. Indeed, it integrates same-sex and opposite-sex pairings, makes sense out of the development of human childhood, and explains the longer lives of humans as compared to primates. Nevertheless, it is possible to think that the story Wright and Low tell is more integrative in that it appears to cohere better with the findings of other sciences, including studies of the brain. In the next section of this chapter, I therefore want to look at some of these.

STUDIES OF BRAINS AND INTELLIGENCE

In the behavioral ecologist account that Low gives, the different functions of the sexes in mating effort and parental effort lead to gender

differences in mental capacities. As befits an evolutionary history in
which, she claims, men search out nubile mates and provide resources
for their own and their families' survival, men are better with numbers, maps, and spatial analysis.[44] As befits the role she gives women
as sedentary nurturers, women notice things, are more sensitive to
others and can recall the location of objects.[45] Hence, men tend to give
directions in terms of streets and miles while women tend to cite
landmarks.

Low's explanations here seem to fit with unrelated studies of
mental characteristics. According to these studies, infant girls who are
only a day old react more intensely than day-old boys to the sound of
another's trouble. As adults, women have an acuter sense of smell
than men; they are more sensitive to touch; and even the hair cells in
their inner ears vibrate more intensely.[46] In tests of the ability to
visualize and rotate three-dimensional figures in their heads men
outperform women by around 67 percent and they do better in maze
performance, angle-matching tasks, and in a test called the block
design test. Twelfth-grade boys outperform twelfth-grade girls on the
Advanced Placement physics exam. Indeed, a study of thirty years of
math and science testing found that boys outnumbered girls in the top
10 percent of scores by three to one. "In the top 1 percent, there were
seven boys for every one girl. In some mechanical–vocational tests,
such as electronics and auto repair, there were no girls in the top 3
percent."[47] Test results of verbal abilities move in the opposite direction. The same thirty-year study that showed boys at the top in math
and science found girls consistently at the top in reading comprehen-
sion and writing skills.[48] Some of these differences are more stable
than others but even those that have decreased in the last thirty years
have not disappeared.

Given the history of intelligence tests, however, we might rea-
sonably be suspicious of such results. In the first part of the twentieth

[44] Low, *Why Sex Matters*, p. 46.   [45] *Ibid.*, p. 47.   [46] Blum, *Sex on the Brain*, p. 68.
[47] *Ibid.*, p. 58.   [48] *Ibid.*, p. 58.

century, Jews were found to perform so much more poorly than gentiles on intelligence tests that scientists insisted that Jews were genetically inferior to gentiles and Congress passed laws that restricted
Jewish immigration into the United States.[49] In contrast, studies
from 1947 to 1984 found that Jews performed better on intelligence
tests than gentiles did. The discrepancy in the results of the two texts
cannot be attributed to improvement in the living conditions of
Jewish immigrants from the first to the second part of the twentieth
century because the findings spanned different economic classes.
Instead, Troy Duster attributes the discrepancy to the conduct of the
testing itself.[50] Might not the same be said for studies of male and
female intelligence?

Take one of the popular versions of the test for differences in the
spatial abilities of men and women. In it, subjects sit in dark rooms in
front of rods placed within large vertically held frames. Their task is to
keep the rod perpendicular to the floor as the researcher tilts either the
frame or the chair in various directions. In five of twelve such studies
examined, no differences were found between those identified as men
and those identified as women. In the remaining seven, those identified as men performed better.[51] Of course, model and block-building
are popularly defined as "boy" activities. Hence, it is perhaps not
surprising that men do better on the test. Girls may have had less
chance to build things and hence be less experienced with spatial
relations and, if so, it remains unclear what the findings mean for
their innate abilities. Basing her own suspicions about the meaning
of the results upon cross-cultural studies, Anne Fausto-Sterling claims
that "sex-related differences in visual–spatial activities are strongest
in societies in which women's social (public) roles are most limited,
and ... these differences tend to disappear in societies in which

---

[49] Troy Duster, *Backdoor to Eugenics* (New York: Routledge, 2003), p. 11.

[50] *Ibid.*, p. 11.

[51] Anne Fausto-Sterling, *Myths of Gender: Biological Theories about Women and Men*, revised edn. (New York: Basic Books, 1992), p. 31.

women have a great deal of freedom."[52] Yet, although one explanation of the differences between male and female scores may involve public roles, another may have more to do with comfort levels: perhaps, for social and cultural reasons women are simply less comfortable in dark rooms than men are, particularly if those conducting the test are male. Women may perform more poorly on the tests for reasons therefore wholly unconnected to their mental capacities.

Studies of the brain are supposed to by-pass these sorts of problems with intelligence tests by looking directly at brain structure and function. Women have been found to possess corpus callosi that are more bulbous than those of men, neurons that are packed more tightly together in the temporal cortex than are those of men, and limbic systems that are more active in a region linked to a quick verbal response than are male limbic systems. The latter, in turn, are more active in a region linked to a quick physical response.[53] Yet, like intelligence tests, studies of the brain have a suspicious history. Anne Fausto-Sterling notes that "scientific" studies once found differences in "Negro" and "Caucasian" brains,[54] claiming that Negroes had smaller frontal lobes than so-called Caucasians, larger parietal lobes than Caucasians, and a left–right asymmetry in lobes that was the reverse of the Caucasian one. These differences, in turn, were said to explain the "undeveloped artistic power and taste" of blacks as well as their characteristic "lack of self-control, especially in connection with the sexual relation."[55]

Even if brain studies are currently more sophisticated, they remain notoriously difficult. The corpus callosum, for instance, is connected in multiple ways to other parts of the brain and is very difficult to isolate in exactly the same way in the different brains.

---

[52] *Ibid.*, p. 35.   [53] Blum, *Sex on the Brain*, pp. 60–61.

[54] See Robert Bennett Bean, "Some Racial Peculiarities of the Negro Brain," *American Journal of Anatomy*, 5, 1906, pp. 353–432. The terms "Caucasian" and "Negro" are Bean's.

[55] Bean, "Some Peculiarities of the Negro Brain," p. 377. Also cited in Ann Fausto-Sterling, *Sexing the Body: Gender Politics and the Construction of Sexuality* (New York: Basic Books, 2000), p. 122.

Hence, it is unclear whether scientists always obtain the sort of measurements that can permit meaningful comparisons. Even more perplexing, perhaps, is the conclusion from a meta-analysis that pooled together the data from a large number of smaller studies. This meta-analysis found "no gender difference in either absolute or relative size or shape of the CC [corpus callosum] as a whole or of the splenium."[56] A similar finding held for Negro and Caucasian brains: blind studies found no group differences that could outweigh individual differences and further casual inspection found no differences at all.[57]

Notwithstanding such suspicions, scientists may ultimately locate indisputable differences in male and female brains as well as clear differences in their intelligences. On the other hand, the expectation of these differences may be another theoretical commitment, similar to the idea of racial difference. Yet, suppose it does turn out that male and female brains differ and that men and women have different mental strengths. The brains of left- and right-handed people also differ but we do not connect these differences to personality traits and abilities. Indeed, for much of our history, we have assumed they are malleable and that left-handed children could and should be taught to write and eat with their right hands. Far from indicating something about identity, differences between left- and right-handers were thought to be entirely erasable. Why, then, should we suppose that structural differences in the brain say anything more fundamental about identities as men and women?

Before we decide on the meaning of test results we acquire from brain or intelligence studies, we should first ask why we are interested in the particular identities we are comparing. We should keep in mind that both people and their brains differ in all sorts of ways and that we can compare and contrast them along different routes, according to different criteria, and with regard to different interests. Why, then, are scientists even interested in differences in male and female brains?

[56] Fausto-Sterling *Sexing the Body*, pp. 131, 135. [57] *Ibid.*, p. 123.

Duster argues that interests in differences between groups usually point to concerns a higher socioeconomic class has about a lower one. "In a culture where race and sex are firmly rooted categories of differentiation and sustained stratification, we should expect both common sense and probing inquiry into the intelligence differences between the races and into the biological destiny of females."[58]

HORMONES, SEX, AND GENDER

"The Big T," Andrew Sullivan writes about testosterone "correlates with confidence, competitiveness, tenacity, strength and sexual drive."[59] It is a "facilitator of risk: physical, criminal, personal" and goes a long way to explaining why there are four times as many male criminals as female ones and why most violent crimes are committed by men.[60] "The Big T" also explains why the sacrifice of quantity of life for intensity of experience is a "deeply male" trade-off.[61] Testosterone "affects every aspect of our society, from high divorce rates and adolescent male violence to the exploding cults of bodybuilding and professional wrestling. It helps explain, perhaps better than any other single fact, why inequalities between men and women remain so frustratingly resilient in public and private life."[62]

For health reasons, Sullivan must inject himself with testosterone every two weeks and his expertise on its results issues from the effects he personally experiences, not only in increased lust but also in mood, physique, and behavior:

> Losing my temper in a petty argument; innumerable traffic confrontations; even the occasional slightly too prickly column or e-mail flame-out. No doubt my previous awareness of the mythology of testosterone had subtly primed me for these feelings of irritation and impatience. But when I place them in the larger

---

[58] Duster, *Backdoor to Eugenics*, p. 22.
[59] Andrew Sullivan "The He Hormone," *New York Times Magazine*, April 2, 2000, downloaded from "New York Times Archives," download, pp. 4–5.
[60] *Ibid.*, download, p. 8.   [61] *Ibid.*, download, p. 12.   [62] *Ibid.*, download, p. 1.

context of my new testosterone-associated energy, and of what we know about what testosterone tends to do to people, then it seem plausible enough to ascribe some of this increased edginess and self-confidence to that biweekly encounter with a syringe full of manhood.[63]

testosterone = manhood

Or course, Sullivan is no scientist, but his account nicely captures some popular assumptions about the connection between testosterone and "manhood." Moreover, scientific studies often support this idea. Thus, critics of David Reimer's gender reassignment often point to the "masculine" hormones that bathed his brain while *in utero* and that must, they think, have had consequences for his behavior.[64] Despite their emphasis on up-bringing in the acquisition of gender identities, John Money and Anke Ehrhardt also point to the exposure to fetal androgens that causes "masculine" behaviors in girls. According to other studies, male songbirds sing and female songbirds do not. Nevertheless, if injected with sufficient amounts of testosterone, females sing like males.[65] Male sparrows are more nurturing than many males of other bird species. Nevertheless, if injected with testosterone, they fly off in pursuit of female sparrows, in complete disregard of their new baby chicks.[66] Female rats curve their backs in the presence of male rats in a submissive manner. Injected with testosterone, however, they "will be more aggressive and try to mount other female rats."[67] As for human beings, Congenital Adrenal Hyperplasia (CAH) is the condition in which fetuses with XX chromosomes are exposed to elevated amounts of androgens, the precursors of testosterone, in the womb. According to a study by Melissa Hines, Charles Brook, and Gerard S. Conway, individuals affected by the condition "are more likely than other girls to prefer

David Reimer (margin note)

examples of "masculine" behaviour in female animals after being injected w/ testosterone (margin note)

---

[63] *Ibid.*, download, p. 3.

[64] See Milton Diamond and Keith Sigmundson, "Sex Reassignment at Birth: Long-term Review and Clinical Implications," *Archives of Pediatric and Adolescent Medicine*, 151, 1997, pp. 298–304.

[65] Anne Moir and David Jessel, *Brain Sex: The Real Difference Between Men and Women* (New York: Delta Books, 1989), p. 27.

[66] Blum, *Sex on the Brain*, p. 172.   [67] Moir and Jessel, *Brain Sex*, p. 26.

toys that are normally preferred by boys (e.g. cars) and less likely to prefer toys that are normally preferred by girls (e.g. dolls). They also show increased preferences for boys as playmates and for boy-typical activities."[68] Hines, Brook, and Conway note that these characteristics "are seen on questionnaires, in interviews, and in direct observation of toy choices." Moreover, they find them "when girls with CAH are compared to unaffected female relatives, as well as to controls matched for background factors like age and parental socioeconomic status."[69] "Jane" is typical:

> She was noticeably rougher and tougher in play. She was an intensely physical, outdoor person. She also went out of her way to seek out the company of boys as playmates. She had no time for dolls, preferring to play with her bother's trucks, cars and building blocks. At school she was a late developer in reading and writing. She would also get into trouble for starting fights.
>
> As a young teenager, she refused to be a bridesmaid at her cousin's wedding. Later, she displayed no interest at all in babies. Alone among her female friends, Jane always refused to baby-sit. She had absolutely no interest in feminine clothes.
>
> When she got married, she had an unromantic, down-to-earth view of marriage. She describes her husband as "my best friend." When she had children, she was devoted in equal measure, to her family and to her career. Her hobby is orienteering, the strenuous cross-country sport where success depends on stamina and an accurate sense of direction.[70]

Studies of both animals and human beings, then, seem to confirm the connection between testosterone and "manhood," or at least masculine attitudes and behaviors. Yet, Fausto-Sterling, for one,

---

[68] Melissa Hines, Charles Brook, and Gerard S. Conway, "Androgen and Psychosexual Development: Core Gender Identity, Sexual Orientation, and Recalled Childhood Gender Role Behavior in Women and Men with Congenital Adrenal Hyperplasia (CAH)," *The Journal of Sex Research*, 41, 2004, p. 75.

[69] *Ibid.*, p. 75.   [70] Moir and Jessel, *Brain Sex*, pp. 29–30.

remains as suspicious of these studies as she is of brain comparisons. CAH-affected girls must be monitored for a potentially life-threatening electrolyte imbalance and can be treated with cortisone to inhibit the overproduction of androgens. Moreover, CAH infants are often born with large, "masculinized" genitals that are often surgically reshaped or "corrected."[71] Fausto-Sterling argues that these surgical corrections and treatments may explain the behavior of those with CAH as much as or more than the presence of testosterone *in utero*. She also simply distrusts the claim that there are differences between CAH-affected females and non-CAH-affected ones. In this connection, she cites studies that either do not find significant patterns of differences between the two groups or find ones that seem peculiar at best. For example, one study reports that CAH-affected children tend to spend more time caring for their pets than do children without the condition. The study thus concludes that although CAH-affected girls are less interested in human infants than are unaffected girls, they are "not less nurturant overall."[72] As Fausto-Sterling remarks, however, this conclusion "would imply that testosterone interferes with the development of interest in infants, but that some general character called nurturance, which could get directed everywhere but to children, existed independently of high androgen levels."[73]

The Hines, Brook, and Conway study as well as Sullivan's report are equally remarkable for the assumptions they make as to what manhood is. The fact that male sparrows injected with "the Big T" fly off rather than attending to their off-spring is meant to show the link between testosterone and male behavior. But why does flying away from one's young mean that one is behaving in a masculine way? If the answer is that the sparrows are flying off to pursue female sparrows and are doing so in an indiscriminate way, why suppose that this activity correlates with being male or behaving as one? The assumptions here are that testosterone makes a sparrow

---

[71] See Moir and Jessel, *Brain Sex*, p. 30.
[72] See Fausto-Sterling, *Sexing the Body*, p. 75. [73] *Ibid.*, pp. 289–290, n. 129.

indiscriminately interested in whatever female sparrows fly by and that a lack of discrimination is somehow masculine. Yet, if Roughgarden and others are correct about male coyness, we might wonder about this correlation. Moreover, if studies since the 1970s are correct, it may be that female sparrows are as interested in female sparrows as male sparrows are. If so, following sparrows would seem to be an indication of the way testosterone increases a sparrow's interest in other sparrows rather than an expression of "manhood." Likewise, it may be that injecting human individuals with testosterone from an external source makes them impatient and increases their "confidence, competitiveness, tenacity, strength, and sexual drive." Nevertheless, it remains equally unclear how these characteristics are meant to correlate with something called masculinity.

There is no reason to dispute the endocrinological differences between men and women. Males have more testosterone on average than females do. Yet, even if they are also stronger on average than females, it is certainly unclear that they are more confident, competitive, tenacious, or sexually driven on average. Moreover, many males are stronger than other males as well. Again, with Duster, we might ask why we should be interested in the strength difference between men and women and not that between men and men. Why not say that increasing the amount of testosterone in a body increases "confidence, competitiveness, tenacity, strength, and sexual drive" without bringing sex or gender into the analysis at all?

Actually, it is far from clear that testosterone does increase confidence, competitiveness, or tenacity, whatever we might say about strength and sexual drive. Tests of male tennis players after a match show that the winner has higher levels of testosterone than the loser. Yet, before the match, tests show that both possess similarly high testosterone levels. Only after the match have the winner's levels gone even higher while the loser's have significantly decreased.[74] This

---

[74] Natalie Angier, *Woman: An Intimate Geography* (New York: Anchor Books Edn., 2000), p. 271.

finding suggests that the anticipation of competition raises levels of testosterone and that success in competition occasions an even greater spike. Conversely, losing depresses testosterone. Hence, it is not clear that increasing the amount of testosterone in one's body increases one's confidence, competitiveness, or tenacity. Rather, the causal chain seems to run the other way: increased confidence, competitiveness, or tenacity increases one's testosterone levels. There is another inference – if fanciful – we might want to draw from these findings. If competition and winning produce high levels of testosterone and if losing a match lowers testosterone, then perhaps we have an additional explanation for why women's bodies, on average, possess less testosterone than men's: constant and intractable identification as a woman is already a losing proposition.

What are we to make of the description of "Jane?" Suppose she was rough and tough as a child and suppose she had no time for dolls, was a late developer in reading and writing, refused to be a bridesmaid at her cousin's wedding and did not like to baby-sit. Suppose as an adult, she has an unromantic, down-to-earth view of marriage and is devoted in equal measure to her family and to her career. Hines, Brook, and Conway understand these behaviors and preferences as interlinked parts of her gender anomaly caused by her exposure to uterine androgens. But how do these features of "Jane's" character link up with one another? What is the connection supposed to be between learning to read later than one's peers and refusing to be a bridesmaid? Moreover, how does whatever link such characteristics are meant to have to one another pertain to sex or gender? Why suppose that a lack of interest in baby-sitting and an unromantic, down-to-earth view of marriage have any relation to sex or gender, let alone to one another? Indeed, if an absence of interest in babies, a lack of romantic sentiments, and an equal devotion to career and family are meant to characterize men, this idea is surely a surprise to many of them, despite their exposure to fetal androgens.

Yet another study focused on the effects of testosterone on women and found that women with high levels of testosterone tended to be career women. In contrast, "lower-testosterone women usually had a great deal more interest in children and in dressing up. They liked makeup; they liked jewelry. They liked cooking better than the high-testosterone women did. They enjoyed interior decorating more."[75] The implication of this study is the same as that of the Hines, Brook, and Conway study: high levels of testosterone move women in a masculine direction, signified here by an interest in careers. In contrast, comparatively low levels of testosterone move women towards more feminine interests, signified here by interests in jewelry and interior decorating. To be sure, it seems bizarre that testosterone could have such definitive tastes. Even if we were to decide that an interest in jewelry is a feminine interest, despite the number of men who share it, we would still want to know why low testosterone would lead one to this interest. Moreover, given the results of the effects of competition on levels of testosterone in the body, it is surely more reasonable to assume that individuals engaged in careers have higher levels of testosterone than those without them just because they are in more competitive environments. If so, the study's causal account is again backwards: higher levels of testosterone do not cause an interest in careers; instead, the pursuit of a career raises levels of testosterone. Likewise, lower levels of testosterone do not cause an interest in jewelry or interior decorating. Instead, a lack of competition lowers testosterone. Perhaps lowering one's competitive urge also leaves space for the emergence of interests in jewelry and interior decorating. Or perhaps researchers have simply been misled by the introduction of sex and gender into endocrinology to suppose all sorts of strange bedfellows, including connections between low levels of testosterone, lack of interest in a career, and a love for bejeweled adornment.

None of the studies we have looked at so far suggests that our hormones need to be understood through the perspective of sex and gender. One can increase the amount of testosterone in one's body by

---

[75] Moir and Jessel, *Sex on the Brain*, p. 184.

injecting oneself with it and doing so may make one more impatient, confident, competitive, tenacious, stronger, and more sexually driven. One can also increase the amount of testosterone in one's body by putting oneself in a competitive environment. Similarly, one can take pills to become less depressed, or one can go running. We do not associate either one of these activities with sex and gender. Why should we associate testosterone levels with sex and gender any more than we connect serotonin levels with sex and gender? Many of our most popular ideas about testosterone are simply circular: testosterone can be thought to lead to typically male behaviors only if certain behaviors such as an interest in careers and a certain degree of impatience, confidence, competitiveness, tenacity, strength, and promiscuity have already been interpreted as male. Similarly, a relative lack of testosterone can be thought to lead to typically female pursuits only if interests in jewelry and interior decorating have already been interpreted as female. If, instead, we associate a relative lack of testosterone with losing a match, we might be led to ask what match women have lost.

In any case, if the question remains why we should necessarily associate testosterone only with the male sex and especially with the masculine gender, moving from humans to rats fails to make the association any clearer. The studies of the effects of injecting female rats with testosterone are supposed to show that testosterone leads to male sexual behaviors insofar as the female rats attempt to mount other rats. Other studies are meant to show the obverse: injecting male rats with estrogen leads them to adopt female sexual behaviors in as much as they present themselves in a receptive position to other rats.[76] Yet, in a series of studies in the 1940s and 1950s, Frank Ambrose Beach already observed the same mounting patterns in uninjected female rats as well as in male and female rats injected with estrogen.[77] The claim, then, that a rat mounting another rat is

---

[76] *Ibid.*, pp. 163–164.

[77] Fausto-Sterling, *Sexing the Body*, p. 209. See Ambrose Beach, "Execution of the Complete Masculine Copulatory Pattern by Sexually Receptive Female Rats," *Journal of Genetic Psychology*, 60, 1942, pp. 137–142.

exhibiting male behavior while a rat presenting itself in a receptive position is exhibiting female behavior is peculiar. It is more likely that both are just exhibiting rat behavior.

As Fausto-Sterling explains, hormone studies are even more exasperating than even the foregoing considerations suggest. For, it is not simply the behaviors to which androgens and estrogens are meant to lead that are identified as either male or female but androgens and estrogens themselves.[78] In 1889, the French physiologist Charles Edouard Brown-Sequard hypothesized that male gonads secreted substances controlling male development and in 1891 reported renewed vigor after he began injecting himself with crushed guinea pig and dog testicles.[79] In the 1920s and 1930s scientists isolated secretions from the ovaries that they considered decisive for the female "character."[80] Accordingly, scientists named the secretions in terms of the site where they had initially found them: androgens for the substances isolated from testes and estrogens for substances from the ovaries. From the beginning, then, estrogens and androgens became the "sex" hormones and were associated with the characteristic behaviors of different genders. Indeed, by linking hormones to sex and linking sex to sexual object-choice, researchers came up with an explanation for homosexuality: it was caused by the presence of estrogen in men.[81] Conversely, interests in properly male activities such as suffrage were caused by the misplaced presence of androgens in women.[82]

Unfortunately, researchers had to modify this elegant theory in 1934 when Bernard Zondek found estrogen in the testicles of a virile stallion.[83] They had to modify it even more thoroughly when they

[78] See Adele E. Clarke, *Disciplining Reproduction: Modernity, American Life Science and the Problems of Sex* (Berkeley, CA: University of California Press, 1998), pp. 125–128.
[79] Nelly Oudshoorn, "Endocrinologists and the Conceptualization of Sex, 1920–1940," *Journal of the History of Biology*, 23 (2), 1990, p. 165.
[80] *Ibid.*, p. 166. [81] *Ibid.*, p. 176. [82] Fausto-Sterling, *Sexing the Body*, p. 154.
[83] Adele Clarke quotes an interview with Bernard Zondek: "To this day, I do not understand how it is that the high concentration of estrogen in stallion testes and blood does not exert an emasculating effect. F[the interviewer]: It is fortunate for the stallion that he has no chance of knowing your trouble." *Disciplining Reproduction*, p. 126.

discovered that androgens and estrogens converted into one another. Other studies in the 1930s, as well as more recent studies, chart the effects of hormones on such phenomena as human growth, fatty deposits, and kidney weight. According to Fausto-Sterling, then, testosterone and estrogen are simply "powerful growth hormones affecting most, if not all, of the body's organic systems."[84] Their association with sex and gender is both confusing and confused.

CONCLUSION

Denise Riley recounts the attempt of Renaissance feminists to restrict their status as women to their mortal bodies and to insist that it did not penetrate to their immortal souls. These feminists were willing to concede that women were composed of "deprived, passive, and material traits, cold and moist dominant humours and a desire for completion by intercourse with men."[85] Nevertheless, they insisted that women's souls were neuter. While their identity as women might be an aspect of their earthly existence, it was no part of their identity in the afterworld. If women were "the inferior of the male by nature," they were "his equal by grace."[86] Women were women only on a temporary basis, then, as part of a temporary existence. In their souls and essence, they were not women at all. By the eighteenth century, this attempt to reserve femaleness for a temporary existence had failed. The identity of being a woman pervaded all of one's identity, penetrating to one's very soul. Theorists such as Rousseau insisted upon it: "The soul of a perfect woman and a perfect man," he famously wrote, "ought to be no more alike than their faces."[87]

Many contemporary researchers seem to agree. Sex and gender are central to every facet of our evolutionary pre-history. They divide our brains and they name our hormones. Indeed, the discovery that testosterone and estrogen are multi-site chemical growth regulators

---

[84] Fausto-Sterling, *Sexing the Body*, p. 193.

[85] See Denise Riley, *Am I That Name: Feminism and the Category of "Women" in History* (Minneapolis, MN: University of Minnesota Press, 1988), p. 24.

[86] *Ibid.*, p. 25.   [87] Cited in Riley, *Am I That Name*, p. 36.

has not undermined their position as sex hormones. Instead, if estrogens and androgens regulate human growth, fatty deposits, and kidney weight, then our growth, weight, and kidneys are gendered as well. As Fausto-Sterling writes, "Chemicals infuse the body, from head to toe, with gender meanings."[88]

Yet, the findings of evolutionary psychology, brain and intelligence studies, and endocrinology raise interpretive complexities. With regard to no part of the evidence to which they refer is there only one story we can tell. We can tell different stories about the evolutionary situation, depending upon whether we focus on differences between males and females or on shared tasks, activities, and interests. We can also tell different stories about the brain. In the first place, scientists disagree. Some have found differences between male and female brains and some have not. Some are able to correlate the differences they perceive with differences in the abilities and intelligences of men and women and some cannot. In the second place, there are probably countless ways to look at brains and countless differences between individuals to examine, including differences between left-handers and right-handers. Hormones also admit of different interpretive gambits. To be sure, their entanglement with masculinity and femininity provides for vexingly circular ideas: attitudes and behaviors are given sexes and genders because sexes and genders are already associated with attitudes and behaviors. Moreover, hormones are seen not only as causes of sexed and gendered attitudes and behaviors, but as sexed and gendered themselves. Yet, even if we confirm endocrinological differences between male and female bodies, it is difficult to see how we get from these differences to Sullivan's syringe of manhood.

We need not make men and women, males and females central to our evolutionary history, our brains, or our hormones. Indeed, we can give community members, individuals, and growth regulators equal billing. But if so, we might question the uses of science in enforcing sex and gender identities. In reflecting on past uses of

<hr>

[88] Fausto-Sterling, *Sexing the Body*, p. 147.

sciences, Duster offers a useful reminder: "In the fifteenth-century
Spain of Torquemada, people routinely raised the question about the
biological differences between believers and heretics, between
Christians and Jews, posited the natural superiority of one group
over the other and invoked the known procedures for coming to
terms with the available knowledge."[89]

[89] Duster, *Backdoor to Eugenics*, p. 3.

5 Rethinking sex and gender identities

A survey of behavioral ecology fails to show that male and female differences provide the sole or even most important motor for evolutionary development, while surveys of brain studies and endocrinology fail to show that brains and hormones are fundamentally sexed. Still, these failures need not lead us to question whether we are men and women at all, or whether there are any differences between men and women. Instead, they raise the question as to why we are so interested in precisely these as opposed to the myriad of other differences and other motors of change. In this chapter, I want to suggest that our identities and identifications as men and women have the same status as identities and identifications as Red Sox and Yankees fans or Irish Americans and Polish Americans. Identities and identifications as men and women are no less partial than the other identities and identifications we possess. Nor are differences between men and women, however different cultures define them, any less situationally restricted than differences between left- and right-handers.

In order to make these claims, I shall argue that, like these other identities and identifications, our identities and identifications as men and women are understandings of who and what we are. As such, they are historically "effected" and intelligible parts of only particular interpretive wholes. As I did in the case of racial identity, I shall use accounts of the socially constructed status of sex and gender to set the stage for my claim. The accounts in which I am interested confront questions about the scope and consistency of constructions of sex and gender. Further, they raise the issue of whether we can or should simply dismantle them.

THE CONSTRUCTION OF SEX AND GENDER

There are many investigations into the construction of sex and gender, most of which focus on the construction of women. Here I take up Denise Riley's 1988 book, *Am I That Name: Feminism and the Category of "Women" in History*,[1] because it is explicit about a problem I want to raise. Riley's aim is to show that histories of women are misleading precisely because they assume that women have a history. In her view, the "arrangement of people under the banners of men and women"[2] is so intertwined with particular cultural conceptualizations of nature, the soul, the social world, and the body that the arrangement is always a specific arrangement. It is peculiar to what we might call a specific language game or discourse and cannot subsist outside of it. The language games are impermeable: women have no history because there is no historical thread that leads from one construction of their identity to another.

Riley focuses on what she sees as three separate and unrelated constructions of women. According to the medieval theology on which early feminists insisted, the identity of individuals as women pertained only to their life on earth. It had no existence in the afterworld or with regard to an individual's immortal soul. To be sure, women's earthly and mortal bodies exuded a greater sensuality and their corporeal existence therefore had the potential to pollute their souls. For just this reason, however, sixteenth- and seventeenth-century feminists took it upon themselves to prove and protect the sanctity and sex- and gender-neuter status of the soul. They sought to prove it through demonstrations of their learning and rationality.[3] They tried to protect it by advocating women's sanctuaries devoted to education and freed from the sensual and soul-polluting temptations of sexual intercourse.[4] These attempts failed. Riley claims that by the eighteenth century the sensuality of women's corporeal nature pervaded their identity and their identity included their souls. Moreover, since

---

[1] Denise Riley, *Am I That Name: Feminism and the Category of "Women" in History* (Minneapolis, MN: University of Minnesota Press, 1988).

[2] *Ibid.*, p. 7.   [3] *Ibid.*, pp. 26–28.   [4] *Ibid.*, pp. 11, 31.

Women associated w/ sensuality

women now simply were their bodily sensuality, their existence and moral character were bound to it. In the second construction of women on which Riley focuses, women's morality was nothing more or less than her chastity. "The whole moral potential of women was therefore thoroughly different, and their relation to the order of moral reason was irretrievably not that of men's."[5]

women's morality = chastity

Riley thinks the introduction of the concept of the social in the nineteenth century brought with it a third set of building blocks for the construction of women. The relevant opposition was no longer that between body and soul or moral reason and corporeal sensuality. Rather it was that between social beings and political ones. Because the social world was conceived of as a household writ large and because women were meant to be uniquely suited for domestic responsibilities, women could properly extend their sphere of domesticity beyond their own families to include a concern for the hygiene, education, sexuality, childbearing, and child-rearing of the population as a whole. Upper-class women thus took up new philanthropic roles that focused on the causes and prevention of illness and delinquency while working-class women became objects for upper-class philanthropy. Nevertheless, Riley thinks that what was most important about this new conceptual constellation linking women to the social world was what it precluded. The new construction of the social world reconstructed women in its image. Yet, it also set women in opposition to a construction of the political sphere which, for its part, became a masculine domain of juridical and government power. To allow women entry into this sphere would have been unreasonably to contaminate important matters of war and peace with feminine questions of health, housing, and care.

upper vs. lower class women

politics = men's sphere

In Riley's account, not only do women have no history; even within a particular historical period they possess no common features. Take the efforts of early twentieth-century British women to gain suffrage and thereby transform themselves from social beings to

[5] *Ibid.*, p. 40.

women seen as belonging to the domestic sphere, not political

political ones. In arguing against extending the suffrage to women, anti-suffragists often claimed that women were different from men. They were meant to have greater talents and affinities for domestic and social work, which would be grievously dissipated were they to trespass onto political turf. When suffragists countered that women's difference from men indicated just how important their participation in politics would be, since it would add new perspectives and raise new issues, anti-suffragists reversed themselves and denied that there was any difference between men and women at all. "As citizens ... they are sufficiently represented already. To give them the franchise would just double the number of voters, without introducing any new interest."[6] Likewise, when suffragists argued that women's lives were influenced by political decisions and therefore that women should possess the right to influence them, anti-suffragists responded that women's nature as generous but impulsive creatures suited them for only an indirect influence, through their more rational husbands and fathers. Yet, when suffragists insisted that women were no more impulsive than certain men – the Irish, for example[7] – anti-suffragists replied that the very impulsiveness of certain men meant that granting women the vote could lead to domestic violence if they were to disagree with impulsive husbands and fathers.[8]

Women, then, are not only "diachronically" but also "synchronically ... erratic."[9] They are both equal to men by grace and thoroughly inferior in body and soul; they are both natural beings and social ones; they are both the same as men and ineradicably different. Given these constructions, Riley concludes that "There aren't any women."[10] There is no continual substrate, "women," who could possess a history. Instead, there are only the constructions of different language games that possess different and even competing purposes.

---

[6] Cited from Anon. in Riley, *Am I That Name*, p. 71.

[7] See speech by Arabella Shore in Riley, *Am I That Name*, p. 77.

[8] See Riley, *Am I That Name*, pp. 67–95. I have somewhat modified the sequences of arguments and replies as Riley states them.

[9] Riley, *Am I That Name*, p. 2.   [10] *Ibid.*, p. 2.

Women have no history
└> constructed

To be sure, this conclusion is not the only one to take from the account that Riley offers. Her argument about women is a version of Foucault's argument about homosexuals: homosexuals have no history but are rather made up at a precise point in the nineteenth century.[11] Likewise, women have no history because who they are is constructed out of radically different building blocks at different times and sometimes out of radically different building blocks at the same time. Yet, Foucault's thesis is not uncontroversial, and we might say the same for Riley's: it is not clear that the discontinuities that Riley finds in constructions of women are really discontinuities. In many cultures and in the popular imagination, women continue to be connected, either more or less, with sensuality, a natural suitability to the domestic sphere, a comparative indifference to reason, and a tenuous hold on the political domain. These connections are not exclusive descriptions of women, nor are they perhaps even predominant ones. Yet, their persistence suggests that we might consider the history of women less as a set of disjunctions than as a series of separate strands, each of which possesses more or less influence at different times. In other words, descriptions of women are elements of an interpretive history. Just as various interpretations of *Hamlet* possess an afterlife that continues to influence how we understand the play and that receive more or less prominence at different times, various interpretations of women have afterlives that continue to influence how we understand who and what they are.

women associated w/ sensuality

Riley's account also leads to what she herself acknowledges as a problem, for if "there aren't any women," what becomes of struggles on their behalf? If we claim that women do not exist as enduring entities, what do we do about the associations and descriptions that do endure? Riley asks, "Does all of this mean, then, that the better programme for feminism now would be – to minimize 'women'? To cope with the oscillations by ... downplaying the category?"[12] This

---

[11] See Michel Foucault, *A History of Sexuality, Vol. I: An Introduction*, Robert Hurley, trans. (New York: Random House 1978).

[12] Riley, *Am I That Name*, p. 112.

question reproduces the question we raised about racial identities. Race is a historically developed means of distinguishing people, one that devolves from, and issues in, shameful practices, actions, and institutions no matter how internalized it becomes as a mode of identity. Why, then, not simply declare that there are no blacks, whites, Asians, Latinos, or Latinas? One answer to this question looks to the historical legacy of identifying people in racial terms and insists that we need to continue to identify ourselves and others in racial terms if we are to ensure that we correct the horrors done by these terms. Another answer to the question sees our "constructed" racial identities as sources of pride. While there may be no races, there are people who possess racial identities and who take them to be central features of their life and self-esteem. Riley seems to think that both are good answers as applied to women. In the first place, in the case of women, as in the case of blacks and minorities, inequalities persist. Hence, she argues, we cannot always take as our political principle the fact that "there aren't any women." In the second place, although feminism ought to direct "an eagle eye" at any use or definition of the term "women" and to question the purposes for which it is used,[13] at times there is no alternative to a politics of identity. Feminists need to be strategic, determining when to insist on the non-existence of women and when, conversely, to struggle for their recognition:

> Feminism must be agile enough to say, "Now we will be 'women' – but now we will be persons, not these 'women'." And, in practice, what sounds like a rigid opposition – between a philosophical correctness about the indeterminacy of the term, and a strategical willingness to clap one's feminist hand over one's theoretical mouth and just get on with "women" where necessary – will loosen.[14]

To illustrate her point, Riley offers the example of women workers. She thinks that feminists ought to continue to argue against the

[13] *Ibid.*, p. 2.   [14] *Ibid.*, p. 113.

idea that "women workers" are more interested in nine-to-five positions or in positions with flexible hours than they are in positions that
pay well. Although the former sorts of position are better suited to
caring for children and husbands, feminists need to insist that women
workers are just as interested in higher incomes as men are. On the
one hand, this insistence leaves "the annoyingly separable grouping
'women workers' untouched." On the other hand, by countering
familiar stereotypes, Riley thinks, the argument "successfully mud-
dies the content of that term."[15]

Joan Wallach Scott expands on this idea in comments on *Equal
Employment Opportunity Commission* v. *Sears, Roebuck & Co.*[16] In
this case, the Commission (EEOC) argued that Sears discriminated
against women by denying them access to its commission sales positions, which were typically its highest-paid jobs. The government's
witness, Alice Kessler-Harris, tried to support the government's case
by pointing to differences in the different job choices different individuals make and thereby dismantling the "annoyingly separable
grouping 'women workers'." As *Sears* noted, however, in a book
Kessler-Harris had previously published, she had argued that women
did prefer work that could be made compatible with domestic responsibilities and in doing so she stressed just this "annoyingly separable
grouping 'women workers'." The government lost the case.
Nevertheless, Scott tries to explain Kessler-Harris' position:

> In relationship to a labor history that had typically excluded
> women, it might make sense to overgeneralize about women's
> experience, emphasizing difference in order to demonstrate that the
> universal term "worker" was really a male reference that could not
> account for all aspects of women's job experiences. In relationship
> to an employer who sought to justify discrimination by reference to
> sexual difference, it made more sense to deny the totalizing effects

[15] *Ibid.*, p. 113.
[16] See Joan Wallach Scott, "The Sears Case," in Joan Wallach Scott, *Gender and the Politics of History* (New York: Columbia University Press, 1988), pp. 167–177.

of difference by stressing instead the diversity and complexity of women's behavior and motivation.[17]

In relation to labor history, then, we are to pursue a politics of identity, taking up the cause of the "annoyingly separable grouping 'women workers'." We are to demand recognition for their unique needs and aspirations and distinguish these from those of male workers. Further, we are to assure that women are not required to cut and prune their working identities to fit a model of working people geared to men. In contrast, in relation to a form of employment discrimination that tries to use differences between men and women to preclude the hiring of women for certain positions, we are to stress the diversity of women and deny that the "annoyingly separable grouping 'women workers'" exists at all. Still, what are the standards for this sort of strategic feminism? How do we know when to emphasize sex or gender identities and when to dismember them? Moreover, how does a strategic feminism counter a strategic sexism? Why not, for example, refer to "women workers" in relation to alleged employment discrimination, as Sears' own expert witness, Rosalind Rosenberg did, and, conversely, stress that "there aren't any women" in relation to labor history? Where do we obtain standards for doing one or the other?

Not all theorists pursue the strategic approach to women's identity that Riley and Scott employ. Kate Bornstein appeals to the possibility of playing with sex and gendered identities and Judith Butler appeals to the possibilities of subverting them. Although both are useful in helping us to rethink the status of our identities as men and women, they raise additional normative questions.

Bornstein is disturbed about identities as men and women because she regards them as club or class memberships that are simply oppressive. They are oppressive, first, because men are members of a higher class than women are; but they are oppressive, second, because everyone is required to be a member of one class or club or another.

[17] *Ibid.*, p. 170.

RETHINKING SEX AND GENDER IDENTITIES 161

"Why," she asks, "do we have to be gendered creatures at all?"[18] In reflecting on her decision to undergo genital surgery, Bornstein insists the motivation for her decision was not that she thought she was really a woman or that she "hated" her penis. Rather, what she hated was "that it made me a man."[19] The possession of a penis does not simply make certain actions and activities possible. It is a club card that brings with it a set of physical and behavioral requirements as well as a list of mandated objects of desire and a certain power relation to other human beings. There are, moreover, no exceptions to possessing one of only two club cards: "In this culture, the only two sanctioned gender clubs are 'men' and 'women.' If you don't belong to one or the other, you're told in no uncertain terms to sign up fast."[20] Yet, in belonging to one or the other, Bornstein thinks we neglect other possibilities. Indeed, she likens gender membership to alcoholism: "It's something we do to avoid or deny our full self-expression."[21]

What are the possibilities that membership in either a male or a female club precludes? Here Bornstein offers a confusing set of prospects. At times she talks about a third gender, a transsexuality somewhere between man and woman and transgressive of both:

There is black on one side of a spectrum, and

white
on the other
with a middle ground of grey, or
some would say there's a rainbow between the two.
There is
left and

right
and a middle ground of center
There is birth on one side,

and death on the other side

[18] Kate Bornstein, *Gender Outlaw: On Men, Women, and the Rest of Us* (New York: Vintage, 1995), p. 58.
[19] *Ibid.*, p. 47.   [20] *Ibid.*, p. 24.   [21] *Ibid.*, p. 45.

And a middle ground of life
Yet we insist that there are two, and   And we insist that this
only two genders: male and female.   is the way of nature.[22]

The insertion of a middle term between men and women cannot
resolve the concern that Bornstein has with gender clubs and oppressive gender codes, however. She points to the *hijras* of India and the
berdaches of American Indian cultures as examples of third genders
that are accommodated and even highly regarded in their respective
cultures.[23] Yet if membership in the classes or clubs of men and
women is oppressive, why will adding new clubs help? Will these
new clubs not have their own set of membership rules and their own
behavioral codes? If we replace alcoholism with another addiction,
do we deny any less of our full self-expression, whatever that is?
Bornstein sometimes abandons the idea of membership in a third
gender and refers instead to a "gender fluidity" that allows one to
take up a limitless number of genders "for any length of time, at any
rate of change."[24] The fluidity is meant to permit us to live beyond
rules because we are constantly leaving one gender for another. Yet,
presumably in taking up a limitless number of genders, we must also
take up the codes and rules of these genders, and hence become subject
to their codes and rules for however long we take them up. How, then,
do we live beyond codes? Why is moving between sets of rules better
than living under one set?

In the end, and despite her question about why we need to be
gendered creatures at all, Bornstein denies that she wants a world
without gender: "I love playing with gender and I love watching
other people play with all the shades and flavors that gender can
come in."[25] On this last of Bornstein's solutions to gender, it is a
performance. In being socialized into either the male or the female
club, one learns to move in certain ways, to wear certain clothes, and
to adhere to certain behaviors, such as making eye contact if one is a

[22] *Ibid.*, p. 49.   [23] *Ibid.*, p. 131.   [24] *Ibid.*, p. 51.   [25] *Ibid.*, p. 58.

RETHINKING SEX AND GENDER IDENTITIES 163

man and ending statements on a high, questioning note if one is a woman. Belonging to the male or female club, then, is simply a question of putting on a male or female act. Drag performances are important for Bornstein because they make this act explicit by revealing the extent to which gender can float free of bodies. Moreover, they exaggerate the codes and rules of gender and in so doing reveal just how artificial they are. Drag intentionally mixes and matches different bodies with different gender traits, performs certain cues on the "wrong" body type, and twists behaviors around "to a point of humor."[26] Bornstein herself contravenes prescribed gender policies: "As part of learning to pass as a woman," she announces about the counseling she went through before her genital surgery, "I was taught to avoid eye contact when walking down the street; that looking someone the eye was a male cue. Nowadays, sometimes I'll look away, and sometimes I'll look someone in the eye – it's a behavior pattern that's more fun to play with than to follow rigidly."[27]

Nevertheless, it is not clear how effective playful performances are as a means of exposing the artificiality of sex and gender. Bornstein need not insist that drag is always transgressive. Yet, she does suggest that it reveals gender to be nothing more than a performance. Because men can "do" women as well as women can, all that being a woman amounts to is this sort of performance. But, even if men "do" women as well as women do, surely part of the humor in the performance is our "theoretical commitment" to the idea that the people performing as women are not women. Indeed, this humor arguably reinforces the theoretical commitment: we "know" that the flamboyantly feminine woman on stage is "really" a man. What is funny is how well he does "female" without having the "genes" for it. What drag shows is the skill with which certain people can artificially reproduce what is natural to others. No more than *berdaches* or *hijras*, then, does drag defy the gender memberships that Bornstein criticizes.

humor in drag

---

[26] *Ibid.*, p. 137.   [27] *Ibid.*, p. 27.

There is, furthermore, an element of chic in Bornstein's analysis. For, if we in the West can play with different wardrobes, what about those who are imprisoned unless they wear a veil? If those in the West can play around with gender codes, giving off male cues in what count as female bodies, what about those who can be stoned unless they strictly follow gender rules? For those for whom the smallest transgression of rigidly defined female roles is grounds for exclusion or even death, highlighting the virtues of drag appears not only utopian but also somewhat tactless. More to the point and like a strategic feminism, it provides no guidance on when we should play with gender and when we should take it seriously. If members of certain societies cannot play with gender without risking their lives and if their sex and gender identities are forced upon them as the prescribed nature of every action they take, do we not need to think about the justifiable scope of gender identities rather than simply fooling around with them? Riley's reflections raise the question about when we should be women and when we should not. Bornstein's comments raise a similar question: when should we play with gender identities and when should we ask directly whether we possess them in the context at issue?

Butler is far more reflective than Bornstein about such normative questions, but ultimately her analysis raises yet more questions. If Riley's and Bornstein's reflections lead to the question of when we should accept or reject, occupy, or vamp on our gender identities, Butler's reflections raise the broader questions of which identities we should subject to these questions, and why. She begins with the disciplining power of what, following Adrienne Rich, she calls a "compulsory heterosexuality."[28] The starting point for scientific studies begins with male and female bodies that are meant to be fundamental, ahistorical facts. Male bodies find their natural expression in masculine identities while female bodies find their natural

[28] See Adrienne Rich, "Compulsory Heterosexuality and Lesbian Existence," in Elizabeth Abel and Emily K. Abel, eds., *The Signs Reader: Women, Gender, and Scholarship* (Chicago, IL: University of Chicago Press, 1983).

RETHINKING SEX AND GENDER IDENTITIES 165

expression in feminine identities. Natural desires, for their part, are all heterosexual. Butler turns this analysis on its head, however. What we begin with are the disciplining practices of a reproductive sexuality that work to maintain a "normal" heterosexuality by creating a binary system in which only two forms of coherent identity are possible and in which those two forms are aligned with only two sorts of body.[29] "Men and women," Butler writes, "exist ... as social norms."[30] In this binary system, combinations of bodies, identities, and desires that contravene the norms count as deviations. Moreover, they are studied and further disciplined as such, as deviations for which we must find the cause as well as the cure. A compulsory heterosexuality thus sets up the matrixes of body, identity, and desire that decide which subjects can count as intelligible and which must be seen, instead, as deviant or ambiguous. As Butler puts the point, "Subjects are constituted through exclusion, through the creation of a domain of deauthorized subjects, presubjects, figures of abjection, populations erased from view."[31]

On this analysis norms are double-edged swords. On the one hand, they are, Butler says, "what binds individuals together, forming the basis of the ethical and political claims."[32] On the other hand, they are a form of violence, providing "coercive criteria" for what counts as evaluatively normal and what is, instead, "deauthorized." Norms determine those whose activities, interests, and attitudes are intelligible because they fit the norm as well as those whose activities, interests, and attitudes are not intelligible because they do not. Consequently, any appeal to norms in the name of undoing violence and coercion is an appeal to standards that are themselves violent and coercive. At the same time, because the subject that is produced

---

[29] Judith Butler, *Gender Trouble: Feminism and the Subversion of Identity* (New York: Routledge, 1990), p. 17.

[30] Judith Butler, "The Question of Social Transformation," in Judith Butler, *Undoing Gender* (New York: Routledge, 2004), p. 210.

[31] Judith Butler, "Contingent Foundations: Feminism and the Question of 'Postmodernism,'" in *Feminist Contentions*, p. 47.

[32] Butler, "The Question of Social Transformation," p. 219.

[handwritten margin note at top: normative violence = produced + reproduced / ↳ Butler: "resignifications"]

[handwritten left margin, rotated: identities: authentic vs non authentic / (ex) drag femininity performed by 1 body (female) is authentic / but not authentic by another body (male is authentic]

through normative violence is not only produced but also continuously reproduced, this constant reproduction opens up the possibility of what Butler calls resignifications. Reproduction allows for "redeployment, subversive citation from within, and interruption and inadvertent convergences with other [power/discourse] networks."[33]

In trying to find an example for this resignification, redeployment, and subversive citation from within, Butler, like Bornstein, points to the ways in which sex and gender provides a form of entertainment, "play, pleasure, fun, fantasy."[34] Moreover, like Bornstein she emphasizes drag performances. In Butler's account, drag performances serve to illuminate an implicit ontology in which certain identities count as real and authentic while other ones do not. A drag identity is viewed as an unreal one, excluded from the mainstream and regarded as less valuable than other identities. In other words, to perform femininity on one sort of body is authentic; to perform it on another is not. By making the arbitrariness of this distinction clear, drag identities expose the violence and exclusion at the core of "authentic" identities. Moreover, drag shows that our implicit ontology is "open to rearticulation"[35] through its "citation" or repetition in the identities it excludes: *[handwritten note: Citation... citing (?)]*

> Although there are norms that govern what will and will not be real, and what will and will not be intelligible, they are called into question and reiterated at the moment in which performativity begins its citational practice. One surely cites norms that already exist, but these norms can be significantly deterritorialized through the citation. They can be exposed as nonnatural and nonnecessary when they take place in a context and through a form of embodying that defies normative expectation.[36]

Butler's argument, then, is that we can appeal to norms and change them at the same time. If certain identities are normal and

---

[33] Judith Butler, "For a Careful Reading," in *Feminist Contentions*, p. 135.
[34] Butler, "The Question of Social Transformation," p. 214.
[35] *Ibid.*, p. 214.   [36] *Ibid.*, p. 218.

others are not, we can simultaneously, as drag does, cite and subvert the standard in question. Yet, even if citing can also be subversive, which identities should we submit to such subversive citation and which should we protect from it? Butler writes, "What moves me politically, and that for which I want to make room, is the moment in which a subject – a person, a collective – asserts a right or entitlement to a livable life when no such prior authorization exists, when no clearly enabling convention is in place."[37] She does point out that both Nazis and anti-apartheid South Africans fall into this space: anti-apartheid black South Africans sought to vote without an enabling convention and Nazis asserted a right to a certain kind of life for which there was no precedent in the Weimar Republic. What, then, is the difference between the two? Butler again appeals to violence and exclusion: whereas the Nazis tried to intensify it, the anti-apartheid movement sought to undo it. She concludes that the task of radical democratic theory is to ask what resources we need "in order to bring into the human community those humans who have not been considered part of the recognizably human."[38]

Still, it is not clear that Butler can specify her appeal here to the "recognizably human" in any way that would allow us to exclude Nazis and include anti-apartheid fighters. As she emphasizes, the idea of the human is itself a norm and, as such, it both circumscribes and excludes. But then how do we know whom and what it legitimately encompasses and whom or what it does not? If our goal is "to bring into the human community those humans who have not been considered part of the recognizably human," then we might think that the worst Nazi war criminals fall into this category and that we should seek to make them part of the recognizably human. Further, we might think that although the Nazis sought to intensify violence and exclusion, we should also think ethically about the violence against, and exclusion of, the Nazis. Should we bring them into the recognizably human community? Should we bring in rapists and serial murderers

---

[37] *Ibid.*, p. 224.   [38] *Ibid.*, p. 225.

as well? On the one hand, Butler is not against leveling "judgments against criminals for illegal acts and so subject[ing] them to a normalizing procedure."[39] Moreover, she thinks this normalizing procedure can be decided on when "we consider our grounds for action in collective contexts and try to find modes of deliberation and reflection about which we can agree."[40] On the other hand, she asks whether we have "ever yet known the 'human'"[41] and is suspicious of agreement and the collective consideration of grounds for action where these involve social integration or common orientations. On the one hand, the norm of "the recognizably human" is meant to allow for standards for action and character that make it possible to condemn and exclude those responsible for genocide and mass murder. On the other hand, any agreement on these standards has to be regarded with suspicion:

> Do we need to know that, despite our differences, we are all oriented toward the same conception of rational deliberation and justification? Or do we need precisely to know that the "common" is no longer there for us, if it ever was, and that the capacious and self-limiting approach to difference is not only the task of cultural translation in this day of multiculturalism but the most important way to nonviolence?[42]

The norm of "the recognizably human" thus possesses and even hones the same double-edged character as the norm of the recognizably male and recognizably female. It provides both a standard for inclusion and exclusion and an objection to processes of including and excluding. Yet, for this reason, it is not clear how we can appeal to the norm of the recognizably human to resolve the "normalizing" violence of our other norms. The questions remain. When should we emphasize our identities as women and when should we reject them? About which identities should we be playful? Which identities should we try to bring into the human community and which should

---

[39] *Ibid.*, pp. 221–222.   [40] *Ibid.*, p. 222.   [41] *Ibid.*, p. 222.   [42] *Ibid.*, p. 221.

we try to keep out? In what follows, I want to return to the conditions of our understanding of texts in order to consider these questions.

UNDERSTANDING IDENTITIES AS MEN AND WOMEN

According to the account I gave in chapter 3, textual understanding moves in a circle. We understand parts of texts in terms of the whole and understand the whole in terms of the parts. Moreover, these circles are historical ones. We approach texts from within historical perspectives that these same texts have contributed to effecting or forming. The same holds for our understanding of one another: we understand one another in terms of identities that are parts of the histories in which we live and, in turn, understand our histories in terms of the identities that we employ for understanding one another. These identities include sex and gender ones. Just as we cannot go back before the point at which the Oedipal complex became a meaning that *Hamlet* can possess for us, we cannot go back before the point at which boys and girls, men and women became identities that individuals can possess for us. Nor are these identities any more limited by our intentions than are the meanings of texts by their authors' intentions. Kate Bornstein may never have formulated an intention to be a man and, indeed, she may have formulated the intention not to be one. Nevertheless, her possession of particular genitalia made her intelligible as one. Just as Freud has come to be contained in *Hamlet* whether Shakespeare put him there or not, being a man has come to be contained in a penis, whether its owner puts it there or not. Bornstein's play, "Hidden: A Gender," which is part of her memoir,[43] provides a direct parallel to the experience that Du Bois had with trading visiting cards:

> I'm four and a half years old, my first day of nursery school ... These
> are the days when the boys and girls have to play separately – so I start
> to go off with the other little girls to play. And this teacher ... says,

---

[43] Part Six of Bornstein, *Gender Outlaw*.

No No Dear, this is the line for the little girls. And I say, I know, I'm a little girl. And you know the look that grownups can give you – the one that says you are loathsome and sick and vile and about to be abandoned. She gives me that look. And I know I'll have to pretend to be a little boy from then on.[44]

Just as it was not part of Du Bois' intention or original self-understanding to be different or a black while trading visiting cards, it was not part of Bornstein's to be a boy while on the playground. Nevertheless, the understanding the teacher has of him as a boy becomes available to him as a way he comes to think he can be intelligibly understood. Moreover, just as Du Bois' new self-interpretation with the racial identity it contains offers him an interpretive framework for understanding and living his life, Bornstein's self-understanding with the sex and gender identity it contains offers her a way of thinking about and ultimately changing her life. What Du Bois and Bornstein understand, then, when they understand themselves in racial or sex and gender terms, are different texts than those with which they begin. These texts are the ones they must take up in new understandings of their futures.

Yet, there is no one interpretive tradition or set of historical relations from the point of which *Hamlet* is uniquely intelligible. Nor is Bornstein uniquely intelligible as a man or a woman. In the first place, there are different ways of being a man and being a woman. Just as we cannot restrict legitimate understandings of texts to one canonical understanding, or restrict legitimate understandings of racial identities to one way of being a certain race, we cannot restrict legitimate understandings of men and women to only one way of being either. One may be a man because of one's brain sex, or one's body sex, or some other way, just as one may be morphologically, culturally, or ethnically black and be so in different ways. In the second place, just as we cannot restrict legitimate understandings of one another to racial understandings, we cannot restrict legitimate understandings of

[44] Bornstein, *Gender Outlaw*, p. 176.

others and ourselves to understandings in terms of sex and gender. Instead, we will understand others and ourselves in various different ways, as professors, chess-players, and so on and all of these identities will have the same interpretive status. If *Hamlet* is no more fundamentally Freudian than it is existentialist and individuals are no more blacks and whites than they are baseball fans and opera buffs, they are also no more men and women than they are a myriad of other identities, including blue-eyed people and scuba divers. All of these identities are equally versions of who and what we are and are valuable only to the extent that they supply interpretations of identity that can be integrated with the context of which they are a part. What is problematic about sex and gender understandings of ourselves and others, then, is just what is problematic about racial ones. The problem is not that these understandings do not articulate identities we possess within certain situations. Instead, what is problematic is that these understandings attempt to monopolize who or what we are, to obscure the equal status of other identities and identifications, and to appear in contexts in which they make no sense and on which they have no purchase. Sex and gender identities, like racial ones, are possible only on a non-dogmatic basis, one that recognizes the equal status of other identities and acknowledge men and women as identities that appear only within specific horizons of interpretation.

It is arguable, however, that identities as men and women are psychologically more fundamental than this analysis gives them credit for being. They may not be central to all scientific endeavors and it may be possible to rewrite sciences currently written in terms of them without them. But these expectations may be naïve when it comes to moral psychology. Our sustained gender identities as men and women are arguably not simply one way of understanding who we and others are, intelligible only within restricted, situational contexts. Instead, these identities function for everyone as basic to our sense of who we are. Thus, Bornstein's sex and gender self-interpretation seems to have been more than the result of simply one interpretive framework applied to understanding and living one or a few parts of her life. Rather, the question of which sex or gender she "really" was became the defining question of her life and the one that has continued to orient the actions and positions she takes. Moreover, if we look at other transsexual memoirs and autobiographies, the suggestion that sex and gender are somehow fundamental in and to all life-situations is even stronger. For these memoirs and autobiographies express the sense that their writers have of possessing authentic sex and gendered selves that are at odds with their external appearance. Thus, Jan Morris begins her memoir, "I was three or perhaps four when I realized that I had been born into the wrong body and should really be a girl."[45] Raymond Thompson writes, "My body didn't exist in the way it was born; for me it only existed in my inner identity as a male."[46] Most poignantly, perhaps, Jennifer Finney Boylan claims that "The awareness that I was in the wrong body, living the wrong life was never out of my conscious mind – *never*."[47] Such statements seem to indicate that interpretations of who we are as men or women have a status that our other self-interpretations as body-surfers and professors, for example, do not have and that they reach to a deeper and more basic level of who we are. Individuals do not come to think that they were born into the wrong racial or ethnic body. They do not realize as children that they should really have been born black although they have white bodies, or that they are Chinese at a fundamental level although they appear to be English on a superficial one. Nor do they think they are "really" a right-handed person in a left-handed body or that they are living the wrong life as a left-hander. Yet Morris goes so far as to associate her sex and gender identity with her soul.[48] She considers whether her "conundrum" might be a consequence of a mid-twentieth-century society that required and elicited strictly differentiated sex and

---

[45] Jan Morris, *Conundrum* (Harcourt Brace Jovanovich, 1974), p. 3.

[46] Cited in Jay Prosser, *Second Skins: The Body Narratives of Transsexuality* (New York: Columbia University Press, 1998), p. 77.

[47] Jennifer Finney Boylan, *She's Not There: A Life in Two Genders* (New York: Broadway Books, 2003), p. 21.

[48] Morris, *Conundrum*, p. 172.

[margin note: some transsexuals see their urge to tran as "bio., imag., spiritual"]

gender roles. Yet, she dismisses the idea. "I believe," she writes, "the transsexual urge ... to be far more than a social compulsion but biological, imaginative and spiritual too."[49] For Morris, the soul that medieval feminists sought to keep neuter is a profoundly sexed and gendered one.

Of course, someone could wish that he or she were a Chinese person although he or she was not, or wish that he or she were a right-handed person although he or she was not. Some transsexuals at least sometimes understand themselves in this way. Thus, Deirdre McCloskey writes of the epiphany she had that she was a woman but she also tells her sister, "I don't think I'm a woman. I want to be one."[50] Wanting to be a man or a woman, however, is very different from thinking that one "really" is one. It is no different from wanting to be a gymnast or a Chief Executive Officer (CEO) without yet being one. Just as one might want to be a man without yet having the normal or, in Butler's sense "normed," body for it, one might want to be a gymnast without possessing the right body or coordination for it and one might want to be a CEO without having the necessary chutzpah. But if wanting to be a woman (or a man) is different from the sense one has that one is a woman (or a man) despite the way one's body is understood by others, what sense of identity is this latter sense? How are we to understand the sense that some transsexuals possess that they are men or women and are trapped in the wrong bodies?

Bornstein thinks this sort of claim is simply "an unfortunate metaphor that conveniently conforms to cultural expectations rather than an honest reflection of our transgendered feelings."[51] In her case, the feelings that led to her genital surgery were feelings of not wanting to be a man rather than either wanting to be or thinking that she was a woman. She also asks, "What does a man feel like? What does a

[margin note: same see it as 2 simple longing wanting to be vs. feeling you are the opp. sex is diff]

[bottom note: Bornstein: genital surgery bc did not want to be a man anymore —]

---

49 *Ibid.*, p. 173.
50 Deirdre McCloskey, *Crossing: A Memoir* (Chicago, IL: University of Chicago Press, 1999), p. 59.
51 Bornstein, *Gender Outlaw*, p. 66.

What does it mean to "feel" like a man or woman? (handwritten)

Jorgensen: seemingly male body (handwritten, left margin)

woman feel like?"[52] These are good questions. In her autobiography, Christine Jorgenson claims that she had "sissified" ways as a young boy; she did not like to fight and sometimes cried.[53] She kept a small piece of needlepoint in her desk and carried her books in what her sister insisted was the way girls, not boys, did. Yet, she does not say that she felt like a woman or that she was in the wrong body. Instead, she and her doctors understood her body as only "seemingly male."[54] Her view seems to be that she had a glandular problem caused by insufficient testosterone and that undergoing genital surgery was a way to correct the condition.[55] To this extent, her story is more about medicine than it is about sex or gender. McCloskey, for her part, compares her "crossing" from being a man to being a woman to other changes in identity one might accomplish, from being an elementary school teacher to being a hospital chaplain and from being a shop-keeper to being a monk.[56] She also compares herself to the kind of foreign traveler who becomes so enamored of a country that he or she decides to live there permanently. As Donald McCloskey, she always liked to dress in women's clothing. After her children were grown, she thought she "might cross-dress a little more. Visit Venice more too." As it turned out, she writes, "I visited womanhood and stayed."[57]

McCloskey: change from man to women like changing professions (handwritten, right margin)

Thinking one has a medical condition that makes one effemi-nate or deciding to become an ex-patriot because one likes Venice are not expressions of some pre-existing or authentic identity. I do not see how we can follow Bornstein and dismiss some people's unshakeable convictions that they have been born into the wrong bodies. Nevertheless, although Morris, Thompson, and Boylan speak of their sense of possessing a fundamental sex and gendered identity that conflicts with their external appearance, it is also important that not all transsexuals speak this way. What memoirs and

Warnke disagrees w/ Bornstein's dismissal of idea that some transsexuals feel like they weren't born in the right bodies (handwritten)

→ but not all feel this way (handwritten)

[52] Ibid., p. 24.

[53] See Christine Jorgensen, *Christine Jorgensen: A Personal Autobiography* (New York: Paul S. Eriksson, 1967).

[54] Ibid., p. 111.

[55] See Jorgensen's letter to her parents in *Christine Jorgensen*, pp. 123–126.

[56] McCloskey, *Crossing*, p. xii.   [57] Ibid., p. xiii.

autobiographies by transsexuals show is just how varied and multiple our senses and understandings of what is most fundamental to who we are can be. Two children brought up as Christians might both find that identity lacking in some way. For one, the sense of the lack might be so important that he or she converts to another religion or discovers that he or she is "really" Jewish or Muslim. For the other, the deficiencies of his or her original religious identity might be of less consequence. Sex and gendered identities are similar. Some people understand themselves as primarily sex and gendered and this sense of who they are is so powerful that they must transform their bodies to express their inner selves if they determine that their present appearance is not adequate as this expression. Others are less invested in their sexes and genders. Perhaps these people understand themselves in primarily religious terms so that what most importantly requires affirming or changing is their religious identities. Others may understand themselves to be fundamentally younger "at heart" than their ages or bodies signal. Hence, like transsexuals, they may seek plastic surgery in order to transform their appearance so that it more nearly fits the younger identities they possess. Yet, while some people must cross religious, age, or sex and gender boundaries to become who they understand themselves to be, others need not and they need not for at least two reasons: either because they already are who they understand themselves most fundamentally to be or because their sense of possessing an "authentic" or "most fundamental" identity is less compelling. In each respect, however, identities as men and women are of a piece with our other identities. We can make them more a part or less a part of our individual moral psychologies just as we can make identities as professionals more a part or less a part of our moral psychologies.

In comparing sex and gender identities with racial identities, Appiah performs a thought-experiment that leads him to a different conclusion.[58] Suppose one were to undergo a series of operations to

[58] K. Anthony Appiah, "'But Would that Still be Me?' Notes on Gender, 'Race,' Ethnicity as Sources of 'Identity'," in *Race/Sex: Their Sameness, Difference, and Interplay*, Naomi Zack, ed. (New York: Routledge, 1997).

surgeries to change racial appearance — does not change one's fundamental identity

alter one's external "racial" appearance, changing the shape of one's nose, darkening or lightening one's skin or making one's eyes more or less round. One would still be the same person, Appiah says. The alterations would not change who one was or one's fundamental identity. But suppose, in contrast, one were to undergo a series of operations to alter one's external sex appearance and gender, restructuring one's chest, reshaping one's genitals, or taking artificial hormones. In this case, Appiah says, one would become a different person. Morris has precisely the opposite view, of course, insisting that in going through her surgery she finally became who she really already was. Indeed she writes of the result of her sex-reassignment surgeries that "I had reached Identity."[59] Yet, in a way, this view simply substantiates Appiah's point. A sex-reassignment operation either changes utterly who one is or makes one utterly who one understands oneself to be. A race-change operation does not. "'Racial' identities," Appiah writes, "are for us – and that means something like, us in the modern West – apparently less conceptually central to who one is than gender ... identities."[60]

Appiah: for changing sex appearance person becomes diff. person...

gender identities is more major to who we are as ppl than race

Yet just as transsexuals understand their transition from one sex and gender to the other differently they also understand the continuity of their lives differently. Indeed, different people would presumably have different answers to Appiah's question about whether they still are who they once were, whether or not they had undergone sex-reassignment surgery. For some people, the narratives of their lives take shape as straight-on trajectories and the adult emerges from the child without dead-ends or detours. For others, surely, when they think over their lives they encounter so many twists, turns, and re-evaluations that they do not understand themselves to be the same people as they once were in any way. McCloskey writes that, "It's strange to have been a man and now to be a woman. But it's no stranger perhaps than having once been a West African and

[59] Morris, *Conundrum*, p. 163.   [60] "'But Would that Still be Me?'," p. 79.

now being an American."[61] For most individuals, in fact, it is probably the case that they understand themselves to be the same people they were in the past in some ways and not in other ways. Moreover, this probably holds for those who know them as well. Think again about the Califia-Rices who met and fell in love as lesbians, parted ways, and then met and fell in love again after both had begun to live as men. Despite taking hormones and undergoing various sex-reassignment surgeries, presumably each still saw those aspects of the other that had initially drawn them together. Sex-change and race-change operations do not differ in kind from one another in their hermeneutic status. Nor, more importantly, do they differ from any of the other changes we may undergo in our views of who we are or ought to be. We can change from liberals to conservatives, for example, from religious people to secularists, or from West Africans to Americans. In all of these cases, we might also revise some of the ways we understand ourselves, our past, and our future. Others presumably understand us differently in some ways as well. But, in most cases, we do not abandon all of our self-understandings. Nor do our acquaintances find nothing of who they previously took us to be. We remain intelligible to ourselves and to others in some of the same ways, just not all of them. In an epilogue to Boylan's memoir, the novelist Richard Russo writes about Grace, the person who had been James Boylan's wife and was now Jennifer's:

> Years earlier, her heart had inclined in the direction of another soul, and now, against the advice of many friends and well-wishers, she'd had the wisdom to understand that when our hearts incline – often in defiance of duty, blood, rationality, justice, indeed every value we hold dear – it's pointless to object. We love whom we love. In the past two years, for Grace, everything had changed and nothing had changed. Her heart still inclined, as was its habit.[62]

---

[61] McCloskey, *Crossing*, xii.

[62] Richard Russo, "Afterword: Imagining Jenny," in Finney Boylan, *She's Not There*, p. 299.

changing sex/gender does not necessarily mean
changing who that person is, through & through; just pronoun change

If we can and often do understand ourselves to be both the same people we were in the past in certain respects and to be entirely different people in other respects, then changing from a man to a woman or the reverse differs only in that it involves a change in pronoun. Of course, it could be argued that the fact that we cannot approach one another except by using masculine and feminine pronouns shows the extent to which individuals are always and primarily men and women, girls and boys. Pronouns always designate us as male or female, men or women in a way that they do not designate us as blacks or whites, parents or non-parents, sports fans, or opera buffs. Indeed, other pronouns behave quite differently. In German, one can be "*du*" to certain people and "*Sie*" to others and the same holds for "*tu'* and "*vous*" in French. Perhaps nicknames have something of the same function in the United States but, in any case, all three instances emphasize the different identities we have in different contexts in a way that "he" and "she," "his" and "hers" cannot. Moreover in languages in which all nouns have one gender or the other, the centrality of sex and gender understandings would seem to be deeply entrenched.

Yet, why should pronouns indicate who we are in any more "conceptually central" a way than the bumper stickers we put on our cars or the name-tags we wear? Like bumper stickers and name-tags, pronouns serve as convenient descriptions. At a conference, a person might wear a name-tag that indicates who he or she is in terms of his or her professional affiliation. At his or her child's school, however, the same person might wear a name-tag that indicates who he or she is in terms of the child of whom he or she is the parent. The same holds of pronouns. Although they indicate one of our identities, they do not show that this identity either exhausts or necessarily grounds who or what we are. Of course, their prominence presents a particular difficulty for remembering the multiplicity of ways we have of understanding who we are – similar, perhaps, to the way the prominence in graduate school applications of students' scores on the Graduate Record Exam (GRE) presents a difficulty for evaluating prospective graduate students. Both are often the first aspects of people that we

Significance of pronouns!

pronouns: Convenient descriptions

know. Nevertheless, we also know enough not to allow our knowledge of GRE scores to exhaust our understanding of an applicant's claim to be a worthy candidate. Nor need pronouns ground or remain central to our understanding of who or what a person is. For her part, Virginia Woolf dismisses them in an aside:

> Orlando had become a woman – there is no denying it. But in every other respect, Orlando remained precisely as he had been. The change of sex, though it altered their future, did nothing whatever to alter their identity ... His memory – but in future we must, for convention's sake, say "her" for "his and "she" for "he" – her memory then, went back through all the events of her past life without encountering any obstacle ... The change seemed to have been accomplished painlessly and completely and in such a way that Orlando herself showed no surprise at it.[63]

opposite idea of Appiah's

Woolf's thought experiment leads in the opposite direction to Appiah's. Orlando is able to understand her life in exactly the same terms she had understood it before her transition from a man to a woman. No reinterpretation of that life is necessary. To the contrary, whereas we might suppose that a religious or political conversion would require one to rethink one's past actions and affiliations, Orlando's change from man to woman is accomplished without erecting any obstacles in considering her past. All that has changed is the pronoun appropriate to referring to him or her, and Woolf says this change is only a convention.

MISUNDERSTANDING AND MISIDENTIFICATION

There is no hermeneutic basis for distinguishing an understanding of others or ourselves in sex and gender terms from an understanding of others and ourselves in any other terms. Some individuals will worry about their identities and identifications as men and women

---

[63] Virginia Woolf, *Orlando: A Biography* (New York: Harcourt Brace & Co., 1928), pp. 138–139.

more than others will, just as some people will worry about their religious identities and identifications more than others will. Some of the people with these latter worries will take on different religious identities and some will not. Some individuals will live their lives more in line with one of their identities than in line with any of the others and some will live their lives in line with more than one or even all of them. Yet, what about misidentification? What about the normative questions that Riley's, Bornstein's, and Butler's analyses raise? When are understandings of individuals as men and women appropriate and when should they cede ground to other interpretations? Why should we be women in histories of labor and not women in our job applications?

In answering this question with regard to racial identities, we returned to textual interpretation and to the hermeneutic circle of whole and part. Many different interpretations of a text may succeed in integrating parts into a unity of meaning but interpretations that fail to do so also fail as interpretations. Hammill's interpretation of Caravaggio's "Sacrifice of Isaac" tries to understand the painting as a "scene of pederastic anal sex."[64] Yet, the interpretation fails to integrate its understanding of Abraham's knife, which it takes to be "strikingly erect," with other elements of the painting including the building in the background, the direction of the angel's finger, and Abraham's position in it. Suppose we look at the Sears case. Is identity as a woman intelligible in the context of selecting a sales force? What about in the context of university teaching?

The entrance of those centrally identified as women into university teaching gave rise to new disciplines such as women's studies. It also led to new ways of looking at both canonical texts and the content of "the canon" itself. Yet the same holds for the entrance of Straussians, Kantians, Marxists, and Republicans into university teaching. They help understand texts from the perspective of esoteric

---

[64] Graham L. Hammill, *Sexuality and Form: Caravaggio, Marlowe and Bacon* (Chicago, IL: University of Chicago Press, 2000), p. 89.

teachings, universal principles, the critique of ideology, and supply-side economics, and can be illuminating in doing so. They also include different books in their canons and develop new fields. Yet, if the entrance of diverse groups into university teaching opens up new perspectives, the validity or enlightening character of those perspectives is independent of the identities of those offering the insights. Typically, in fact, only when insights seem forced or tendentious do questions about the identity of those offering them arise. If a scholar's interpretation of a text makes it a sexist one in a way that fails to make a coherent whole of the text, it can be interesting to ask why the scholar developed the interpretation he or she developed and one answer to this causal question might refer, legitimately or illegitimately, to his or her sex and gender. Of course, it might, instead, refer legitimately or illegitimately to his or her political identity.

Identity as a woman, a liberal Democrat, a religious person, a Straussian, or a Kantian might make a difference to the subjects one teaches, the canon one accepts, and the textual meanings one discovers. Yet, the worth of one's discoveries does not depend upon those identities but upon the ability of the interpretation to illuminate the text and to do so in ways that others find valuable. Similarly, if one is part of a sales force, one's sex, gender, or political affiliation might make a difference to the products one wants to sell or to the way that one sells them. Yet, just as clearly, it might not. McCloskey writes of telling the dean of his college that he intended to become a woman. Both McCloskey and his dean were economists, both were members of the business college at their university, and both were adamant proponents of the free-market. When McCloskey advised the dean of his intended transformation, the dean quipped, "Thank God ... I thought ... you were going to confess to converting to socialism!"[65] For a free-marketer, becoming a woman is far less momentous than becoming a socialist precisely because it has less to do with one's economic perspective.

[65] McCloskey, *Crossing*, p. 93.

What about identities as men and women in medical contexts? Surely it is important to understand certain people as female patients for purposes of determining proper nutrition, susceptibility to certain diseases, or conditions such as pregnancy. Yet, is it? We have already considered the confusion over menopause caused by understanding individuals primarily as women and childbearers. Are the confusions to which understandings in terms of sex and gender lead not as dangerous as those to which understandings of people in terms of race are? If we understand individuals as blacks or non-blacks in the context of screening for sickle cell anemia, we risk a series of misdiagnoses. Given the mixing of the United States population, identities as blacks and non-blacks would seem to be particularly inappropriate to medical contexts. But dogmatically insisting on these identities also means that we can overlook the possibility of sickling in individuals from southern India and the Arabian Peninsula while looking for it in the Xhosa of South Africa. Medical contexts are similarly inhospitable to sex and gender identities. Does screening for ovarian cancer in women under the presumption that they all possess ovaries make any more sense than looking for sickling in Xhosans? Does urging individuals as women to take calcium because women are at risk for osteoporosis mean that we overlook the risks of osteoporosis for individuals as men? In deciding which medical tests to conduct or preventative therapies to encourage, should we not rather ask what characteristics specific individuals possess rather than who or what they are (among the many whos and whats they are)? If we are interested in medical research into the causes and risks of being left-handed, ought we not look at the medical histories of left-handers? Similarly, if we are interested in the nutritional needs caused by pregnancy ought we not research outcomes for those who have been pregnant and offer nutritional advice on this basis?

Pregnancy raises a particularly fraught set of answers to questions of identifying patients as women, for many feminists have argued that a refusal to look at pregnant people as women leads to inequities. In the 1974 case of *Geduldig* v. *Aiello*, the Supreme Court upheld a California medical insurance program that excluded pregnancy[66] and in 1976 it upheld similar pregnancy exclusions in private insurance plans in *General Electric Co.* v. *Gilbert*. In both cases, the court took the physiology of non-pregnant persons as its standard for normal conditions and saw pregnancy as an "additional risk."[67] Insurance companies, it said, had leeway in deciding which additional risks they were willing to cover. Moreover these risks could legitimately include such procedures as vasectomies and prostatectomies without also including pregnancy. Feminists protested, arguing that allowing policies to exclude coverage for conditions related to pregnancy failed to acknowledge facts of biology unique to women and therefore also failed to provide sufficient protection for women in the workplace.[68] Particularly outrageous, these feminists said, was the comparison of pregnant and non-pregnant persons for clearly only women can be pregnant persons.

The Pregnancy Discrimination Act was a response to this outrage. According to the law, "women affected by pregnancy, childbirth, and related medical conditions shall be treated the same as other persons not so affected but similar in their ability or inability to work."[69] In 1987, the court gave its interpretation of this law in upholding a California statue that required employers to give pregnant women reasonable leaves of absence but that did not stipulate such leave for others. Here it said that the intent of the Pregnancy Discrimination Act was to guarantee women's right "to participate fully and equally in the workforce."[70] For many feminists this decision corrected the 1974 and 1976 decisions. It singled out women for special treatment and it established conditions that would allow women to compete with men

equality in workforce & yet feminists want special treatment when pregnant

[66] *Geduldig* v. *Aiello* 417 US 484, 497 n. 20 (1974).

[67] *General Electric Co.* v. *Gilbert* 429 US 125 (1976).

[68] See Deborah L. Rhode, *Justice and Gender: Sex Discrimination and the Law* (Cambridge, MA: Harvard University Press, 1989), p. 117.

[69] See Rhode, *Justice and Gender*, p. 119.

[70] *California Federal Savings and Loan Association* v. *Guerra* 758 F2d 390 (CA 1985) Also see Rhode, *Justice and Gender*, p. 120.

on an equal footing in the workplace.[71] In fact, in California, pregnant women were not only to be treated in the same way as "other persons not so affected but similar in their ability or inability to work;" they were to be treated better.

Yet, for precisely this reason, the salutary effects of the law are less than obvious. By singling certain job holders out as women and by allowing them to be treated differently than others, the law suggests that women require special rights and accommodations in order to hold jobs others can hold without them. Hiring them can seem likely to employers to be more expensive than hiring others and, worse, women can seem to be constitutionally unsuited to responsible working lives.[72] Hence, the better way to accommodate pregnancy and working is to regard reproduction and child-rearing in ways that are neutral with regard to identities as men or women. One can equate absences from work due to pregnancy with absences from work for other legitimate reasons and insist through such legislation as the Family and Medical Leave Act that these reasons include emergencies connected to workers' family lives. Further, rather than arguing for maternal leaves and reinforcing the idea that raising children is a female job, one can argue for and support parental leaves that are neutral with regard to whether the parent is male or female.[73] Indeed, it is possible to ask just how understanding workers as women is meant to be relevant to pregnancy or child-rearing. Pregnancy is a condition. Given its current essentiality to the reproduction of the species, we can surely argue that it should be accommodated in social, political, and economic life, whoever undertakes it: whether a woman, an opera buff, or Matt Califia-Rice. By the same token, raising

---

[71] See Marjorie Jacobson, "Pregnancy and Employment: Three Approaches to Equal Opportunity," *Boston University Law Review*, 68, 1988, pp. 1023–1045.

[72] See, for example, Wendy Williams, "Equality's Riddle: Pregnancy and the Equal Treatment/Special Treatment Debate," *New York University Review of Law and Social Change*, 13, 1983, pp. 325–380.

[73] Iris Marion Young disagrees but usefully surveys the 1980s feminist debate in *Justice and the Politics of Difference* (Princeton, NJ: Princeton University Press, 1990), pp. 175–178.

children who are both physically and psychologically healthy would seem to be a necessity for any society interested in its reproduction and long-term future. For this reason, we can demand accommodations that allow for strong and viable families. Neither pregnancy nor child-rearing, however, needs to be understood in sex and gender terms. Instead, those who are pregnant and those who are raising children are adequately understood as, respectively, pregnant people and parents. An employer who understands a pregnant employee as a woman is thus engaged in sex and gender profiling in just the way that the police officer who understands a person as a black or Hispanic is engaged in racial profiling. If the latter identification fails to contribute to fighting crime, the former fails to contribute to questions of worker productivity or parental leave. Why not equally irrelevantly understand a worker as an Episcopalian?

Riley and Scott are therefore justified in their suspicion of "the annoyingly separable group 'women workers'." Still, the answer to the question as to when we are to be women workers and when we are not depends not on strategy, but on context. We are workers at work, not women. Understanding individuals at work as women is tantamount to understanding the devil in *Damn Yankees!* as Milton's Satan. Neither allows for an integration of part and whole.

As in the case of race, however, there is a caveat to this analysis based on the length of history for which racial, sex, and gender identities have been mistakenly found in contexts in which they make no sense. Thus, we might insist on identities as women in order to assess progress in overcoming disparities in income, wealth, and power that were themselves caused by misunderstanding individuals as women in contexts in which these identities could not be intelligibly integrated. Disparities are particularly clear in the case of income. Historically, working women were segregated into jobs that paid less well than men's jobs and disparities remain between traditional women's work such as nursing and traditional men's work such as truck driving. Women also continue often to be paid less well than men doing the same job. Because women typically earn less money than men at every stage of their working lives, these disparities cannot be explained by pointing to hours or days off work spent fulfilling family responsibilities. Actually, according to Vicki Schulz, even in that part of their working life in which women have children at home, they do not take a great deal of time off. Women with pre-school children work as hard as men, if not as hard as women without pre-school children.[74] These disparities in income render it excusable to understand individuals as women for the purposes of analyzing and correcting the inequities that issue from the historical use of the identification as women, just as it is excusable to understand individuals as blacks for the purposes of analyzing and correcting inequities that issue from the historical use of the identification as blacks or African Americans. Yet, the excuse does not mean that it is intelligible to understand people as women in any and every context. We can also hope that the historical after-effects that excuse the understanding of individuals as women in the context of social justice issues will not always excuse it. After all, they rest on mistaking workers, citizens, parents, and the like for women.

To be sure, a caveat to this analysis recognizes that some individuals regard pregnancy and childbirth as the defining moments of their lives, as the moments that provide the framework for the rest of their lives and hence offer them, and perhaps others, a good perspective for understanding who they are. Defining moments for other people might be different, however: a stint of duty in Vietnam, the death of a parent, a particular career choice, and so on. The common characteristic of these moments, however, is that their meaning is individual rather than social. I may most often present myself as Irish, a mother, or a baseball fan. Where one of these identities provides the shape of my life, the identity may define me for others as well, at least for the most part. Nevertheless, not all those with Irish ancestry, children, or season tickets to the Red Sox need to understand

[74] Vicki Schulz, "Life's Work," *Columbia Law Review*, 100 (7), 2002, p. 1986.

themselves or present themselves to others as Irish, parents, or fans. The same holds for identities as women.

These considerations suggest that understandings and self-understandings as men and women are limited to the same conditions as understandings and self-understandings as blacks, whites, Asians, Latinos, or Latinas. They are incidental and recreational in the way that our understandings of one another as sports fans are; they are ceremonial in the way that our understandings of one another as Irish Americans are, and they are restricted in the way that our understandings of one another as siblings are. Just as one might understand oneself or others as Red Sox fans during the World Series, one might understand one's infant child as a girl in giving her a name, for example, or painting her room. And just as one might wear green on St. Patrick's Day to indicate that one is Irish, one might wear a dress or a skirt on certain occasions to indicate that one is a woman. One might also intelligibly understand individuals as males and females in that context in which procreation is a possibility. While reproduction takes place in contexts other than heterosexual intercourse, heterosexual intercourse remains one route to it. Hence, one might profitably understand someone else in sex and gender terms in a context in which one needs to know what to do in order either to avoid or to encourage egg fertilization.

The coherence of understanding others as men or women in the context of procreation is often taken as a justification for restricting marriage to unions between men and women. In chapter 6, I want to see if this link is hermeneutically justified and I also want to consider the uses of identities as men and women in the military.

6 Marriage, the military, and identity

The hermeneutic conditions of sex and gender identities mean that they are intelligible ways of understanding who we are only under certain conditions with regard to specific interpretive wholes. Hence, individuals are men and women in no more or less incidental or unrestricted a way than they are blacks, whites, athletes, or scholars. Acknowledging the incidental character of Irish American identities in the United States went hand in hand with recognizing their lack of significance for social institutions and practices. Sex and gender identities, however, continue to possess significance for and within at least two influential social institutions: the armed forces and civil marriage. Eligibility for service in the military is still understood in terms of sex and gender insofar as men must register for the draft while women must not. Since 1940, however, public opinion has favored drafting women when men are drafted and even to many of those who support women's exemption, the justification for the exemption is less than compelling.[1] What has been thought to be more compelling is an understanding of individuals as men and women for purposes of limiting service in the military to heterosexuals. Since heterosexuals are those who engage in sexual activity with individuals who possess a different sex and gender identity from their own, the armed services must identify their service members and recruits in sex and gender terms. A similar understanding of individuals holds for the institution of civil marriage. The federal Defense of Marriage Act and statutes in many states understand marriage as the union precisely of one man and one woman. Racial understandings of

---

[1] See M. C. Devilbiss, *Women and Military Service: A History, Analysis and Overview of Key Issues* (Maxwell Air Force Base, Alabama, AL: Air University Press, 1990), p. 56.

participants in civil marriage or the armed services no longer retain any legitimacy. The question I want to ask in this chapter is whether sex and gender understandings make any sense in the context of marriage or the military.

Asking this question is not the same as asking whether marriage or the military are institutions we should value or try to preserve. Claudia Card compares the struggles for the right of gays and lesbians to marry (although not to join the military[2]) with a hypothetical struggle on the part of a certain group to own slaves if the group had been arbitrarily prohibited from doing so.[3] She thinks that, like slavery, marriage, "is a deeply flawed institution." Hence, "even though it is a special injustice to exclude lesbians and gay men arbitrarily from participating in it, it would not necessarily advance the case of justice ... to remove the special injustice of discrimination."[4] Nevertheless, it is possible to be unconcerned with preserving the institutions of either marriage or the armed services and still be concerned with the question of whether the participants in them are intelligible as men and women. For, if we can plausibly understand the participants in the institutions in these ways then the social influence of the institutions suggests that sex and gender identities will also maintain a more central role in our understandings of one another than I have argued that their partial and non-exclusive status warrants. Conversely, if it turns out that the participants in marriage and the military cannot plausibly be understood in sex and gender terms, then reinterpreting these participants should help de-center sex and gender identities in general. The question thus remains as to whether we can plausibly understand those who want to marry or those who join the military as men and women.

[2] See Claudia Card, "The Military Ban and the ROTC: A Study in Closeting," in Claudia Card, *Lesbian Choices* (New York: Columbia University Press, 1995), pp. 169–193.

[3] Claudia Card, "Against Marriage and Motherhood," *Hypatia: A Journal of Feminist Philosophy*, 11 (3), 1996, download from *Genderwatch*, http://proquest.umi.com.

[4] Card, "Against Marriage and Motherhood," download, p. 3.

Answering this question will depend upon how we understand the institutions in which these individuals seek to participate. These institutions form the whole for which men and women are meant to be the parts. Does an understanding of these parts as men and women allow for an integration of part and whole? How shall we understand the wholes or contexts that marriage and the military form? I shall begin with an attempt to understand what marriage is.

THE NATURAL-LAW UNDERSTANDING OF MARRIAGE

Defenders of what is sometimes called traditional marriage define civil marriage as the union of one man and one woman. According to this definition, sex and gender identities are crucial to the meaning of civil marriage because civil marriage is inseparably tied to procreation and the raising of children. This tie does not depend on whether a particular marriage actually issues in children. Nor does it matter that a relationship between two men or two women might include them. Rather, civil marriage is an institution set up to protect and nurture the children that the sexual intercourse between a man and a woman might produce and this purposive structure for the institution holds whether or not the intercourse was intended to or does produce them. In this view, then, there is a crucial difference between different-sex unions and same-sex unions since the former has the capacity for unintended consequences in pregnancy and childbirth while the latter does not. Where such consequences ensue, children need the stability of a married mother and father. In particular, they need an institution geared towards binding fathers to the families they have helped to create. The New York Court of Appeals affirmed this sort of analysis in refusing to grant same-sex couples a right to marry under the New York state constitution in *Hernandez* v. *Robles*:

> Heterosexual intercourse has a natural tendency to lead to the birth of children; homosexual intercourse does not ... The Legislature ... could find that an important function of marriage is to create more stability and permanence in the relationships that cause children to be born. It thus could choose to offer an inducement – in

the form of marriage and its attendant benefits – to opposite-sex couples who make a solemn, long-term commitment to each other.[5]

While mothers typically stay with the children to whom they have given birth, without the inducement of the benefits of marriage, defenders of restricting marriage to opposite-sex couples fear that men will not. "Marriage is the way every society attempts … to give every child the father his or heart desires," Maggie Gallagher insists.[6] To be sure, one might wonder why extending the benefits of marriage to same-sex couples should affect the value of the benefits and inducements for opposite-sex couples. But defenders of a ban on marriage between same-sex couples claim that such an extension would. Gallagher writes, "Good fathers are made, not born. When family and sexual norms are weakened, it is … children's access to fathers … that is put at risk."[7] How establishing marriages between same-sex couples would weaken family and sexual norms, however, is never made clear.

Gallagher and others also maintain that opposite sexes are important to raising children because their qualities complement one another. Children, they say, are best raised in intact nuclear families with female mothers and male fathers whose inherent qualities as men and women balance one another.[8] Moreover, they insist that there is too little evidence to determine the long-term psychological health and well-being of children who are raised in families headed by two men or two women.[9] Again, New York's highest court

[handwritten right margin: allegedly, same-sex couples weaken family/sexual norms — why never revealed]

[handwritten left margin: idea that household w/ 1 mother & 1 father is best bc opp. sexes complement ea other]

[handwritten bottom: concern of long-term psych. health & well being of kids]

---

[5] *Hernandez* v. *Robles* 7 NY 3d 338 (2006), Lexis pagination, p. 6.

[6] Maggie Gallagher, "Normal Marriage: Two Views," in Lynn Wardle *et al.*, eds., *Marriage and Same-Sex Unions: A Debate* (Westport, CT: Praeger, 2003), p. 18.

[7] *Ibid.*, p. 17.

[8] See, for example, Dwight D. Duncan, "The Federal Marriage Amendment and Rule by Judges," *Harvard Journal of Law and Public Policy*, 27, 2004; Teresa Stanton Collett, "Recognizing Same-Sex Marriage: Asking for the Impossible?," *The Catholic University Law Review*, 47, 1998, pp. 1262–1263 and both David Organ Coolidge and George Dent at "The University of Chicago Law School Roundtable," 7 *University of Chicago Law School Roundtable*, 2000, pp. 41, 47.

[9] See Judge Cordy's dissent in *Goodridge* v. *Department of Public Health* 440 Mass. 309 (2003).

agrees: "Intuition and experience suggest that a child benefits from having before his or her eyes, every day, living models of what both a man and a woman are like."[10] Further, "Social science literature reporting studies of same-sex parents and their children … do not establish beyond doubt that children fare equally well in same-sex and opposite-sex households. What they show, at most, is that rather limited observation has detected no marked differences. More definitive results could hardly be expected, for until recently few children have been raised in same-sex households, and there has not been enough time to study the long-term results of such child-rearing."[11]

Yet, what are the differences between men and women that are meant to provide for the psychological health of children? Who are the living models of what both a man and a woman are like? What are men and women like? George Dent admits that "No law forbids an effeminate man to marry a masculine woman."[12] But if so, why can an effeminate man not marry a masculine man or an effeminate woman not marry a masculine woman? Indeed, no law forbids an effeminate man from marrying an effeminate woman or a masculine man from marrying a masculine woman. So what are the complementary qualities that make a difference to raising children? Since most defenders of traditional marriage concede that men and women can take nontraditional roles in a marriage, the issue is even more perplexing. If different sexed members of a couple can both be effeminate in their attitudes and behavior, whatever this idea of effeminacy is supposed to signify, and if different sexed members can take on whatever roles in the marriage that work best for them, why is this not the case for members of an identically sexed couple? Indeed, why do we need the identities of different-sexed or same-sexed at all? Is the point not simply that children do well if their parents complement each other in certain ways?

As thus far stated, the link between marriage and the necessity of opposite-sex participants is unclear for other reasons as well. In the

---

[10] *Hernandez* v. *Robles*, p. 359.   [11] *Hernandez* v. *Robles*, p. 360.
[12] "The University of Chicago Law School Roundtable," p. 47.

MARRIAGE, THE MILITARY, AND IDENTITY 193

first place, we need not understand pregnant individuals as pregnant women. In the second place, if we avoid talking about pregnant women and refer to pregnant people instead, it is still not clear that it is possible to argue that the point of marriage is to compensate for the vulnerability of children and people who can become pregnant. Were we to do so, how would we justify the legality of marriages to sterile partners or older partners who cannot become pregnant? Moreover, even if marriage were first established to compensate for the vulnerability caused by pregnancy, it is surely possible to ask whether its meaning might not develop with the meaning of other social and historical practices and institutions. To the extent that, as a social institution, marriage participates in the histories of the societies of which it is a part, it would be odd to think that its meaning must be limited to the intentions of those who first established it. Making this assumption would be as odd, in fact, as it would be to think that the meaning of a text must be limited to its author's intentions. Just as texts take on new meanings from new perspectives as part of different interpretive traditions, so too, surely, does marriage. Finally, if the point of marriage were really to compensate for pregnancy, why would a better strategy for a person (married or unmarried) who found herself pregnant be immediately to have sexual intercourse with as many men as possible in the hope that at least one of them would assume that the child was his and contribute to its support? Among the Canela of Brazil, "all men with whom a woman had sex when she became pregnant, and including the period just prior to when she was detectably pregnant, are expected to provide food for her child. Hence, it is scarcely surprising that just as soon as she suspects she is pregnant, a Canela woman, like a groupie after a rock star, attempts to seduce the tribe's best hunters and fishermen."[13]

Of course, if the Canela strategy is a plausible one, we might agree with those who trace the roots of marriage to the need to combat

---

[13] See Sarah Blaffer Hrdy, *Mother Nature: Maternal Instincts and How They Shape the Human Species* (New York: Ballantine Books, 1999), p. 247.

marriage used to control women & their sexuality

such strategies. Rather than a mechanism for protecting women, marriage is a mechanism to control women and their sexuality. Through marriage, a man prohibits his wife from sleeping with multiple partners and thereby assures himself that the children he nurtures and supports are his own.[14] Yet, in this case, we would expect defenders of limiting marriage to opposite-sex partners to applaud weddings between same-sex partners since these have the potential to help in this endeavor. The more lesbians there are who are engaged in state-sanctioned monogamous relationships, the fewer there are whose sexuality men need to control. Moreover, the more gay men there are who are engaged in state-sanctioned monogamous relationships, the fewer there are who are available to muddy the lines of descent.

There is, however, another approach to defending the restriction of marriage to one man and one woman, that of "natural law," which tries to make the connection between marriage, procreation, sex and, gender tighter and less instrumental. Robert P. George calls marriage "a two-in-one-flesh communion of persons that is consummated and actualized by acts that are procreative in type, whether or not they are procreative in effect (or are motivated, even in part, by a desire to procreate)."[15] By "acts that are procreative in type," George means the sort of acts that can create children. Such acts can be performed by sterile different-sexed couples and by older different-sexed couples for whom the creation of children is no longer possible. In these cases, the acts remain the type of act by which children can be created in other circumstances, whereas the acts are not of a type that can be performed by men with men or by women with women. Moreover, for George and others in the natural-law tradition, the creation of children is not instrumentally related to marital acts but is, instead, a gift that

Children = a gift of "marital acts"

[14] See Carmen Shalev, *Birth Power: The Case for Surrogacy* (New Haven, CT: Yale University Press, 1989), esp. chapter 1.

[15] Robert P. George, "Neutrality, Equality and 'Same-Sex Marriage'," in Warole *et al.*, eds., *Marriage and Same-Sex Unions*, pp. 120–121. Also see John Finnis, "Law, Morality and 'Sexual Orientation'," *The Notre Dame Law Review*, 69, 1994, pp. 1049–1074.

supervenes on them. As George puts the point, acts that are procreative in type "belong to the only class of acts by which children can come into being, not as 'products' that their parents choose to 'make,' but rather as perfective participants in the organic community (i.e. the family) that is established by their parents' marriage."[16]

According to this understanding of civil marriage, then, marriage is not tied to procreation and hence to different-sexed couples as a means of tying fathers to families. Rather, it is procreative because it has unity or a two-in-one-flesh communion at its foundation and because this unity rests on acts that are procreative in type on which children may supervene. George's grounds for this claim are biological: in the kind of act in which reproduction is possible, a couple becomes a single organism. A mated pair of one man and one woman is necessary to reproduction and for purposes of reproduction, then, the pair forms one organism. Because marriage is a two-in-one-flesh communion and because in acts that are reproductive a man and a woman form a single organism, it is only such acts that make marriage the "unitive" value it is. Two additional points follow for George. First, the value of acts that are procreative in type is irrespective of the pleasure they may or may not involve.[17] Second, no acts that are not procreative in type are, properly speaking, marital ones because they cannot lead to the same unity.[18] For George, masturbation and sodomy are valueless whether they occur outside of marriage or inside of it since, in both cases, they can serve only instrumental ends of sensory pleasure, friendship, or the like. He also thinks it is a mistake to conceive of genitalia as mere "plumbing" and of bodies in general as a means to extrinsic ends. Rather bodies are part of the "personal

---

[16] George, "Neutrality, Equality and 'Same-Sex Marriage'," p. 123.

[17] See Robert P. George and Gerard V. Bradley, "Marriage and the Liberal Imagination," *Georgetown Law Journal*, 84, 1995, pp. 308–310.

[18] Hadley Arkes goes further, insisting that they are not sexual acts at all. Indeed they "may be taken as minor burlesques or even mockeries of the true thing" (Hadley Arkes, "Questions of Principle, Not Predictions: A Reply to Macedo," *Georgetown Law Journal*, 84, 1995, p. 323).

bodies not to be treated as "instruments for personal pleasure"

reality of human beings. To treat them as instruments for personal pleasure is to destroy the integrity of body, mind and spirit."[19]

The natural-law account of marriage suggests that there is a cost to undoing the link between marriage and acts that are procreative in type: namely, erasing the line marriage establishes between communion and any other sensory experience. If marriage is no longer connected to the one-flesh union of two individuals possible only in acts that are procreative in type, and hence possible only for a different-sexed couple, then there is no reason not to open the institution, not only to same-sex couples, but to bigamists, polygamists, and others.[20] As Hadley Arkes asks, "If the notion of marriage were separated from the teleology of the body – if it were separated from the fact that only two people, a man and a woman, could beget a child – then *on what ground of principle could the law confine marriage to 'couples?'*"[21] Marriage becomes an institution open to any group of people interested in an intimate relationship involving sex, friendship, and the hope of self-fulfillment. "While we are at it," Arkes continues, "we might ask how the law, on these new premises, rules out marriage between parents and their children."[22] What is lost, according to George, in provoking a "redefinition" of marriage in this way is a basic element of morality. Over time marriage will not only lose its capacity to provide security for children but will also lose its value as a human good. As George writes:

how do we limit marriage to couples? or do non-relatives? etc.

> The law ... will teach either that marriage is an intrinsic human good that people can choose to participate in, but whose contours people cannot make and remake at will ... or the law will teach that marriage is a mere convention that is malleable in such a way that individuals, couples, or, indeed, groups can choose to make it whatever suits their desires, interests, subjective goals and so on.

[19] See Arkes, "Marriage and the Liberal Imagination," p. 314.
[20] See Richard G. Wilkins, "The Constitutionality of Legal Preferences for Heterosexual Marriage," in Warole *et al.*, eds., *Marriage and Same-Sex Unions*, p. 233.
[21] Arkes, "Questions of Principle," p. 325, emphasis in the original.   [22] *Ibid.*, p. 325.

The result … will be the development of practices and ideologies that truly do tend to undermine the sound understanding and practice of marriage.[23]

George is aware that the philosophical and theological roots of this understanding of marriage might seem to preclude its relevance to the on-going legal debates over civil marriage between same-sex partners. To the extent that the natural-law account is an essentially religious one, it cannot constitutionally be imposed on those who do not share it. Yet, George insists that the law is not and cannot remain neutral with regard to marriage. Laws already underwrite the ethical value of mutual commitment in marriage, for example, by establishing legal conditions on and procedures for leaving it. George and other natural lawyers suggest that the same holds for its value as a two-in-one-flesh communion. Like mutual commitment, it is a good that requires cultural recognition and institutional support:

> The law would embody a lie (and a damaging one insofar as it truly would contribute to the undermining of the sound understanding and practice of marriage in a culture) if it were to pretend that a marital relationship could be formed on the basis of, and integrated around, sodomitical or other intrinsically nonmarital (and, as such, self-alienating) sex acts.

What are we to make of this analysis of the necessity to civil marriage that its participants be defined as one man and one woman? George suggests that his account is the only "sound understanding and practice of marriage." Is this suggestion plausible? If we look at American constitutional history, the answer seems to be "no." Indeed, George's account is arguably more hostile to our historical understanding of traditional marriage in the United States than is marriage between same-sex partners. The natural-law account of marriage emphasizes the unique "unitive" value of acts procreative in type. Yet

---

[23] George, "Neutrality, Equality and 'Same-Sex Marriage'," p. 128.

given the American tradition of pluralism in the pursuit of individual goods, it is surely non-traditional to dismiss other routes to union or other values a particular marriage might have for its members. Even more non-traditional would be an attempt to use the law to impose one way of valuing marriage or one route to that value. George's claim that legally enforceable exit conditions on marriage already ground its particular ethical values does not make his account more plausible, for if we can understand marriage differently than he does, we will also understand the point of its exit conditions differently as well.

Is there, then, an alternative to George's understanding of marriage? Suppose we take the legal history of civil marriage in the United States as a key to its meaning. The instrumental account of this meaning that ties marriage to procreation and the raising of children cannot make sense out of the legitimacy of a myriad of marriages, including those that do not issue in children. The natural-law account does not make sense in light of an American commitment to the plurality of conceptions of the good. How, then, might we understand marriage? Moreover, how might we understand the right to marry? What is the meaning of American actions and legal decisions in regard to both?

"FORMAL AND RIGHTFUL" MARRIAGE

In the early nineteenth century, one of the ways in which the former American colonies tried to establish their distance from England was to move away from the state regulation of marriage.[24] Americans, excluding slaves, entered marriage in various ways, through marrying each other on their own, without the presence of church or state officials, and common-law marriage, as well as by secular and church authorities, if they could be found.[25] Central to marriages between non-slaves was a couple's decision to live as a married couple and to

---

[24] See Michael Grossberg, *Governing the Hearth: Law and the Family in Nineteenth Century America* (Chapel Hill, NC: University of North Carolina Press, 1985), pp. 69–71.
[25] See Nancy F. Cott, *Public Vows: A History of Marriage and the Nation* (Cambridge, MA, Harvard University Press, 2000), pp. 30–31.

establish a joint household, followed by their community's acknowledgment of them as a married unit. What distinguished slave marriages from non-slave marriages, then, was not the regulation of the
state before the wedding but the legal and community recognition of
the union after people "took up" with one another. Although some
slave owners allowed slaves to take part in wedding ceremonies such
as "jumping the broomstick," these ceremonies had no binding consequences. Husbands, wives, and children might live apart on adjacent
farms and see each other only at their owner's discretion.[26] They
might be sold away from one another at any time and, in any case,
they had no control over the ways they or their wives were sexually
used by owners or overseers. For these reasons, writing for the North
Carolina Supreme Court in 1838, Thomas Ruffin denied that slaves
could be united in "rightful and formal marriage ... Concubinage,
which is voluntary on the part of the slaves, and permissive on that of
the master ... is the relation, to which these people have ever been
practically restricted, and with which alone, perhaps, their condition
is compatible."[27] A slave preacher was more succinct. Typically he
ended his "wedding" ceremonies: "Till death or buckra part you."[28]

After the Civil War, slave unions could finally acquire official
recognition and slaves took advantage of the opportunity in droves.[29]
Why? What is important about the legal acknowledgment of one's
intimate relation to someone else? What does the recognition of a
couple as legally married do for that couple in the United States?
Obviously, it helps to express their mutual love for, and commitment
to, one another but commitment ceremonies without the authority of
the state can arguably do the same. If a wedding ceremony is a public
expression of love, why need the state be involved at all? Moreover,
while federal law includes 1,049 places where civil marriage confers a

---

[26] See Margaret A. Burnham, "An Impossible Marriage: Slave Law and Family Law,"
Law and Inequality, 5, 1987, p. 196.

[27] Cott, *Public Vows*, p. 34.   [28] Grossberg, *Governing the Hearth*, p. 132.

[29] Cott, *Public Vows*, p. 88.

special status, right, or benefit on those who participate in it,[30] two unmarried but committed partners might work out a series of contracts with one another to enjoy most if not all of these rights and benefits. Given adequate financial means, they could adopt one another's children to obtain the rights of parents; they could prepare wills and health care proxies designating each other as heirs and responsible parties, and they could work out contractual relations to govern their shared finances. Although the possibility of joint insurance policies and health care benefits through one partner's employment would vary according to state and employer, individuals could, again given the financial means, purchase separate insurance policies and health insurance for dependents who did not qualify. In splitting up, cohabiting couples could not avail themselves of the laws of divorce with regard to child support issues and the division of property. Nevertheless, they could employ principles of equity jurisdiction. What, then, is so special about civil marriage that many former slaves would travel long distances to have their marriages made legal? Why are many same-sex couples interested in civil marriages as well?

Civil marriage can be understood as an institution that, barring violence, creates a zone of privacy for intimate choices. In the contemporary United States legalized marriages grant couples two capacities: they can pursue those behaviors that in their estimation best solidify their particular bond and, at the same time, they can present themselves to the public world in a way that compels official recognition of their legitimate investment in one another's lives, in whatever way they conduct their particular relationship. Married couples thus possess a kind of immediate legitimacy that slaves were forced to do without and that even a set of legal documents cannot duplicate. If one is married, one is automatically the parent of the children born into the marriage; one is the default heir of one's spouse unless other arrangements have been made; one is also the default person in

---

[30] See Evan Wolfson, "All Together Now," in Warole *et al.*, eds., *Marriage and Same-Sex Unions*, p. 4.

emergencies where one's identity as someone's spouse permits immediate access to police officers, doctors, and the like. To be sure, cohabit-
iting couples can no longer be sold away from one another as slave
couples could be. Nevertheless, marriage provides a kind of shorthand
communication of the legitimacy of one's involvement and concern in
someone else's life and affairs, and it is this shorthand that is not
available to those who simply cohabit.

The 1930s dispute over Abraham Lincoln Erlanger's estate is a
case in point.[31] Erlanger and a woman who called herself Charlotte
Fixel-Erlanger had been living together for ten years when Erlanger
died in 1930, a multi-millionaire. In deciding whether Fixel-Erlanger
was entitled to inherit his estate, the court heard testimony from
149 witnesses, examined 834 evidentiary exhibits, and reviewed a
6,965-page record.[32] Witnesses recounted private conversations and
described how Fixel-Erlanger helped the frail Erlanger to eat; they
detailed walks the couple had taken and commented on their entertainment style. Fixel-Erlanger's lawyer even entered Fixel-Erlanger's
credit card receipts into evidence and produced evidence of her regu-
larly selecting Erlanger's suits. The details of the Erlangers' private life
served to convince the court that their relationship merited recognition as a common-law marriage. Had the couple been formally wed to
one another before Erlanger's death, however, Fixel-Erlanger would
have been entitled to an inheritance no matter how the couple had
behaved towards one another and the details of their relationship
would have escaped public scrutiny.

William H. Hohengarten uses the New York case of *Braschi* v.
Stahl Associates Co. to make a similar point about privacy and pub-
licity.[33] The case concerned the question of whether Miguel Braschi
could be evicted from a rent-controlled apartment after the death of his

---

[31] *In re Estate of Erlanger* 145 Msic 1 (NY 1932). Also see Ariela R. Dubler, "Wifely
Behavior: A Legal History of Acting Married," *Columbia Law Review*, 100,
pp. 957–1021.

[32] Dubler, "Wifely Behavior," p. 992.

[33] William M. Hohengarten, "Same-Sex Marriage and the Right of Privacy," *Yale Law
Journal*, 103 (6), 1994.

partner, to whom he was not married. In deciding that he had a right to remain in the apartment, the court determined that "in the context of eviction, a ... realistic and ... valid view of a family includes two adult lifetime partners whose relationship is long term and character-ized by an emotional and financial commitment and interdepend-ence."[34] At least for purposes of rent-controlled apartments, then, legal marriage is not a prerequisite to official recognition of a relation-ship. At the same time, the court suggested an exacting set of tests for deciding whether a given non-marital relationship met its standard for a family. These tests included assessments of "the exclusivity and longevity of the relationship, the level of emotional and financial commitment, the manner in which the parties have conducted their everyday lives and held themselves out to society, and the reliance placed upon one another for daily family services." The judges conceded that "the presence or absence of one or more of [these factors] is not dispositive since it is the totality of the relationship which should ... control." Nevertheless, evaluating the "totality of the relationship" involved estimating "the dedication, caring and self-sacrifice of the parties."[35] In contrast, if a couple is married, the question of their dedication to one another, caring and self-sacrifice is neither a neces-sary nor a legitimate area of inquiry. It is enough that they are married.

At least part of the reason, then, that civil marriage is an attrac-tive option for many couples is that it is able to offer an immediate and no-questions-asked mark of legitimacy. Take as a point of compari-son, the affidavits of plaintiffs in *Hernandez* v. *Robles*.[36] Mary Jo Kennedy writes that when her partner was rushed to the hospital for emergency surgery, they had first to "fill out revised forms to make sure that [Kennedy] could consent to treatment for her if necessary."[37] When his partner was dying Nevin Cohen "was not always given the same information or asked the same decision-making questions in a

[margin handwritten note: married couples not questioned over their legitimacy of their commitment, etc.]

---

[34] 543 NE2d 49 (1989), p. 54.   [35] 543 NE2d 49 (1989), p. 55.

[36] Available at lambdalegal.org.

[37] *Hernandez* v. *Robles*: Memorandum of Law in Support of Plaintiff's Motion for Summary Judgment, p. 16, n. 12, available at lambdalegal.org.

way a spouse would be."[38] Raising children in cohabiting households also requires a level of state intrusion not required for married couples. Freeman-Tweed writes "When our son ... was born, I was the first person to hold him. But it would take over two years, during which Lauren and I had to submit to intrusive interviews and background checks before I could legally adopt him and have the rights that other parents have automatically."[39] Her partner Lauren continues, "We hired an attorney and paid her over $800 to prepare wills, health care proxies and guardianship papers ... We had to have friends write letters on our behalf ... we had to be fingerprinted; and we had to have a New York State probation officer come into our home to decide if it was "a suitable environment."[40]

In avoiding the need for these sorts of inquiries and inspections civil marriage permits an off-loading of questions into the details of private lives onto a common coinage that compels public recognition and respect. It confers onto committed couples public rights to an immediate and no-questions-asked involvement in one another's lives and with regard to whatever responsibilities and relationships these lives entail. Thus, whereas George endorses as marriages only those unions that achieve a two-in-one-flesh communion, the difference between slave and non-slave marriages and between marriage and cohabitation suggests a different understanding. Whether married couples are friends, enemies, lovers, or the particular kind of lover George supports, the fact that they are married precludes most inquiries by public authorities. The law is meant to protect individuals from violence and coercion both inside and outside of marriage. Nevertheless, civil marriage entails a publicly recognized right to an involvement in one's partner's life and to protection from state inference into the relationship, short of protecting the individuals within it from violence and coercion.

To be sure, if this understanding of modern marriage is a plausible one, then it is not an unproblematic institution. Card thinks that

___

[38] *Ibid.*, p. 16, n. 12.   [39] *Ibid.*, p. 16, n. 12.   [40] *Ibid.*, p. 16, n. 12.

current laws in fact fail to protect spouses, and particularly wives, from injury and death at the hands of those to whom they are married. Hence she suggests that the state ought either to get out of the business of licensing relationships altogether or to take greater care in licensing marriages by engaging in more inspections and inquiries of those who plan to wed. As a society, she writes, we need to think more carefully about "the dangers of legally sanctioning the access of one person to the person and life of another."[41] The immediate, state-sanctioned recognition of a right to an involvement in someone else's life works two ways, then. On the one hand, it transfers a set of rights to couples, including the right of immediate access to one's spouse and children in emergencies. On the other hand, it allows such an immediate access to one's spouse and children that laws against spousal abuse and child endangerment often come a step too late.

Card and other critics of marriage also argue that in legitimizing certain relationships, marriage delegitimizes others.[42] Certain relationships have title to a publicly respected zone of privacy while others do not. Currently precluded from this zone are not only relationships between same-sex couples, but also, among others, polygamous relationships, incestuous relationships, bigamous relationships, intimate but non-cohabiting relationships, and what might be called serially non-monogamous relationships in which a person has a series of intimate relations with others who have intimate relationships of their own but not with one another. Thus if state-licensed marriages bestow official recognition on certain relationships, we can ask on which relationships it should it bestow this recognition, and how. Should these relationships be required to take a certain form? Should the granting of marriage licenses be contingent on individuals' passing certain psychological tests designed to measure propensities towards violence? How should we understand the right to marry and those who possess it? Put more hermeneutically, what is the meaning

[41] Card, "Against Marriage and Motherhood," download, p. 6.
[42] See Michael Warner, *The Trouble with Normal: Sex, Politics and the Ethics of Queer Life* (New York: Free Press, 1999), esp. p. 96.

of the right to marriage? If texts develop their meaning in the course of their interpretive histories, what is the meaning of the right to marriage as it has developed in our legal history? Is a right to marry held only by certain individuals with certain identities?

MARRIAGE RIGHTS

After the Civil War, at the same time that states legalized marriages between former slaves, many states also passed anti-miscegenation statutes outlawing marriages between whites and non-whites. Despite the Fourteenth Amendment such bans were held to be constitutional on the assumption that the amendment dealt only with civil and political rights, not with "social equality."[43] Courts also upheld the statutes on the basis of nature. In 1871, for example, the Indiana Supreme Court cited a Pennsylvania case validating racially segregated railroad cars to make an even stronger case for racially segregated marriages. The Pennsylvania decision said that "The fact of a distribution of men by race and color is as visible in the providential arrangement of the earth as that of heat and cold."[44] Consequently, the Indiana court inferred that prohibiting marriage between those of different races derived not from "prejudice, nor caste nor injustice of any kind, but simply to suffer men to follow the law of races established by the Creator himself."[45]

Following a similar logic, the California legislature passed a law in 1850 banning legal marriages between whites and Negroes and in 1905 amended the law to add a prohibition on marriages between whites and mulattoes or Mongolians, by which it meant individuals with Japanese or Chinese ancestry. In 1933, after the California Supreme Court upheld the legality of a marriage between a white and a Filipino, the legislature promptly added "Malay" to its list of those whites could not wed. However, in 1948, in the case of *Perez* v. *Sharp*, a majority of the California court found that the 1850 statute

---

[43] Grossberg, *Governing the Hearth*, p. 137.

[44] *The West Chester and Philadelphia Railroad Co.* v. *Miles* 55 Pa. 209 (1867), p. 213.

[45] *Ibid.*, p. 405.

and its amendments violated the California constitution. In so doing, without disputing racial segregation laws then in effect, the court set a precedent for a line of United States Supreme Court decisions that linked the right to marry to capacities for choice and consent. Civil marriage, the California court said, was "a fundamental right of free men."[46] More importantly for our purposes, it was not a right merely in the abstract; instead the right was one "to join in marriage with the person of one's choice."[47] This finding served as the basis on which the court was able both to invalidate a ban on interracial marriages and to uphold statutes mandating separate facilities, including separate railway cars, for whites and other races. According to the judges, as long as there was some railroad car one could occupy, it was no impingement on one's fundamental rights to be banned from occupying a particular railroad car. The same did not hold of spouses. The law could not claim that, as long as there was someone one could marry, it was no impingement on one's fundamental rights to be banned from marrying a particular person. "Human beings," the opinion said, "are bereft of worth and dignity by a doctrine that would make them as interchangeable as trains."[48]

no more restrictions on race for marriage in Virginia

In 1967, in *Loving v. Virginia* the United States Supreme Court finally followed California's example and invalidated all restrictions on the right to marry that were based on racial classifications.[49] The state of Virginia had argued that its ban was legitimate since it applied to whites and non-whites equally. Whites could not marry non-whites and non-whites could not marry whites. Yet, the court appealed to "the very heavy burden of justification" that it said was "traditionally required of state statutes drawn according to race" and denied any "legitimate overriding purpose independent of invidious racial discrimination" that could justify classifying participants in marriage according to race.[50] Defenders of limiting the right to marry to opposite-sex partners often appeal to this link to the history of racism to

---

[46] *Perez* v. *Sharp* 32 Cal. 2d 711 (1948), p. 714.   [47] *Perez* v. *Sharp*, p. 715.
[48] *Perez* v. *Sharp*, p. 725.   [49] *Loving* v. *Virginia* 388 US 1 (1976), p. 12.
[50] *Loving* v. *Virginia*, p. 10.

distinguish *Loving* from current court cases over marriage between same-sex partners. Indeed, four years after *Loving*, the Minnesota Supreme Court upheld Minnesota's prohibition against such marriages in the face of a *Loving*-inspired challenge brought by same-sex partners.[51] In *Hernandez* v. *Robles* in 2006, the New York court reiterated what it saw as the narrow racial scope of the *Loving* ruling: "Although the Court characterized the right to marry as a 'choice,' it did not articulate [a] broad 'right to marry the spouse of one's choice.'" Rather, the Court observed that "the Fourteenth Amendment requires that *the freedom of choice to marry not be restricted by invidious racial discriminations.*"[52]   racial vs. sexuality discriminations

Yet, the subsequent history of Supreme Court marriage cases belies this narrow reading of *Loving*. In 1978, *Zablocki* v. *Redhail* extended the right to marry from interracial couples to non-custodial parents who were too poor to pay to support their children from previous relationships[53] and in 1987, *Turner* v. *Safely* extended the right to prison inmates.[54] To be sure, these later decisions focus on the rights of prison inmates and indigent, non-custodial parents to marry without specifying whom they have a right to marry. Nonetheless, unless prison inmates and indigent, non-custodial parents have a right to marry, a person who wanted to marry a prison inmate or indigent, non-custodial parent would be deprived of the right to marry a particular person, the deprivation that *Perez* said would suppose that people were "as interchangeable as trains." Other ppl, like inmates allowed to marry

Hernandez v. *Robles* notwithstanding, then, the history of marriage litigation suggests that in the United States the right to marry has come to mean a right to marry the person of one's choice as long as that person consents to do so. Indeed, so fundamental to marriage are choice and consent that California had to acknowledge their logical force even under conditions of legally enforced segregation. This freedom of choice and consent were first unjustifiably withheld from

↳ right to marry: w/ person's consent

---

[51] *Baker* v. *Nelson*, 291 Minn. 310 (1971).   [52] *Hernandez* v. *Robles*, p. 371.
[53] *Zablocki* v. *Redhail* 434 US 374 (1978).   [54] *Turner* v. *Safely* 482 US 78 (1987).

slaves, second, unconstitutionally withheld from interracial couples, third unconstitutionally withheld from prison inmates and, fourth, unconstitutionally withheld from indigent, non-custodial parents. In eliminating these restrictions, the principle guiding the development of marriage law is that people who are free are free to marry whom they want to marry, provided those whom they want to marry also consent. In American legal history this understanding of the right to marry has gradually won out over attempts to tie it to certain sorts of identities. Although anti-miscegenation bans understood couples in racial terms and although other regulations stressed identities as prison inmates or indigent non-custodial parents, in determining that these identities were irrelevant to the right to marry, legal decisions suggest that the identities entailed by its meaning are identities as autonomous choosers and consenters. *Idea of choice/consent not congruous w/ who we fall in love w/ or attracted to*

One might argue that the ideas of choice and consent make little sense with regard to intimate relationships. We do not choose those whom we love or even those to whom we are sexually attracted. In marrying, then, we can often act against our best interests, subjecting ourselves to an open-ended term of unhappiness, violence, and even death. For this reason, Card thinks that no one should choose marriage and, more importantly, that no one should struggle to open it up to couples now barred from marrying.[55] *Card: No one should be married* Nevertheless, the choice and consent at issue in the right to marry are not choices to love or to be sexually attracted to someone. They are rather choices about long-term investments in, and involvements with, another person. *we can love and not marry* We can love someone and choose not to marry him or her. The right that the meaning of civil marriage in the United States gives us is the right to marry the person we choose. *right to marry who we choose*

Yet, if the identities entailed by the right to marry are identities as free choosers and consenters, and if the right therefore fails to involve either whites or non-whites, prison inmates or non-inmates or indigent or non-indigent parents, it also fails to involve either men

[55] Card, "Against Marriage and Motherhood," p. 6.

[handwritten: human beings not interchangeable like railway cars = denying personal right]

or women. If human beings are not interchangeable in the way that railway cars are (or were supposed to be), then to deny someone his or her choice of a spouse, however we understand that spouse, is to deny him or her a "vital personal right." Courts have allowed that these choices can be restricted for purposes of health and particular states have placed restrictions on marriages of people younger than what those states consider to be the age of consent. Yet, they have also repeated the claim in *Zablocki* v. *Redhail* that such gate-keeping laws cannot "interfere directly and substantially with the right to marry."[56] Hence, neither understandings of participants in marriage as blacks and whites nor understandings of participants as men and women are intelligibly related to the meaning of that right as that meaning has developed in the United States. This logic is the one that courts in Massachusetts and New York City followed in deciding that bans against marriage between same-sex partners violated the Massachusetts and New York constitutions. In *Goodridge* v. *Department of Public Health*, the Massachusetts Supreme Court understood the right involved in marriage to be "at the core of individual privacy and autonomy," and it concluded that the right "would be hollow if the Commonwealth could, without sufficient justification, foreclose an individual from freely choosing the persons with whom to share an exclusive commitment in the unique institution of civil marriage."[57] Although her decision was overturned by the higher courts, the trial judge in *Hernandez* v. *Robles* agreed ruling that "The 'liberty at stake' is the freedom to choose one's spouse. Thus, for the State to deny that freedom to an individual who wishes to marry a person of the same sex is to deny that individual the fundamental right to marry."[58] *[handwritten: denying gays fundamental right to marry]*

What does this understanding of the participants in civil marriage as free choosers and consenters rather than as whites, non-whites,

---

[56] *Zablocki* v. *Redhail*, p. 387.
[57] *Goodridge* v. *Department of Public Health* 440 Mass. 309 (2003) pp. 328–329.
[58] *Hernandez* v. *Robles* Supreme Court of New York, New York Country, 794 NYS 2d 579 (2005), p. 601.

parents, men, or women mean for the potential ills to which those opposed to a right to marry for same-sex couples point? If we extend marriage rights to individuals irrespective of these identities, must we also permit polygamy, bigamy, or marriages between parents and children? Both bigamy and marriages between parents and children would seem to be precluded by understanding the participants in marriage as free choosers and consenters. In a bigamous relationship one of the two partners does not know that the other is married to one or more other people as well. Yet, if the partner has no knowledge of these other relationships, it is hard to see how he or she could be understood as a free chooser of or consenter to the arrangement. Nor is it clear how children below the age of consent can be free choosers or free consenters to another's choice. Indeed, defenders of a ban on marriage between same-sex partners emphasize children's need for nurturance, guidance, and parental authority. Hence, although these defenders worry that lifting bans against marriage between same-sex partners leaves no principled protection against incestuous marriages between parents and children, the very capacities for choice and consent that they imply children do not possess would seem to provide just such a principle. We might disagree on when children reach the age of consent. Yet, in detailing children's need for protection as a basis for civil marriage, defenders of a ban on marriage between same-sex partners already provide the principle for prohibiting marriages between parents and their young children. In any case, incestuous marriages of any sort are ruled out by the legitimate gate-keeping functions of marriage laws insofar as these are concerned with health considerations.

Of course, if we understand marriage as a way of off-loading inquiries into private relationships onto a common coinage that commands immediate respect and if we understand those with a right to marriage as free choosers and consenters, little in this understanding seems to preclude an extension of marriage to consensual groups or to serially intimate relationships. Indeed, polygamous marriages are traditional in much of the world and serially intimate relationships are

Why shouldn't polygamists/ polyamorous ppl be allowed to marry?

part of certain gay and lesbian communities. Why should the participants in these relationships not have a right to the common coin of
marriage? Why should three or more individuals not have a right to
marry one another? One can also imagine a web of long-term relationships that *A* has with *B* and *C* and that *B* has with *A*, *D*, and *E*. Why
should *A* not be able to marry *B* if *B* knows that *A* is also married to *C*
and why should *B* not be able to marry *A* if *A* knows that *B* is also
married to *D* and *E*? In this case, both parties can be said to consent
freely to the arrangement. *Why not? mormon church & freedom of practicing of religion*

One might try to argue against a ban on polygamous marriages
on the basis of the history of the Mormon Church and the constitutional guarantee of the free exercise of religion. In other words, one
might argue that in prohibiting polygamous marriages the law targets
a specific religion in a way that the state's legitimate defense of the
health, safety, and welfare of it citizens cannot justify. This argument
is a difficult one to make, however, since the Mormon Church no
longer includes polygamy as one of its authorized practices. One
might also argue that while the development of marriage law in the
United States clarifies marriage's contours, rights, and identities, that
law has yet to address fully the question of its binary character.
Instead, in the case of Utah, the federal government made accepting
this binary character a condition of admission into the Union. For this
reason, the move from a dyadic to a triadic or serial structure for
marriage would have to look to a different pedigree than the one to
which marriage between same-sex partners has access. Although this
latter pedigree is one gradually articulating the identities of those with
a right to marriage, it has left the question of the number of identities
untouched.

To be sure, this analysis is insufficient as an argument for
excluding polygamy and serial forms of intimacy. If marriage is plausibly understood as the right of free choosers to an immediately
respected form of legitimate intimacy, this understanding may well
encompass not only marriages between same-sex couples but other
forms of marriages as well. This concession, however, is unlikely to be

satisfactory for many critics of marriage since civil marriage, even under these conditions, would continue to legitimize certain intimate relationships at the cost of delegitimizing others. Marriage, Michael Warner says, "is the zone of privacy outside of which sex is unprotected."[59] The meaning of marriage and the logic of marriage rights may dictate opening the institution to same-sex couples. At the same time, the very legality of civil marriage gives the state license to intrude on other relationships, to outlaw prostitution and bigamy, and to condemn promiscuity, for example. Hence, Warner thinks we should imagine "a world capacious enough in its recognition of households to be free from ... invidious regulatory institutions."[60] Yet, presumably such a world would still need mechanisms for deciding who should legitimately have mostly unquestioned access to whom and under what conditions. Questions about inheritance, hospital visitation rights, and the possibility of staying in a long-inhabited home would still arise, as would questions about distributing common property if a household splits up. For these reasons, removing the common coin of marriage would doubtless lead to more rather than less intrusions by the state into private relationships. All relationships would be subject to the scrutiny that the Erlangers received. If all households are freed from state licensing, then none are free from intrusive monitoring and regulation.

Nevertheless, we need not defend civil marriage as an institution, even one open to more forms of intimate relationship than it now includes, in order to point out that nothing about it leads to an understanding of its participants as men and women. Instead, understanding participants in the institution of marriage in sex and gender terms is as distorting as understanding them in racial terms. If we return to the hermeneutic circle of whole and part and take the history of marriage and marriage rights to be the whole into which we must integrate the parts, then, while we can integrate the identities of free choosers and consenters, we cannot integrate the identities of races, inmates,

---

[59] Warner, *The Trouble with Normal*, p. 96.   [60] *Ibid.*, p. 105.

non-custodial parents, or sexes and genders. For this reason, the struggle to legalize marriage between same-sex partners may be more
important than its critics think. If successful, it will eliminate from
a socially influential public institution the plausibility of understandings of its participants as men and women. What matters to marriage
is the choice to enter into it, not the economic or social status of those
that do so and not their political, racial, religious, sex, or gender
identities. The same holds for another important public institution,
the armed services.

GAYS IN THE MILITARY

It might seem that current law understands members of the armed
services in terms of sexual identities rather than in terms of sex and
gender ones: heterosexuals and closeted homosexuals are welcome
whereas open homosexuals are not. Under the "Don't Ask, Don't
Tell" policy, officials are not supposed to question either applicants
for military service or those currently serving in the military about
their sexual orientation. If applicants or service members reveal
homosexual orientations, however, or if they are discovered engaging
in homosexual conduct, they can be rejected from the armed services
or discharged. Yet, it is difficult to see how we can describe sexual
orientations or sexual conduct as heterosexual or homosexual without
thinking about those engaged in it or oriented toward engaging in it as
either two men, two women, or one of each. Sexual acts with a man are
normally not grounds for rejection or discharge if one is oneself a
woman and the same holds for sexual acts with a woman if one is a
man. They are grounds for rejection or dismissal if one engages in
sexual acts with a man and is a man or if one does so with a woman
and is a woman. To this extent, sex and gender remain the lens
through which the military understands service members and potential service members even though it addresses its policies to
homosexuals.

To be sure, it is not quite clear what the military means by
homosexuals. The "Don't Ask, Don't Tell" policy defines a homosexual

[handwritten: defining "homosexual acts"]

as "a person ... who engages in, attempts to engage in, has a propensity to engage in, or intends to engage in homosexual acts."[61] It defines "homosexual acts," in turn, as "any bodily contact, actively undertaken or passively permitted, between members of the same sex for the purpose of satisfying sexual desires and ... any bodily contact between service members of the same sex that a reasonable person would understand to demonstrate a propensity or intent to engage in" such homosexual acts.[62] At the same time, a service member can rebut the charge of homosexuality by, among other demonstrations, showing that his or her homosexual conduct is "a departure from the member's usual and customary behavior," that it is "unlikely to recur," and that he or she "does not have a propensity or intent to engage in homosexual acts."[63] Thus, not all homosexual acts constitute grounds for dismissal. Instead, it is evidently only homosexual soldiers who cannot engage in homosexual acts.[64] The Ninth Circuit Court of Appeals made this clear in the case of *Watkins* v. *US Army* by deciding that "If a straight soldier and a gay soldier of the same sex engage in homosexual acts because they are drunk, immature or curious, the straight soldier may remain in the army while the gay soldier is automatically terminated."[65] But, how, then, are homosexual and non-homosexual soldiers to be distinguished? How many homosexual acts make one a homosexual? What sorts of acts? *[handwritten: what's the diff now bw homo- & non-homo soldiers?]*

The military policy on homosexuality trades on the same sort of ambiguity that courts employed in the nineteenth century in deciding cases of racial identity. Just as courts deciding racial prerequisite cases *[handwritten: → similar to cases of racial identity in 19th cent.]*

---

[61] Title 10, Armed Forces, Subtitle A, General Military Law, Part II, Personnel, Chapter 37, General Service Requirements 10 USCS §654 (2005) section f(1).

[62] 10 USC §654, section f(3A) and (3B).

[63] 10 USC §654, section b(1A), (1B), and (1E).

[64] The pre-1993 policy makes this delineation explicit by noting that the intent of opportunity for rebutting the charge of homosexuality "is to permit retention only of non-homosexual soldiers who, because of extenuating circumstances, engaged in, attempted to engage in or solicited a homosexual act," *Watkins* Cited in v. *United States Army* 847 F.2d 1329 (1988), n. 11. Also see Martha Nussbaum, "A Defense of Lesbian and Gay Rights," in Martha Nussbaum, *Sex and Social Justice* (Oxford: Oxford University Press, 1999), p. 188.

[65] *Watkins* v. *United States Army*, p. 1339.

defined white in whatever way would permit them to exclude those they wanted to exclude, the military policy defines homosexuality in ways that allow it to retain or eject service members at will. Miriam Ben-Shalom asked in 1974 why she was not being discharged. The answer, "We have no arguments with you, so don't worry about it," implies, as Card points out, "that if they did have 'arguments' that were insufficient for a discharge, they could trot out the policy against lesbians."[66] We can also look at the case of Perry Watkins, a soldier who served in the army during the Vietnam War and who repeatedly told superiors that he was a homosexual. Although many soldiers were dismissed on the basis of their sexual orientation, he was not. After the war, however, when he tried to re-enlist, the Army tried to discharge him on the basis of his homosexuality. Here the one "homosexual act" the Army pointed to was that of squeezing another soldier's knee (although the person whose knee was touched could not remember which "black" soldier had squeezed it).[67] The Army thus implied that declaring oneself to be a homosexual was not enough to be one during combat, although squeezing someone's knee was sufficient to be a homosexual during peacetime.[68] Watkins was not the only target of this discrepancy. In general, the military is less concerned with homosexuality during wartime while the number of discharges on the basis of homosexuality increases during peacetime.[69]

The ambiguities involved in the military's view of who and who is not a homosexual would, as Martha Nussbaum writes, "be the stuff of high comedy, or even farce"[70] except that, as in the case of ambiguities in racial understandings, they determine people's lives. Whatever understanding one has, however, of who is a homosexual, this understanding also requires understanding individuals in sex and gender terms. Of course, given that the military acknowledges that

[66] Card, "The Military Ban and the ROTC," p. 176.
[67] *Watkins* v. *United States Army*, n. 2.
[68] See Card, "The Military Ban and the ROTC," pp. 175–176.
[69] Randy Shilts, *Conduct Unbecoming: Gays and Lesbians in the US Military* (New York: St. Martin's Press, 1993), p. 6.
[70] Nussbaum, "A Defense of Lesbian and Gay Rights," p. 188.

you can apparently engage in homosexual acts w/out being homosexual

one can engage in homosexual acts without being a homosexual, determining the sex and gender of a service member and his or her sexual partner is not sufficient for determining that service's member's "sexual identity." Still, it is a start. Hence, as in the case of registering for the draft, military service and the identities entailed by it are still understood in sex and gender terms. The question then is whether this understanding is a plausible one.

The primary ground on which federal policy defends its prohibition of military service on the part of openly homosexual individuals involves their potential threat to "high morale, good order and discipline and unit cohesion," where by "unit cohesion" it means "the bonds of trust among individual service members."[71] The argument for the "Don't Ask, Don't Tell" policy is not that the presence of homosexuals presents a threat to this group cohesion but rather that knowledge of their presence does. The idea here is that military effectiveness requires that military units operate as a cohesive force and that introducing into a unit individuals whose acknowledged sexual orientation differs from that of the majority will disrupt cohesion. "Open homosexuals would paralyze a unit, and degrade unit cohesion and erode combat effectiveness."[72] This argument is odd, however, for at least two reasons. In the first place, one of the first tasks of military training is to break down individuals' primary group loyalties in order to reform them into a new group with principal allegiances to one another. Indeed, as Elizabeth Kier points out, groups composed of individuals who are too similar to one another in attitudes and values can be dangerous to the overall military mission. Desertions in the Confederate Army, for example, were highest in companies composed of individuals from the same general location.[73] As a consequence, "few modern armies attempt to create homogeneous groups on the

---

[71] 10 USC, §654, section a(6), a(7).

[72] Air Force Chief of Staff, General Merrill McPeak, in testimony before US Senate Committee on Armed Services, July 20, 1993, in *Policy Concerning Homosexuality in the Armed Forces* (Washington, DC: Government Printing Office, 1995), p. 710.

[73] See Elizabeth Kier, "Homosexuals in the US Military: Open Integration and Combat Effectiveness," *International Security*, 23 (2), 1998, p. 16.

basis of common ethnicity, race, class, regional origin, age, personality traits, or upbringing."[74] In the second place, even where socially cohesive groups are not a direct threat to military effectiveness, they are less efficient than groups whose cohesion rests on other grounds. Kier takes the sort of cohesion crucial to military effectiveness to be "task cohesion,"[75] or cohesion constructed out of the need to accomplish specific purposes. Groups that are cohesive in this way are more efficient than socially cohesive groups because they do not devote any of their attention to maintaining personal relations or social communication and because, since they have no personal investment in the interpersonal relationships, they do not hesitate to correct any actions on the part of their members that may be counter-productive.

The question, then, is why federal policy should suppose that the integration of openly gay or lesbian individuals into the military would be any different than the integration of different ethnicities, races, classes, or those of different ages, regional backgrounds, upbringings, and attitudes. Indeed, if unit cohesion is enhanced by diversity, one would suppose that the military would be interested in whatever diversity it could find: not only the diversity of homosexual and heterosexual identities, but those with identities as Northerners and Southerners, Red Sox fans and Yankees fans, intellectuals and deep-sea divers. Despite widespread concerns that the racial integration of the American military would diminish cohesion and effectiveness, it did not. As one enlisted person explained when he was interviewed in 1951, "when it comes to life or death, race does not mean any difference."[76] In another 1951 interview, a service member said "Concerning combat, what I've seen an American is an American. When we have to do something we're all the same."[77] In the early 1990s service members made the same point about women. One said "we don't see it as male and female, we see it as a team"[78] and another

[74] *Ibid.*, p. 22. [75] *Ibid.*, p. 17.
[76] Cited in Kier, "Homosexuals in the US Military," p. 26.
[77] Cited in Kier, "Homosexuals in the US Military," p. 26.
[78] Cited in Kier, "Homosexuals in the US Military," p. 27.

in basic training said, "there was some initial flirtation between the sexes, but that was quickly moved to the back burner as the trainees realized that teamwork was essential if everybody wanted to graduate."[79] In the context of basic training or combat, then, individuals' primary understanding of one another is not as blacks and whites or men and women but as Americans and team members. Yet, if race and sex identities as blacks, whites, men, or women do "not mean any difference" why should identities as homosexuals or heterosexuals? Why would the integration of African Americans, Irish Americans, Latinos, Latinas, Asians, Northerners, Southerners, and Westerners increase task cohesion, and the integration of gays and lesbians diminish it?

Tarak Barkawi and Christopher Dandeker argue that neither the integration of African Americans nor the integration of women into the armed services serves as a good indication for the harm to unit cohesion that the integration of openly homosexual service members can cause. Like Kier, they point to the need to break down primary group loyalties in order to reform recruits into a cohesive unit with principal allegiances to one another. Yet, they stress that the identities that are reformed in this way are specifically masculine. Recruits must be transformed into soldiers who are competitive, aggressive, and willing to kill. Such a transformation, Barkawi and Dandeker contend, produces what they call "warrior masculinity." This masculinity is not undermined by the recruitment of women because they can undergo the same transformation. "Indeed," Barkawi and Dandeker write, "the contemporary image of the service woman is precisely not that of 'traditional femininity' but of someone who is just as tough and capable as male soldiers given the limitations of physical strength." The same, they think, is not true for homosexuality, for it is not "compatible with socially derived constructions of warrior masculinity."[80]

[79] Cited in Kier, "Homosexuals in the US Military," p. 28.
[80] Tarak Barkawi and Christopher Dandeker, "Rights and Fights: Sexual Orientation and Military Effectiveness," *International Security*, 24 (1), 1999, p. 185.

Yet why not? Barkawi and Dandeker criticize Kier for not making a distinction between "sex" and "gender." Women's biological
"sex" does not, in their view, mean that they cannot be made masculine in the "gender." Since they acquire a feminine gender through
acculturation and socialization in the first place, re-acculturation and
re-socialization can transform it. But if women can be made masculine
why cannot homosexuals? By the idea of masculinity, Barkawi and
Dandeker designate traits of aggressiveness, competitiveness, and
willingness to kill. We can certainly question whether this designation is a fair one, given the many other traits we might prefer to label
masculine. Still, if we accept it and if we also agree with Barkawi and
Dandeker's refusal to link masculinity with what they refer to as male
or female "sexes," it becomes entirely unclear why it should be linked
to sexual preferences. Barkawi and Dandeker try to make this connection between masculinity and heterosexuality by noting both the
prevalence of prostitution around military bases and the marching
songs that refer to women as whores.[81] By masculinity they therefore
mean not only aggressiveness, competitiveness, and a willingness to
kill but also a willingness to pay for sex and to sing songs demeaning to
women. Of course, it still remains unclear why these traits should be
labeled masculine ones since many men do not view themselves and
are not viewed by those who know them as aggressive, competitive or
willing to kill, pay for sex, or sing songs demeaning to women. Other
people might possess some of these traits and preferences and not
others. Indeed, we might mix and match all of these characteristics:
we can understand ourselves and be understood by others as masculine, unwilling to fight, competitive, not aggressive, and interested
sexually in just about anyone who comes along.

In any case, if prostitution and marching songs make no difference to the integration of female service members, why suppose that
they would make a difference to the integration of open homosexuals?
Barkawi and Dandeker refer to the heterosexuality of a warrior

[81] Barkawi and Dandeker, "Rights and Fights," p. 184.

identity, but what is this? How is the question of whom one would be willing to sleep with connected to the question of whom one would be willing to kill? Even those who are against allowing openly homosexual individuals into the armed services concede that they have been and continue to be effective soldiers. The Army consistently commended Perry Watkins from the time of his enlistment in 1967 until it sought to discharge him in 1982. Moreover, Kier points out that "discharge proceedings against homosexuals are filled with testimony of many of these individuals' outstanding records, dependability and dedication to their jobs."[82] In these cases, the discharged homosexuals had apparently adopted warrior masculinities although doing so did not save their careers. By defining masculinity in terms of a set of heterogenous traits and a specific sexual orientation, Barkawi and Dandeker embroil themselves in the same morass of perplexing identity determinations that plague the way the armed services try to define homosexuality.

Suppose we were to rethink the military policy by looking at the point of the armed services, just as we looked at the meaning of marriage and marriage rights. In its "Policy concerning homosexuality in the Armed Services" the military insists that there is no constitutional right to serve.[83] At the same time, it states that "The primary purpose of the armed forces is to prepare for and to prevail in combat should the need arise."[84] The tasks of preparing for and prevailing in combat require a number of skills, assets, and tools. During the Vietnam War, the military developed smaller and lighter weapons that could be used by Vietnamese soldiers who were smaller than their American counterparts. Given the availability of these sorts of weapons there is no longer any rationale for distinguishing the possible combat roles of men and women. There is also no rationale for distinguishing homosexuals and heterosexuals in their potential "to prevail." The military tries to distinguish between the valor of

---

[82] Kier, "Homosexuals in the US Military," p. 6.
[83] 10 USCS §654, section a(2).   [84] 10 USCS §654, section a(4).

individual homosexuals and the effect of open homosexuals on unit cohesion. It need only look at the testimony in *Perry* v. *United States Army* to see that this rationale will not wash. In 1975, Watkins' fellow service members testified that "Watkins's homosexuality was well-known but caused no problems and generated no complaints."[85]

CONCLUSION

Card asks the same question about the "Don't Ask, Don't Tell" policy that she asks about the definition of marriage as the union of one man and one woman: namely why anyone, particularly gays or lesbians, should care given that both the military and marriage are suspect institutions. However, while she does not think we should fight to open up marriage to same-sex couples, she thinks that we should fight to make the military accessible to them. Why? Her reasoning holds for both institutions. "What is at stake is one's dignity in communities in which one lives daily."[86]

Reserving marriage for opposite-sex couples and military opportunities for heterosexuals and closeted homosexuals betrays an untenable conception of identity as monolithic. While we can understand those who want to marry each other as free choosers and consenters nothing about either marriage or the right to marry makes it plausible to understand them as African Americans, Irish Americans, baseball fans, prison inmates, men, or women. We cannot view civil marriage as a union for the purposes of procreation if we want to make sense out of the legality of marriages in which children are not possible, intended, or forthcoming. Nor can we view civil marriage as a two-in-one-flesh communion if we want to make sense out of the legality of a host of other marriages. If, instead, we understand civil marriage as the publicly recognized zone of privacy for an intimate relationship there is no reason to limit its legitimate participants by their preferences, sexual or otherwise. It is equally odd to suppose that armed

[85] *Watkins* v. *United States Army*, p. 1331.
[86] Card, "The Military Ban and the ROTC," p. 191.

service members are men and women. There is no right at issue in this case, as the military makes clear. Nevertheless, if the point of the military is "to prepare for and to prevail in combat should the need arise," it is at least worth asking whether the participants the military should try to recruit are not those able to prepare and prevail. The identification of service members and potential service members as homosexuals or heterosexuals and, hence, men or women, reflects a misunderstanding of who or what these service members and potential service members are. They are not men and women and hence not homosexuals and heterosexuals any more than they are baseball fans and Barbie-doll collectors, chess players, and race car drivers. Imposing sex and gender identities on the military imposes identities that make no sense in the context and forces out identities that do make sense: those of willing warriors.

7 Hermeneutics and the politics of identity

hermeneutics: science of searching for hidden meaning in texts

The idea of a hermeneutic circle of whole and part might seem to be an odd idea to bring to issues of identity. Indeed, one might argue that David Reimer's troubles began because of his parents' and physicians' presumptions about the need to integrate parts and wholes. Hermeneutic premises project unity on texts and look to a standard of coherence as a criterion for revising interpretive projections of meaning that cannot be integrated with one another. If one's understanding of a part of the text cannot be integrated with the meaning one has projected for the whole, one has to revise either one's understanding of the part or one's understanding of the whole. In David's case, the loss of part of his body suggested to his parents and physicians that they revise the whole of his sex and gender identity. This same need for revision in the name of coherence explains surgeries on the genital parts of intersexuals so that the whole of their bodies can coherently mean one sex and gender. It also explains sex-reassignment surgeries on the part of individuals who think that their inner and outer selves do not cohere with one another. Such appeals to coherence might even try to justify attempts to "cure" homosexuals on the theory that their sexual desires are at odds with their sexes and genders and need to be revised to be consistent with them.

Nevertheless, were we to apply the hermeneutic circle in such a narrow and dogmatic way, we would have to ask whether we should bleach the skins of ethnicities who act white or Anglo or bring up infants who lose their thumbs as animals. Instead, the hermeneutic circle supports a radically situational account of identity. The assumptions behind David Reimer's operation and upbringing were, first, that identity as a boy undergirds or is a part of all life-contexts and, second, that it requires a penis. Yet the second assumption overlooks the variety of ways we can understand individuals as boys or men. There are no necessary and sufficient conditions that exhaust what it is to be a baseball fan. Rather, the identity is elastic, open to differences in degree, and subject to variations in the habits, incomes, and life-conditions of different individuals. In contrast to this elastic approach to identity, David Reimer's sex identity was meant to depend upon only and absolutely the absence of a penis when it was determined that he should be raised as a girl and his gender identity was meant to depend only and absolutely on the absence of certain behaviors when it was determined that he was really a boy. To be sure, the medical profession can stipulate a strict definition of diseases such as anorexia nervosa, reserving the designation of anorexic for those who eat less than a certain number of calories a day. Yet this definition is consciously stipulative and tailored to helping doctors treat a disease. Furthermore, its justification depends entirely on whether it does help in treating the disease and the medical profession can redefine the contours of the identity if it does not. In contrast, doctors and psychiatrists do not agree on a stipulative definition of men and women. Instead, they simply assume that strict definitions exist and disagree on what they are. Nor does the medical profession sufficiently reflect on its own agenda in attempting to define men and women or boys and girls. Do doctors serve patients by surgically correcting their bodies so that they cohere with standard male and female models or by educating both patients and the public on the range of variation? Must individuals always endure painful surgeries in order to wear a dress coherently or might we use the possibilities opened up by the structure of understanding to stretch the boundaries of sex and gender identities so that they are more flexible and less dogmatic?

Nor need we buy into the first assumption behind David Reimer's operation and upbringing, that identity as a boy is a coherent element of all life-contexts. In whatever way individuals are boys and men, girls and women they are also more and other than boys and men, girls and women. They may be baseball fans, philosophers, poker-players, gourmets, and countless other identities as well. Seen hermeneutically, lives are lived as a series of different contexts of which different identities are parts. Moreover, lives loop. In thinking about our future, we think about who we are, which identities we have that we want to maintain, and which we want to revise or discard. At the same time, in trying to understand who we are, we do so in terms of a continuum that contains both our past and our future. Our task as individuals is to develop and organize our identities in ways that give our lives the meaning we want for them. Of course, some individuals may find that being men is the most important identity they possess or desire. In this way, being a man may count as one of David Copp's self-esteem identities[1] or, in other words, as the central identity around which these individuals organize their lives. For others, identities as baseball fans or philosophers might be a more significant aspect of their self-esteem identity and provide a better key than their sexes or genders to who they most importantly are. Our question, however, has not been so much about the place of identities in our moral psychology as it has been about what identities are, whatever place they have in our moral psychology. And the answer to that question is that identities, themselves, are answers to questions – questions about who or what we are and, crucially, questions that are always asked in particular contexts to which only certain possible answers make sense.

To be sure, it may be difficult to see what content an answer such as "I am a man" can have if we strip "manhood" of its associations with traits such as aggression and a lack of interest in children. In this regard, it is easier to see the sense of answers such as "I am a philosopher" or "an Irish or African American," since these answers link individuals to traditions, disciplines, and ancestral histories whereas the former seems to link individuals only to a set of disputable stereotypes. Nevertheless, for some individuals being a man is the most important identity in their moral psychology and for some of these, because of they way they understand what being a man is, the

---

[1] David Copp, "Social Unity and the Identity of Persons," *Journal of Political Philosophy*, 10 (4), p. 369.

possession of a penis will be crucial. Hence, they will undergo painful operations in order to acquire a penis if they do not have one or
consider it a special feature of their bodies if they do. For others, a penis
will be less crucial to their identity and they may not undergo an
operation or give that particular body part pride of place at all.

The point about these assessments, however, is that we develop
them ourselves in the course of living our lives, in trying to figure out
what we care about. David Reimer's tragedy was that other people
viewed it as their prerogative to make these assessments for him
and that they made them in not only dogmatic but also imperialist
ways. They deemed the possession of a particular appendage to be
necessary to the coherence of the whole of identity as a man; nor
could they conceive for David any identity other than a sex or gender
one. Accordingly, they intervened in his life in a disastrous way. As
David himself put their problem, "It's like your whole personality,
everything about you is all directed – all pinpointed – toward what's
between the legs. And to me, that's ignorant. I don't have the education that these scientists and doctors and psychologists have, but to
me it's very ignorant."[2]

REVISITING THE POLITICS OF IDENTITY
Yet, parents inevitably attempt to mold their children's identities.
In imparting their values they try to make them liberal Democrats
or conservative Republicans. They take them to baseball games to
try to develop a love of the sport; they give them ballet lessons and
they put them on soccer teams. These efforts may fail; the identity
a parent wants to centralize in the children's moral psychology
may become inconsequential for them or even non-existent.
Nevertheless, much of the literature on identity focuses on the question of the obligations of social and political institutions to help
parents in these endeavors and to support centrally identity-forming

[2] Cited in John Colapinto, *As Nature Made Him: The Boy Who Was Raised as a Girl*
(New York: HarperCollins, Perennial Books Edn., 2001), p. 262.

communities.[3] Should liberal democracies allow for collective rights that permit individuals with particular American Indian tribal identities to engage in activities such as fishing or whale-hunting while individuals with other identities cannot? Should liberal democracies allow members of particular religious groups to exempt their children from mandatory schooling if such schooling puts their religious identity at risk? If we support the prerogative of parents to try to mold their children so that they take certain identities to be central to them, do we not need to support and work to preserve the communities that sustain these identities? If we admit that someone can make being Amish the central identity of his or her life and if we also admit that this person can try to make being Amish the central identity of his or her children's lives, then we would seem also to have to support governmental policies that work to sustain the Amish way of life, for one cannot be centrally Amish without the existence of an Amish community of which one is a part. Do we not also need to allow whatever dispensations are necessary to enable American Indian cultures to survive? Furthermore, why should trying to develop our children's identities as boys and girls or men and women be any different from trying to develop their identities as Navajo or Amish? If we need to support collective rights on the part of the Amish, do we not need to support the efforts of doctors and parents to preserve the sex and gender communities we currently possess? Must we not make the same claim for racial communities?

Indeed, if the argument of this book makes sense, then all of our identities have the same hermeneutic status as ways of understanding others and ourselves. Hence, if the government supports the Amish community as a way of supporting those that make their Amish

<hr>

[3] See Kwame Anthony Appiah, *The Ethics of Identity* (Princeton, NJ: Princeton University Press, 2005); Amy Gutmann, ed., *Multiculturalism: Examining the Politics of Recognition* (Princeton, NJ: Princeton University Press, 1994) and Amy Gutmann, *Identity in Democracy* (Princeton, NJ: Princeton University Press, 2003); Will Kymlicka, *Multicultural Citizenship: A Liberal Theory of Minority Rights* (Oxford: Oxford University Press, 1995); Susan Moller Okin *et al.*, *Is Multiculturalism Bad for Women?* (Princeton, NJ: Princeton University Press, 1999).

identities their central ones, it would appear that it should support
all of the communities that sustain all of the identities different
people might make central to their lives, including the communities
of major league baseball and neo-fascism. Conversely, we could
decide that given the status of all identities as understandings and
self-understandings of parts within contextual wholes, the government should not be in the business of supporting any of them. Which
way should we go?

Calling the second option "benign neglect," Will Kymlicka
denies that we can adopt it.[4] To begin with, governments decide on
the language of courts, legislatures, and schools. In doing so, they
cannot help but favor one identity over others – say, Anglophone
identities in the United States over Latino or Latina ones. Kymlicka
points out that English is not simply a natural outgrowth of the
language the majority of the US population uses. If it were, we
would have to change the language with shifts in immigration and
majority populations. Moreover, English was never simply a natural
outgrowth. In adding states to the union the federal government delib-
erately declined to accept territories unless or until English speakers
outnumbered non-English ones in the territories in question. It drew
state boundaries in ways that guaranteed a majority of English speakers, as in the case of Florida. It delayed statehood until sufficient
numbers of Anglophones moved into the territory in question, as in
the case of Hawaii. And, where English speaking was not likely to
become dominant, it established a different sort of political unit, as in
the case of Puerto Rico.[5] In these ways, then, the government worked
actively to support English-speaking communities over non-English-
speaking ones.

Kymlicka also insists that governmental support for certain
identities over others goes beyond language. Governments favor certain identities when they decide on public holidays such as Christmas
and when they decide on the contours of the work-week, selecting one

[4] Kymlicka, *Multicultural Citizenship*, p. 108.   [5] *Ibid.*, pp. 28–29.

that works for Christians, for example, instead of one that works for Muslims. Governments also decide on public uniforms for the police and military that can be more restrictive for certain expressions of identity than they are for others and they design state symbols that reflect certain identities, not others.[6] Indeed, one might say that certain state symbols – for example, state flags involving Confederate symbols – are not simply instances of a benign neglect of other identities but, instead, instances of an outright disrespect for them.

If, in even the best instances, governments cannot help but favor certain identities over others, how are they to decide which to favor? Kymlicka argues that because decisions on language, internal boundaries, public holidays, work-weeks, and state symbols inevitably support the majority culture, what is necessary is "similar support for minority groups through self-government and polyethnic rights."[7] Groups that are entitled to self-government, he thinks, are those such as American Indian groups whose cultures and territories were invaded by what has become the majority culture. He also thinks that ethnic and religious groups such as Jews, Muslims, and those with different heritages deserve some accommodations: consideration in designing state symbols, perhaps, as well as exemptions from holiday closings and uniform codes.

Yet, even if we restrict our examination to their effect on religious and ethnic identities, such measures raise problems. A state flag that looks neutral to African Americans in the southern United States may appear to other groups to be a complete erasure of their culture. To some French citizens, French laws that prohibit girls from wearing headscarves to school may appear necessary as a way of sustaining France's secular culture, while to others they may appear to be an attempt to undermine Muslim traditions and a Muslim identity. Moreover, some communities, and perhaps all communities, constrain their members in certain ways. David Reimer suffered a particularly drastic form of cultural constraint when surgeons cut into his

---

[6] *Ibid.*, p. 115.   [7] *Ibid.*, p. 115.

body to make it conform to a standard sex and gender community. Women in some countries suffer the same sort of invasive cultural practice when they must undergo clitordectomies, "marriage by capture," and even murder if they are accused of adultery.[8] But there are less drastic versions of cultural constraint as well. According to a 1939 ordinance of the Santa Clara Pueblo, children born of unions between male members of the Pueblo and female non-members are themselves full members of the Pueblo. In contrast, children born to female members and male non-members are not. If a Pueblo woman knows that having children with a Navajo man will deny her children the right to live at the Pueblo, hunt or fish on the land, use irrigation water, and share in economic benefits, is she really free of a cultural constraint to marry within the tribe?[9] On one reading, Santa Clara women are denied at least some of the social and political rights that the Pueblo grants to men. Should liberal societies grant these sorts of cultures the sort of accommodations that Kymlicka advocates?

Kymlicka tries to deal with such cases by distinguishing between "external protections," which attempt to reduce a minority culture's vulnerability to majority decisions, and "internal restrictions," by which minority cultures curtail the basic civil or political rights of some of their members.[10] He thinks that liberal societies should support the former, establishing those collective rights necessary to protect minority cultures and, hence, minority identities against the encroachments of the majority culture. But he thinks that liberal societies cannot support cultures that impose restrictions on their members. Kymlicka does not think denying support need lead to forcible intervention into the culture. Nevertheless, he thinks that liberal societies can use incentives meant to encourage a liberalization of illiberal communities. Still, as many commentators have pointed out, the distinction between external protections and internal

[8] See Susan Moller Okin, "Is Multiculturalism Bad for Women?," in Okin, *Is Multiculturalism Bad for Women?*, p. 18.

[9] See *Santa Clara Pueblo* v. *Martinez* 436 US 49 (1978).

[10] Kymlicka, *Multicultural Citizenship*, p. 152.

restrictions is often far from clear. Take the example of Québécois language laws that prohibit French-speakers and immigrants from sending their children to English-speaking schools.[11] Is this example one of external protections, allowing for the survival of a French-speaking culture in the English-speaking Canadian nation? Or is it instead an instance of internal restrictions that forbid French-speaking parents a right to send their children to the schools to which they want to send them? The membership laws of the Santa Clara Pueblo raise the same question. If the cost of a woman's marrying a non-Santa Claran man is the disenfranchisement of their mutual children is this cost a way of preserving and protecting the Pueblo or an internal constraint on its inhabitants?[12]

If we cannot use a distinction between external protections and internal restrictions to separate identities and cultures worthy of support from identities and cultures that are not, what can we use? And if we cannot find any criterion does the impossibility of "benign neglect" mean that governments must support all and every identity that any given individual happens to find central to his or her life? Much of the debate on issues of multiculturalism and collective rights assumes that we must pick between two alternatives: either we pursue a politics of difference that allows for the recognition of select identities such as the Amish and the Pueblo or we pursue a politics of benign neglect that leaves all minority identities to flounder equally within a majority culture. Yet, if the account of identity and identification I have argued for in this book makes sense, then selective recognition and benign neglect are not the only options open to us, for the minority and majority status of our identity shifts depending on the particular context in which we are involved at a given time and the identities that are part of that context. Both selective recognition and benign neglect misconceive identity. We can be understood in many ways and therefore possess many identities. We may be Amish in certain

[11] See Charles Taylor, "The Politics of Recognition," in Gutmann, ed., *Multiculturalism*, pp. 52–53.

[12] Also see Appiah, *The Ethics of Identity*, pp. 79–80.

situations and hence in the minority; but we may be European Americans in other situations and hence in the majority. The question of which identities are to be recognized and which neglected depends on which are intelligible parts of the context of concern and interpretive framework at hand.

None of our identities penetrates every aspect of our lives. If I am with my child I may be, for that period of time, a mother and if I am playing in a chess tournament I am not a mother, unless, perhaps, I am playing chess with my child. Similarly, if I am pregnant, I am a pregnant person, again for a limited period. Indeed, given how limited this period is, it is a least somewhat bizarre that the capacity to become pregnant should be so hegemonic with respect to identity. How often, we might ask, do contemporary human beings reproduce or, at least, want to reproduce? And how much of a life does it really compose? Individuals in advanced Western countries have some control over their reproductive lives and where individuals in developing countries do not, they nonetheless often aspire to it. Hence, it seems quite odd that we continue to define individuals in terms of their reproductive role. Indeed, if the norm in the West is approximately two children per family then we are defining certain people as females or women on the basis of eighteen months of their lives. Even if we identify individuals as females and women for somewhat longer because we suppose that they have a greater responsibility for child care and we equate femaleness with child-rearing, we are still defining them in terms of a continually interrupted and, indeed, limited span of time. And yet this identity is meant to be who and what one is at every moment and in every sphere. Surely, if we go by length of time alone, we would be better defined as workers or sleepers.

The same holds for being Amish, a Québecois, or a Santa Clara Pueblo Indian. Neither is all that one ever is. Indeed, it is conceivable that one's Amish, French, or Santa Claran identity is more prominent to outsiders than it is to oneself. For neither outsiders nor insiders, however, can an individual possess only one identity, any more than a text can possess only one meaning. Instead, just as we approach texts

from within different interpretive wholes and therefore can understand their meaning in different ways, we approach individuals from
within different wholes and therefore can understand their identities
in different ways. If the whole is the context of marriage, then those
individuals will possess identities – put otherwise, they will be intelligible as – certain sorts of people different from those they are in the
context of the military, asthma-research, or childbearing. If the whole
is the context of religion, then they will be intelligible as Amish and
Quakers, Catholics and Wicca. Given this account of identity, however, we need to rethink the conclusions of two central texts in the
literature on the politics of identity: Charles Taylor's defense of
French language laws in Quebec in his "The Politics of Recognition"
and the 1970s Supreme Court ruling in *Wisconsin* v. *Yoder*,[13] dealing
with the exemption of Amish children from schooling.

FRANCOPHONES AND THE AMISH

Taylor argues that certain restrictions on inhabitants of the Canadian
province of Québec are justified as means of ensuring the survival of
French-speaking culture in Canada.[14] Neither Francophones nor
immigrants are to send their children to English speaking-schools;
all signs are to indicate what they are about in the French language
and all businesses with more than fifty employees must be run in
French. In reviewing the restrictions, Taylor argues that "One has to
distinguish the fundamental liberties, those that should never be
infringed and therefore ought to be unassailably entrenched, on
the one hand, from privileges and immunities that are important but
that can be revoked or restricted for reasons of public policy ... on the
other."[15] What justifies Québec's public policy in restricting certain
language and schooling privileges is the goal of ensuring not only that
the French language remains a resource available to those who want to
make use of it but also that in the future there will be a community of

---

[13] *Santa Clara Pueblo* v. *Martinez* 436 US 49 (1978); *Wisconsin* v. *Yoder* 406 US 205.
[14] Taylor, "The Politics of Recognition," p. 52.
[15] Taylor, "The Politics of Recognition," p. 59.

people who do want to make use of it. In *Wisconsin* v. *Yoder*, the US Supreme Court appealed to a similar logic of cultural preservation in exempting Amish adolescents from formal schooling after the eighth grade. "Compulsory school attendance to age 16 for Amish children," it said, "carries with it a very real threat of undermining the Amish community and religious practice as they exist today."[16]

Such policies and exemptions understand identity in monolithic and absolutist ways, however. Whatever other reasons support Québec language laws or Amish exemptions from schooling, reasons that try to preserve a cultural or religious identity do not. In the first place, they allow for only one kind of a Francophone or Amish identity and, in the second place, they allow individuals to be only Francophones or Amish. Surely one can have a Francophone identity in different ways, whether because one speaks French exclusively, or because one speaks it at home, or because speaking French contributes to one's life in some other way. Just as it was odd to reduce David Reimer's male identity to the presence or absence of his penis, it is odd to reduce the question of a French-speaking identity to conducting one's business in French or sending one's children to a French-speaking school. Nor does either necessarily contribute to enhancing a French-speaking identity. Parents might send their children to French-speaking schools not because they have identities as Francophones and want to ensure that their children have identities as Francophones but simply because they have identities as snobs. One can also possess identities in addition to a Francophone one, including, for example, a parental identity concerned with the capacity of one's children to flourish in an English-speaking nation.

One can also surely be Amish in more than one way. It would be as odd to assume that all Amish share every belief as it would be to assume that all Catholics do. Moreover, one can be Amish and a student. The Supreme Court agreed with the Amish that missing two additional years of schooling was not likely to damage the psychological or physical

[16] *Wisconsin* v. *Yoder*, p. 218.

health of the adolescents, burden the surrounding society, or render them unable to support themselves. Yet, why not reverse the question? How would an additional two years of schooling undermine the Amish community? Moreover, if it would, why pick an adolescent's Amish identity as the identity to try to preserve over other identities he or she might possess or, indeed, come to possess as a result of staying in school? Suppose a greater amount of knowledge and exposure to other forms of life renders an Amish teenager a skeptic about the Amish way of life. Will some skeptic society of America now demand help to preserve that culture? Individuals, even if they are Amish are no more Amish than they are schoolchildren and as schoolchildren they should be treated in the same way as other schoolchildren under the jurisdiction of the state. The context of education is different from the contexts of religion and life-style, and if the individuals in question are Amish in the latter contexts they need not be in the former one.

Francophones, too, are no more Francophones than they are businessmen or parents. If and only if sufficient numbers of individuals want identity as a French-speaker to be either one part or a central part of their lives or their children's lives does the identity have a "right" to survive. And even if it survives it will be neither monolithic nor constant. People will be intelligible as French-speakers in different ways and they will be intelligible as other identities in other contexts. Moreover, support for identities outside of the contexts in which they have their meaning is a misapprehension of the hermeneutic conditions of identities – or, in other words, understandings – of who we are. Such support is no less dogmatic than discriminatory laws that require individuals to be races in the context of citizenship or than practices that assume individuals are blacks in the context of driving.

These conclusions suggest a different way of thinking about the politics of identity. For the important question now is not whether the state has an obligation either to support us in our identities as Francophones or Amish or to treat them with benign neglect. Rather, the question is how governments can help to accomplish two different tasks: to curtail the public determination of identities to the particular contexts in which particular identities make sense and to secure the public framework of rights within which we can sort and shape the identities we take to be important to our private flourishing. On this view, the questions we should be asking are not whether Amish adolescents should go to school or what sort of schools Francophone children should attend. Rather, we should also ask how a government can guarantee to individuals that they can be both Amish and school-children or both Francophones and members of an English-speaking nation. Moreover, if we ask this question, certain obvious answers present themselves: the Amish might establish private schools that meet state guidelines without posing a threat to an Amish identity and the Québec government might certify the right of parents to choose their children's schools while helping the Francophone community to set up Saturday or Sunday schools for French language and culture on the model of Hebrew schools or the Chinese and Japanese schools to which some Chinese Americans and Japanese Americans send their children on weekends.

In addition to a monolithic view of an Amish identity, however, the ruling in *Wisconsin* v. *Yoder* betrays a monolithic view of the identity that it thinks education is meant to help to develop. The court reasoned that the Amish do not participate in the welfare state, do not make use of social security funds, and do not become burdens on the state. Hence, their continuing education is not neces-sary in the way that is for a child whose future is not so assured.[17] Yet this analysis supposes that the sole point of education is to make sure that individuals can support themselves as workers. Others, however, understand the identities that education is meant to develop differently – as democratic citizens, for instance – and they therefore deny that an eighth-grade education is sufficient.[18] Instead, children arguably need to develop an understanding of their rights,

---

[17] See *Wisconsin* v. *Yoder*, p. 225.
[18] See Richard Arneson and Ian Shapiro, "Democratic Autonomy and Religious Freedom: A Critique of *Wisconsin* v. *Yoder*", in Ian Shapiro, *Democracy's Place* (Ithaca, NY: Cornell University Press, 1996), p. 146.

responsibilities, and opportunities as citizens as well as a capacity for critical reasoning that allows them to assess opinions and views either similar to or different from their own.[19] In addition, children arguably need some understanding of science, if only to be able to evaluate environmental threats to their way of life or to assess the implications of certain governmental policies. They could also use an understanding of world history, the history of the United States, and the history of democratic institutions, if only to recognize their own position within these histories.[20] Of course, many children complete high school without acquiring these understandings and skills. Nevertheless, as Richard Arneson and Ian Shapiro point out, "The failure of citizens ... to provide education adequate for preparing youth for future citizenship does not justify a decision ... to cease upholding and enforcing these norms."[21] Rather, if part of the goal of education is the development of individuals who can be competent members of a democracy, then the two years that Amish children miss may well be crucial.

How are we to decide between these accounts of the identities that an education is meant to help to develop? Are American schools meant to produce workers or citizens? Obviously the answer here is that education can surely produce both, but this answer confirms the dogmatic character of the court's decision on the Amish. Not only are Amish adolescents both Amish and schoolchildren; as schoolchildren they are more than future self-supporters. Instead, education in the United States is meant to serve at least two goals: that of preparing students to take up identities as workers in a global economy and that of preparing students to take up identities as citizens in a multicultural society and democratic polity. If, for the individuals in question, their present identities as Amish preclude their future identities as workers in a global economy, their Amish identities do not preclude their future identities as citizens. In deciding as it did, then, the court

---

[19] See Amy Gutmann and Dennis Thompson, *Democracy and Disagreement* (Cambridge, MA: Harvard University Press, 1996), p. 65.

[20] *Ibid.*, p. 147.   [21] *Ibid.*, p. 148.

imposed a dogmatic and monolithic understanding on both the adolescents in question, which it saw only as Amish, and on school-children in general, which it saw only as future workers. Recognizing that the adolescents must be understood to be more than Amish and that schoolchildren must be conceived of as more than future workers does not prohibit the Amish from setting up their own private high schools, ones that they could presumably tailor to fulfill the goals of democratic education and their own religious and cultural identity needs. Recognizing multiple identities *does* prohibit a US court from imprisoning the Amish or schoolchildren in any one of their multiple identities.

INCOMPATIBLE INTERPRETATIONS

It is not difficult to see how education can incorporate the goals of creating reliable workers, competent citizens, and, in the case of religious schools, possible believers. But can recognizing a multiplic-ity of identities not often overburden institutions and practices? Can differing interpretations of who and what we are not sometimes pre-empt one another? Take the identities of being both a Christian Scientist and a parent with a very ill child. For Christian Scientists, illness is the result of spiritual alienation and imperfect understanding so that, for them, prayer is a valued form of medical intervention.[22] For most Western doctors, medical care involves more scientifically informed forms of intervention. Since their religion does not allow Christian Scientists to receive conventional medical treatment, the issue arises as to what state authorities are to do when Christian Scientist parents withhold medical care from their gravely ill minor children.

In this instance, we cannot decide the question by tailoring the identity to the framework of interpretation within which it is an identity, for part of the problem is how to understand that framework.

---

[22] See Anne D. Lederman, "When Religious Parents Decline Conventional Medical Treatment for Their Children," *Case Western Reserve Law Review*, 45, 1995, p. 918.

Nor can we allow for both frameworks of interpretation. When we recognize the multiple ways in which we can understand *Sense and Sensibility*, we come to admire the novel all the more and to marvel at its countless interpretive meanings. When we recognize the different ways we can understand a dying child, we are caught in a relativist nightmare. Is the context for understanding the child that of health or religion? Which contextual interpretation of the identity of the child should be decisive: that of medicine within which the child is a diseased corporeal body or that of Christian Science within which the child is a soul alienated from God? Moreover, what is the proper context for understanding the potential death of the child? For Western medicine it is an avoidable event, looming only because of the parents' irrationality. For Christian Scientists, "What appears to be an ending is merely a passing, ascending to a realm of higher understanding."[23] Consequently, the focus of Western medicine on the body alone is misdirected.

It may be that taking seriously the different interpretations of a text that stem from different contexts and different textual relations serves to deepen our understanding and appreciation of the text. Yet, texts do not require us to act, whereas deciding how to proceed in the context of medical care does. What, then, should doctors do when parents refuse to permit them to care for their children? Shapiro offers a possible way out of the problem. First, he distinguishes between a child's basic interests which include his or her needs for food, shelter, education, and the like and the child's best interests, which involve interests that the family thinks are important to his or her religious, ethical, or spiritual development, or to his or her particular talents and special needs.[24] Second, like John Locke, Shapiro argues that responsibilities for children's interests are fiduciary ones.

---

[23] Pam Robbins and Robley Whitson, "Mary Baker Eddy's Christian Science," in *Christian Science: A Sourcebook of Contemporary Materials* (Boston, MA: Christian Science Publishing Company, 1990), cited in Lederman, "When Religious Parents Decline Conventional Medical Treatment," p. 918.

[24] Ian Shapiro, *Democratic Justice* (New Haven, CT: Yale University Press, 1999), p. 86.

Parents are to represent their children's interests until the children are able to represent their own and they are to exercise authority over their children only in their children's interests.[25] For some time, Western governments have also had a fiduciary responsibility towards children's interests, not only providing for their education but also looking out for their physical safety and working to protect their health and nutrition.

In Shapiro's scheme, state and parental responsibilities complement one another. Parents are the primary custodians of their own children's best interests and have ultimate authority over them. They are the secondary custodians of their basic interests. Hence, where the state fails to protect these basic interests parents can and must legitimately intervene. For its part, the state is the primary custodian for children's basic interests and secondary custodian for their best interests. In the case of some basic interests, such as health and nutrition, the state usually gives up day-to-day control to the parents, subject to the proviso that the state has ultimate authority in this area and can intervene if the parents fail to discharge their tasks. The same holds for children's best interests. Where parents neglect these interests or fight over what the child's best interest involves, the state must become the judge.

Using this scheme of fiduciary responsibility for best and basic interests, Shapiro declares that "we should not be troubled when the preferences of Christian Scientists to withhold essential medical care from children are overridden by courts." Rather, "these are instances where parents' conceptions of a child's best interests lead to a violation of the child's basic interests." Since the state has ultimate fiduciary responsibility for basic interests, it can and should intervene.[26] Shapiro does not deny that Christian Scientist parents' actions are directed at their children's best interests as they understand them – in this case, their interests in spiritual salvation. Nevertheless, he thinks that their concerns are properly overridden by the state since

[25] *Ibid.*, pp. 73–75.   [26] *Ibid.*, pp. 93–94.

it is responsible for the children's basic interests – in this case, their interests in physical survival.

Nevertheless, this division of duties raises more complicated interpretive issues than Shapiro acknowledges. For, from a Christian Scientist perspective, in rejecting medical care for their children, Christian Scientist parents are securing their children's basic interests in compliance with their secondary fiduciary duty to be taken up when the state cannot or will not fulfill its primary fiduciary role in this area. The Christian Scientist parents, in other words, may understand their duty as parents in the same way as Shapiro understands it: namely, as a duty that directs them to protect their children's best interests in all circumstances and to protect their basic interests when the state fails to do so. Yet, in withholding medical care, they take themselves to be doing just that: looking out for their children's best interests in spiritual salvation and for their basic interests in spiritual survival, precisely because the state will not.

Our understanding of education can encompass different dimensions as an institution multiply geared to developing well-qualified workers, democratic citizens, and, in some cases, religious believers. In contrast, medical care cannot attend to the body without damaging the soul according to Christian Scientists and cannot attend to the Christian Scientist soul without damaging the body according to Western medicine. The two different understandings of the child as ill patient and alienated soul thus lead to two different but ultimately inadequate responses: non-action in the face of imminent harm or failure in properly respecting a minority identity. We can ask why individuals should be Amish in the context of education and we can understand them to be both Amish and high-school students either at public schools, if their elders will allow it, or in private, Amish schools, if they will not. Yet, it is more difficult to se how children can be both gravely ill children and Christian Scientists since in the eyes of their parents their being Christian Scientists precludes their being gravely ill and in the eyes of the medical profession their being gravely ill precludes their being Christian Scientists.

The contextual solution to the problem – namely that the children are patients in the hospital and Christian Scientists at church – also fails. For a devout Christian Scientist parent, the very fact that his or her child is ill – or, in their view, alienated from God – indicates that the relevant identity in the hospital is a religious one.

In 1996, Congress passed legislation that requires states to provide medical treatment for dangerously ill minor children but also permits the states to allow for religious exemptions to findings of parental abuse and neglect in instances in which the parents objected to or failed to seek medical help.[27] Perhaps we can take this law as an example of the sort of compromise that might be necessary in such cases. To be sure, ultimately the law favors what Kymlicka might see as a majority identity. In the end, the children receive treatments as medical patients, not Christian Scientists. Nevertheless, it is possible to view the law as trying to go as far as it can in recognizing and respecting a minority identity and the hermeneutic perspective it frames on who its children are. Perhaps more importantly, the law asks that minority culture to recognize and respect the different identities its members have. They are not only Christian Scientists and not only parents with their own understandings of the basic and best interests of their children. In addition, they are members of a technologically advanced Western society, just as the Amish are also citizens of a democracy and Canadian Francophones are members of an English-speaking nation. We are all required to balance the different identities we possess and to bear the consequences of whatever incompatibilities they involve. Hence, the 1996 law may be the best accommodation Christian Scientists can expect. At the same time, we should recognize that there are different ways of being members of a technologically advanced Western society and that the religious way that Christian Scientists adopt may not be an unimportant one. In fact, in taking it seriously, non-believers might deepen their own

[27] See Janna C. Merrick, "Spiritual Healing, Sick Kids and the Law: Inequities in the American Healthcare System," *American Journal of Law & Medicine*, 29, 2003, pp. 269–299.

thinking about what human life is and they might use religious views to work out their own views on a number of issues including physician-assisted suicide, artificial means for extending life, and so on. Intervening to save the gravely ill children of Christian Scientist parents does not mean that we cannot respect and even learn from their perspective on who their children are.

The same holds for the possible insights of frameworks and contexts of which other identities are a part. There are also different ways of being members of a democracy and we can try to learn from those who understand the identity differently than we do.[28] We need not tolerate identities that encourage violence as part of who they are, if for no other reason that identities that require violence cut short the possibility of learning from alternative understandings. Still, the idea of alternatives in understanding is as important to our thinking about our identities and our lives as it is to our thinking about our texts. Recognizing the multiplicity of ways of understanding who and what we are opens us to multiple allegiances and tells against our encasing ourselves in one identity, no matter how important that identity is to us or to the politics of difference. In addition, our multiple identities, allegiances, and differences allow us to try accommodation in public policy and to refuse to see it as simply the product of defeat.

To be sure accommodation smacks of appeasement. We certainly should think more than once about appeasing certain sorts of identities including dogmatic or fundamentalist ones, neo-Nazi ones, or ones for which violence is a given. But we cannot start our political thinking from the ground up, deciding in advance which identities we want the world to contain. Rather, we already have identities and we are already parts of different practices and institutions. In this world into which we are thrown, the virtues of recognizing the multiple ways we can understand who and what we are reflect democratic virtues. They allow us to acknowledge the equal status of our different

---

[28] See Georgia Warnke, *Legitimate Differences: Interpretation in the Abortion Controversy and other Public Debates* (Berkeley, CA: University of California Press, 1999).

identities and to be sensitive to the different contexts in which they have their meaning. In addition, these virtues allow us to listen and learn from identities we do not possess. Governments and laws may not always be able to accommodate all the understandings that issue from the perspective of different identities. Yet, if we refuse to entrench ourselves in only one of our identities and if we take seriously their interpretive status, we can at least listen to others. In the end, this point may be the one Butler is making in asking whether we have "ever yet known the human."[29] I would say that we have, but also that there is always more to know.

[29] Judith Butler, "The Question of Social Transformation," in Judith Butler, *Undoing Gender* (New York, Routledge, 2004), p. 222.

Conclusion

The claim I have tried to make is that identities are parts of contexts and make sense only within the contexts of which they are a part. Just as the question of who Elinor Dashwood is makes no sense outside of the context of *Sense and Sensibility*, the question of who someone is or whether someone is black or white, male or female, Amish or student makes no sense unless we know with regard to what. Moreover, depending upon how I understand the whole of the text of which Elinor Dashwood is a part, I will understand who she is differently. If I place the novel in the context of onanism, I may understand her as an incestuous lover. If I understand her in the context of democracy I may understand her as a model of independence. Likewise, if I understand an ill child in the context of Western medicine, I will understand him or her as a medical patient. If I understand him or her in the context of Christian Science, I will understand him or her as an alienated soul. In concluding this book, I want to expand on two remaining issues. First, if one of the points of the book is to emphasize the different ways both identities and the contexts of which they are a part can be interpreted, why accept my interpretations of such institutions as marriage, education, and the military? Second, if one of the points of the book is to support liberal goals of non-discrimination, comparisons between literary interpretation and identity might seem to be total overkill. For what actually is the difference between the traditional liberal thesis that a person's race, sex, and gender are irrelevant in public life and my claim that race, sex, and gender are unintelligible except within limited contexts? Put otherwise, what is the difference between restricting all identities to the contexts in which they can be intelligible and insisting that some are simply not relevant within certain domains? I shall begin with the first question.

The point at which we began this investigation focused on the issue of what gender, race, and sex are. The conclusions of that inquiry are two-fold. First, to understand what gender, race, and sex are we need to apply the hermeneutic (and Wittgensteinian) idea that to understand what something is to understand the way of life of which it is a part. Second, however, we need to specify what we mean by a way of life. For, the problem with gender, race, and sex is that when the way of life of which they are a part is too broadly conceived, none of them makes sense. The way of life conditioned by the institution of slavery does not preclude contradictions and exasperations in providing consistent standards for who is black, white, non-white, and so on. Nor does the way of life conditioned by gender differentiation avoid difficulties in saying what being a man or woman involves. Even sex, which would seem to be a bedrock conception, can be understood in contradictory ways, depending on whether one bases it on chromosomes, hormones, or shoulder structure. Hence, if race, gender, and sex are to be intelligible identities, the contexts of which they are a part must be more precisely defined.

I have argued that these contexts are situational and only occasional wholes. Indeed, I have argued that they are primarily festive and ceremonial ones. To be sure, the situation in which one is trying to have a baby allows for identities as males and females but surely this is the epitome of a festive occasion. For other situations, I have used the identity of Irish American as an example. Being African American is part of celebratory situations in which one acknowledges one's ancestors, remembers their struggles, and thanks them for their achievements. Nevertheless, with regard to institutions such as education and marriage, prerogatives such as citizenship, and practices such as medical care and driving, racial identities stick out like sore thumbs.

Of course, the strength of this claim depends upon how we understand the institutions, prerogatives, and practices at stake. Just as who Elinor Dashwood is depends upon how we understand her story, who the participants in marriage are depends upon how we understand marriage. Moreover, just as we can understand who we are differently depending upon the context in which the issue arises, we can also understand marriage in more than one way. In considering the practices, prerogatives, and institutions I have looked at in this book, then, I have not tried to provide canonical interpretations of their meaning but, instead, to discover what they do not or cannot mean. Here, the question is whether certain interpretations make a hash of the integration of part and whole. The interpretation of marriage as the union of one man and one woman is an example. In resting on procreation, this interpretation is unable to integrate current legal marriages between those who cannot have children. In resting on natural law, it violates the separation of church and state that is necessary to marriage's integration with some of our other practices. In disregarding *Loving* v. *Virginia* as a precedent to expanding those with a right to marry, it omits a range of other cases including *Zablocki* v. *Redhail* and *Turner* v. *Safely*.

Nevertheless, if marriage cannot be understood as the union of one man and one woman, clearly it can be understood in more ways than one and the understanding I have offered is only a possibility rather than the last word. I have understood marriage as an institution that allows couples to off-load public scrutiny of, and inquiry into, their private relationship and to imprint that relationship on a common coinage that commands immediate respect. This understanding makes sense of some of the court cases we have examined and it also makes sense of the interest some same-sex couples have in achieving the right to get married. There are doubtless other ways of understanding what marriage is. Nevertheless, some ways, like some interpretations of *Sense and Sensibility* or Caravaggio's "Sacrifice of Isaac" simply will not work.

Yet are comparisons of this sort really necessary? Why not simply claim that race, sex, and gender are irrelevant to marriage? In one sense, using the hermeneutics of whole and part shows us why racial, sex, and gender identities are irrelevant: they are irrelevant because they make no sense, because they cannot be interpretively integrated into the context into which their "irrelevant" use tries to thrust them. In another sense, to the extent that identities are ways of understanding who and what we and others are, they are less than simply irrelevant to certain situations; they are not part of the situation at all. Elizabeth Dashwood does not exist outside of the context of *Sense and Sensibility*. Females and women likewise do not exist outside of certain stories and do not figure in every context in which we live our lives. The same holds of blacks and whites, Asians, Latinos, and Latinas. We are these identities only in their contexts. We need to remember the incompleteness, contextuality, and limited duration of all our multiple identities.

Index

Made in the USA
Lexington, KY
18 September 2011